ALSO BY MICHAEL HOFFMAN

Secret Societies and Psychological Warfare

The Occult Renaissance Church of Rome

Adolf Hitler: Enemy of the German People

Usury in Christendom:
The Mortal Sin that Was and Now is Not

Twilight Language
Michael Hoffman

Independent History and Research
Coeur d'Alene, Idaho

2021

Twilight Language

Copyright ©2021 by Michael Hoffman

All Rights Reserved.

The scanning, uploading and distribution of this book without permission is a violation of Title 17 of the Copyright Law of the United States and subject to criminal and civil penalties.

With the exception of excerpts in reviews, and fair use in compliance with the Copyright Law of the United States, no part of this publication may be reproduced, stored in a a retrieval system, or transmitted in any form by any means, digital, photocopy, mechanical, recording or otherwise.

ISBN: 978-0-9909547-5-0

www.RevisionistHistory.org

Independent History and Research
Box 849 • Coeur d'Alene, Idaho 83816

Printed in the United States of America

Second Printing: December 2021

The cover illustration depicts Isis and Nephthys officiating at the embalming by Anubis of Ramesses II (circa 1300 BC).

In memory of
James Shelby Downard [1]

---

[1] Photo © WiNG Publications. Used by permission.

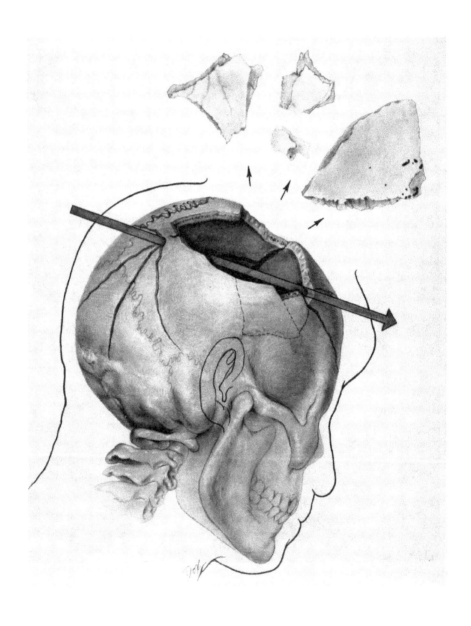

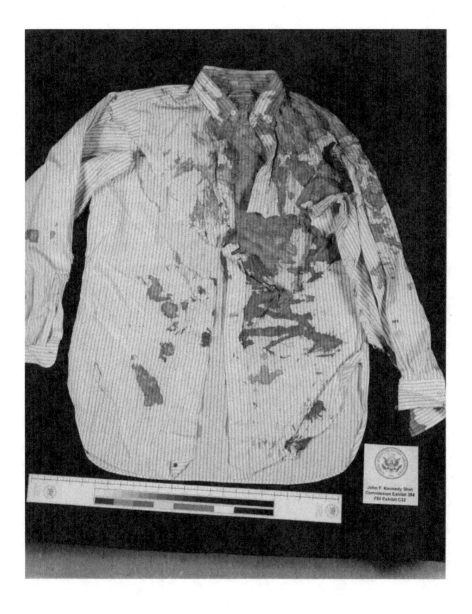

"...everything around them has been built from blood, the earth and the heavens fashioned—literally—from the dismembered body of a murder victim.

"The universe as crime scene: it is an unsettling story, full of strangeness, violence, and contradictions, a tale whose truths must be felt rather than merely explained and understood."

Neil S. Price

```
ABRACADABRA
ABRACADABR
ABRACADAB
ABRACADA
ABRACAD
ABRACA
ABRAC
ABRA
ABR
AB
A
```

Abracadabra is an Aramaic word
often written in the form of a triangle, denoting:

I create as I speak.
With words I create.

Dr SYNTAX AT FREE MASON'S HALL.

Massive Ordnance Air Blast (MOAB) is a non-nuclear US Air Force super-bomb.

The etymology and original meaning of the name Moab is unknown. The word is foreign to Hebrew. In the Old Testament Moab is the name of the incestuous son of Lot (Genesis 19:37). In the Plains of Moab, opposite Jericho (Numbers 22:1 ; 26:63 ; Joshua 13:32), the children of Israel had their last encampment before they entered the land of Canaan. Moses died in the land of Moab (Deuteronomy 34:5 Deuteronomy 34:6).

The MOAB bomb was developed by Albert L. Weimorts of the United States Air Force. In German the word *wei* denotes white. In French the word *mort* denotes death. Weimort = White death. [2]

---

[2] ...the Massive Ordnance Air Blast...nicknamed the "mother of all bombs." (*New York Times*, Dec. 25, 2005, Section 1, Page 41). Moab is the county seat of Grand County and a regional center of southeastern Utah. Known variously as Grand Valley and Mormon Fort, the majority of its residents have been Mormons since its founding in 1880.

"The society of the spectacle had begun everywhere in coercion, deceit, and blood, but it promised a happy path...

"Now it no longer says: 'What appears is good, what is good appears.' It simply says, 'It is so.' It admits frankly that it is no longer essentially reformable, though change be its very nature in order to transmute for the very worst every particular thing. It has lost all its general illusions about itself."

Guy Debord
The Society of the Spectacle
Preface to the Fourth Italian Edition

"Debord's early distinction between the concentrated and diffuse forms of spectacular organization is abandoned in favor of a single category: the integrated spectacle...'When the spectacle was concentrated, the greater part of surrounding society escaped it; when diffuse, a small part; today, nothing. The spectacle has spread itself to the point where it now permeates all reality...this reality no longer confronts the integrated spectacle as something alien...

"Possessing 'all the means necessary to falsify...perception,' the spectacle 'is the absolute master of memories just as it is the unfettered master of plans which shape the most distant future.'

"...Debord argued that the 'vague feeling that there had been a rapid invasion which forced people to lead their lives in an entirely different way is now widespread...many see it...as something inevitable...the cycles of...simulation...'"

Sadie Platt
The Most Radical Gesture

"For Facebook and Google and Instagram and Twitter, the business goal quickly became maximizing and monetizing human attention via addictive dopamine hits. Attention, they meticulously found, is correlated with emotional intensity, outrage, shock and provocation. Give artificial intelligence this simple knowledge about what distracts and compels humans, let the algorithms do their work, and the profits snowball. The cumulative effect — and it's always in the same incendiary direction — is mass detachment from reality...

"With each passing second online, news stories, graphic videos, incendiary quotes, and outrages demonstrate their stunning utility to advertisers as attention seizers, are endlessly tweaked and finessed by AI to be even more effective, and thereby prime our brains for more of the same. They literally restructure our minds...

"And if you live in such a madhouse all the time, you will become mad. You don't go down a rabbit-hole; your mind increasingly is the rabbit hole — rewired that way by algorithmic practice...But the thing about algorithms and artificial intelligence is that they don't rest, they have no human flaws, they exploit every weakness we have, and have already taken over. This is not a future dystopia in which some kind of AI robot takes power and kills us all. It is a dystopia already here — burrowed into our minds, literally disabling the basic mental tools."

Andrew Sullivan
Substack.com

The largest and longest-lived of the devils was the Great God Power, who sanctioned all behavior that was successfully conducted.

Contents

Preface..24
Prologue: A Black Jack Progression: 2(00)1 — (20)21.................27

Part I: Parallel Latitudes   58

Twilight Language: An Interview...59
The Psychic Highway...117
The Willard Factor...122
Anubis: Overlord of the Cosmic Graveyard............................141
"Little Egypt"..147
FLDR..157
Pike Bites the Dust..162
The Moab Monolith..166

Part II: A Slow Music   174

King-Kill/33 Fifty-Eight Years Later......................................175
9/11 Terror as Alchemical Ritual..235
The "Literary Game" of the Rosicrucian Brotherhood 246
The Tarot Card Killer...254
Virginia Tech Terror 33..268
"Batman Massacre" Aurora Colorado....................................275
Necromancy in Parkland..287
End-Time Burnout...293
The Joker...303
El Paso Cielo..306
Satanic Pederast Rings in Legend and Reality......................310
Route 91 Harvest Massacre...322

Part III: Pharmakos   336

Preface

"It was (Martin) Heidegger who first had the audacity to trace the accumulating ills of modern society to a steady deterioration of human sensibilities with regard to the wonder of things in their sheer radiant existence, the miracle of Being that gives all things that are.

"The cultures of the West gradually lost their capacity to mediate and develop this sensibility, the core of truly human existence; the consequent hollowing out of our traffic with beings is manifest both in the way our care for what is has curdled into the manipulation of things as tools, and in the way our communities have devolved into impersonal structures of social management and exploitation. All this, as a result of a fall away from the authentic expression of Being..." [3]

This work, *Twilight Language,* could perhaps serve as a transcendent voyage to a reawakened comprehension of how our experience of Creation has been purloined, and how our human *being* can be restored.

The acquisition of comprehension leading to an "authentic expression of being," is possible, but so arduous and daunting given our inhabitation in and of this time, that it is mainly, if not exclusively, a blessing bestowed by grace unearned, rather than a titanic labor undertaken by *ubermenschen*.

> And as the smart ship grew
> In stature, grace, and hue,
> In shadowy silent distance grew the Iceberg too. [4]

In these pages we are engaged in the study of the nature of reality, in search of a counter-modern retrieval of radiant human *being* amidst the wonders of Creation, against the defection encoded in and abetted by Twilight Language which, in a preponderance of cases, is a departure from authentic apprehension and expression of verisimilitude, into a degraded burlesque of communication which repudiates the ontological search for knowledge of ourselves as images of the divine, within the natural world of wonder.

---

[3] Paul DeHart, *Aquinas and Radical Orthodoxy*, p. 6

[4] Thomas Hardy, "The Convergence of the Twain"

Human beings have been partakers of this debased language which has been codified by the western secret societies such as the early Rosicrucians, and further eroded by post-modern advertising, radio, "rock," cinema, Internet and news media. Inside this psychic pressure cooker, true apprehension of Being and Creation is rendered unobtainable. As a consequence of this Intentional Processing, men and women are radically diminished — experiencing the reduction of their existence to the level of post-human consumers of imitation phenomena, rather than instauration as *imago Dei* living the immanence of divine creation.

The decay is reflected in indices of rising levels of loss of memory and cognitive acuity, divorce, abortion, suicide and "random violence," as well as in our profound disengagement from human relationships and communion, amidst an artificial world simulated by signs conveying constant messages of avarice, degeneration, incapacity, sterility and death.

Twilight Language is the visible spectrum of the occult imperative. It is rendered invisible through our willful forgetfulness — the price we pay to maintain a sliver of comfort and self-satisfaction within the sorcerous system of things.

Consumption of the knowledge and branding of Twilight Language (as opposed to the study and analysis of its function as neuro-linguistic programming), is an act of enthrallment, not liberation. Participants in The Process situate greater knowledge of Twilight Language in a continuum of thrilling jolts to their seriously impaired and dulled autonomic nervous systems, like narcotic addicts who increase their dosage to obtain the same level of serenity first experienced with the ingestion of a lower dose.

Consequently, this book can either be an empowering map for sleuths seeking emancipation from simulation, or a further descent into psychological and spiritual bondage on the part of those who partake of this writing mainly to obtain a more thrilling shock of recognition concerning their own demise — a shock that will eventually dissipate and require yet another unprecedented jolt, and then another, and another...

Many of the people stewed in morbid conspiracy theory suffer the effects of the mental contagion they imagine they are decoding. The Process ends when the nervous system becomes too anesthetized and stupefied to experience further stimulation. This is the Black Jack state of 2(00)1.

Theater of the Clown Priests of Zuni

"...the clowns--priests annually elected from the membership of the Kâ'-kâ, and disguised as monsters, with warty, wen-eyed, pucker-mouthed pink masks and mud-bedaubed equally pink bodies. First appear the dancers, some fifty of them, costumed and masked with such similarity that individuals are as indistinguishable as the birds or the animals they conventionally represent are from each other. Large-jawed and staring-eyed demons of one kind or another marshal them into the open plaza of the village under the guidance of a sedate unmasked priest bearing sacred relies and prayer-meal. One of the demons sounds a rattle and howls the first clause in the song stanza; then all fall into line, all in equal time sing the weird song, and go through the pantomime and dance which invariably illustrate its theme.

"When four verses have been completed, the actors, bathed in perspiration, retire to their *estufa* to rest and pray, while the priest-clowns appear with drum, cabalistic prayer-plumes and the paraphernalia of guess-games.

"They begin the absurdest, most ingenious and witty of buffoonery and raillery, generally managing, nevertheless, to explain during their apparently nonsensical dialogues, the full meanings of the dance and song — the latter being often couched in archaic or jargonistic terms utterly incomprehensible to others than the initiated among the audience..." [5]

---

[5] Clowns, Priests, and Festivals of the Kâ'-kâ, "Zuñi Breadstuff," Millstone 10, no. 8 (1885): 141-44.

Prologue

A Black Jack Progression: 2(00)1 — (20)21

This book is not a how-to manual to prevent being alchemically processed by the Cryptocracy. One cannot prevent a disease that has already metastasized. Neither is it a "wakeup call." Since the Gateway Year 2001, the majority of Americans have been processed as initiates. They are "Masons on sight," i.e. members of the secret society without knowing it.

A "wakeup call' presupposes that people are asleep. They are only partly so. In their waking stages they intuit that the Cryptocracy in the United States engages in human sacrifice and occult process. This thrills them and they keenly anticipate more thrills.

At this stage in history, America is a carnival-sideshow thrilldrome and "We the People" vie for a front row seat. Eternal salvation, the pursuit of truth and freedom—all that takes a back seat, despite the rhetoric.

The alchemical processing of humanity is ahead of schedule. People are becoming less human and far more numb and easily misdirected, as the Reign of Dead Matter appears on the horizon.

Reality, facts and truth are dispensable in the high echelons of the Cryptocracy. Sorcery entails a calculus in which reality, facts and truth are whatever the sorcerer declares them to be.

According to allegations in Ariel Sabar's book *Veritas: A Harvard Professor, a Con Man and the Gospel of Jesus's Wife* (Random House, 2020), one of the principals who was allegedly instrumental in promoting the "Jesus Had a Wife" papyrus fragment hoax, was Karen King, Hollis Professor of Divinity at Harvard University. In a review of Sabar's book, James Lasdun states concerning King's alleged co-conspirators in the hoax:

"She had little interest in hearing what Sabar had found out...Nor did she offer any mea culpas when her fragment was discredited. You could read this as the product of a lofty post modern sensibility, unbound by crude categories of true and false. King's statements over the years certainly support that. 'History is not about truth but about power relations,' she wrote in one paper. Sticklers for the former were guilty of 'fact fundamentalism.'

"But such relativism, for her, was never an end in itself. It was always in the service of a larger goal, and from the beginning of her career that goal was unabashedly religious...A gospel revealing Mary Magdalene as not just Jesus's disciple but also his wife would restore...forfeited sexuality. If it turned out to be genuine, so much the better. But even if it didn't, might it not do some good all the same..." [6]

In the non-Gnostic, orthodox Christian theology of the Bible this legerdemain falls under two categories. The first is *mendacium officiosum* (the officious lie; the helpful lie; lying "for our own good" to "assist us into illumination").

Jacob conveyed to his father Isaac the "helpful" lie that he was his first born son (Genesis 27:19). The seventeenth century theologian Thomas Brooks notes that Jacob told Isaac an officious lie, after which: "Jacob hardly ever had a merry day, a good day after it; for God followed him with a variety of troubles, and his sorrows came posting in, one after another, even to his dying day, that both himself and others might see what bitterness is wrapped up in officious lies...(St.) Augustine stoutly asserts that we are not to tell an officious lie though it were to save all the world....

"Nepos reported of Epaminondas, a nobleman of Thebes and a famous warrior, that he would never lie in jest nor in earnest, either for his own or another's gain. This refined heathen will one day rise in judgment against such kind of Christians who take a pleasure in officious lies."

The most common occult lie is *mendacium perniciosum*, pernicious lying intended to defraud or cheat. There is no occult imperium without rampant *mendacium perniciosum*. If it is successfully conducted it becomes a "truth" of consensus "reality." This is the might-is-right winner's creed. The Christian counter-culture says otherwise: it is better to be a loser in this world than a liar. Jeremiah loathed and

---

[6] James Lasdun, *London Review of Books*, September 24, 2020, p. 8. The *New York Times* lent support to the papyrus hoax, cf. *Times*, September 19, 2012. The "Jesus Had a Wife" papyrus fragment was allegedly forged and conceived by Walter Fritz, a German-American, who, according to Mr. Sabar's book, produced "hot wife" pornographic films starring Fritz's wife, a series of men, and on occasion, Fritz himself. Mrs. Fritz "had her own website that jointly celebrated 'sluthood,' and, of all things, the teachings of Jesus. The latter are given a distinctly Gnostic spin: 'That's why Jesus says: The Kingdom of Heaven Is Within You! It means: find your own reality within, then you will know it all.' References to Aleister Crowley...and even Karen King's translation of the Gospel of Mary, appear in the couple's online writings and videos." (Lasdun, p. 6).

abominated liars to such an extent that he chose to live in the wilderness than among them (Jeremiah 9:2-8).

What is "the Reign of Dead Matter"?
Is it "inevitable"?

In the summer of 2020 Elon Musk expressed anxiety to Maureen Dowd of the *New York Times* over the possibility that Silicon Valley oligarchs may be "summoning the demon." In this connection he informed Dowd that he believed machines will surpass human intelligence before 2025, at which time "things" will start to "get...weird." [7]

Machines = Dead Matter.

"Inevitable"? Can the present be colonized by "the future"? If so, then yes. But what is the future if not a unit of measurement of time, and as Frank Wilczek has observed, "...measurement is a disruptive process, which disturbs the thing being measured."

Concerning His followers, Jesus Christ proclaimed, "He that believeth on me, the works that I do, shall he do also; and greater works than these shall he do..." (John 14:12). Jesus must have had very few actual followers in the America of the twentieth century, because after the Creation and Destruction of Primordial Matter (atomic incineration) at the 33rd degree Trinity Site in New Mexico (the "Land of Enchantment"), in 1945, it was the Killing of the King rite at masonic Dealey Plaza, near the Triple Underpass and on the 32nd degree of north parallel latitude, on November 22, 1963, that *catapulted our nation into a psychic Oz from which we have yet to emerge. The virtuoso managers of the once-and-future-America-as-crime-scene, have gone from victory to victory,* in what until recently was supposed to have been "a Christian nation."

If this writer has learned anything over the course of more than forty years of sleuthing secret languages and coded messages, mass shootings and serial killings, it is that a unit of the Cryptocracy inside the United States government propitiates dark forces with human sacrifices, such as occurred

---

[7] *New York Times,* July 25, 2020. In the play and movie "Harvey" by Mary Chase, a character named Dowd has an evanescent fairy companion, a giant rabbit who renders him invulnerable to harm.

with Son of Sam, Hillside Strangler, Double Initial, Columbine High School, the Aurora Colorado theater, and in Las Vegas, in front of the shimmering pomps and sleazy props of Pharaonic Egypt.

Law enforcement in this country did not arrest and convict the actual killers of John or Bobby Kennedy, Martin Luther King or Malcolm X. The elite perpetrators of the September 11, 2001 attacks, the rapists and suffocaters of the little girls of Rochester, New York; the planners of the Aurora shootings, the perps and commanders of the Las Vegas mass-murder, have all walked free.

Except for the Swartzentruber Amish and members of cognate "primitive" Anabaptist groups, certain non-Amish off-grid wilderness folks, and that rare breed who can live *in* a city without being *of* the city, the vast majority of those who reside in North America, the British isles, Ireland, Europe, Canada, Australia and New Zealand, are occult-processed to such an extent that they have the status of occult initiates.

The masses of people have been immersed in enough twilight language communication that many can see it for what it is, though in most cases they will not admit this to themselves or others.

This is not a book of who to blame for this state of affairs: Jews, blacks, immigrants, rednecks, Rothschilds or Republicans. The "blame," if one may use such a word in this context, is fairly evenly distributed among the millions of human beings who choose to comprise the United States of Amnesia, of Apathy; of eerie indifference.

"Just a Little Bit Crazy"

Howling Madness Spouted After Sept. 11, 2001

"We Have Forgotten How to Hate"

"Today I will surprise you by complaining about how we have forgotten how to hate. The proper response to the cowardly brutes who perpetrated the horrific attacks against America is to hate them with every fiber of our being and purge ourselves of any morsel of sympathy which might seek to understand their motives. The only way to react to incorrigible evil is to wage an incessant war against it...and to hope they find no rest, neither in this world nor in the next...the purpose of our hatred is not revenge, but preservation of justice...we track them down because G-d at Sinai entrusted us with the promotion of justice, turning the jungle into a civilized society....

"Only if we hate the truly evil passionately will we summon the determination to fight them fervently. Odd and uncomfortable as it may seem, hatred has its place...Let us make sure, therefore, that we never make the mistake of forgiving those whose sin is so inextricably woven with their rotten character that the two can never be separate."

— Shmuel Boteach, the Lubavitcher Rabbi of Oxford University.

Americans Will Welcome a Police State

"Probes from the 1970s investigations led by Sen. Frank Church...have crippled intelligence gathering and covert operations...Human intelligence capabilities suffered as CIA agents wishing to pose as journalists or recruit informants with criminal backgrounds face a daunting internal approval process...unshackle our intelligence agencies.

"The absurd rules aimed at...preventing U.S. involvement in assassinations have no place...Americans will greet wider surveillance, detention for questioning...and many other precautions with relief and unified public support."

— Daniel J. Popeo, Washington Legal Foundation

Don't Rule Out Using Nuclear Weapons

"In the excellent words of Paul Wolfowitz, deputy secretary of defense, we must 'end states who sponsor terrorism.'...It must be fought with the most effective weapons we possess (a few weeks ago, Rumsfeld refused, correctly, to rule out nuclear weapons). And it must be fought in a manner that secures victory as quickly as possible...regardless of the countless innocents caught in the line of fire. These innocents suffer and die because of the action of their own government in sponsoring the initiation of force against America..."

— Leonard Peikoff, Ayn Rand Institute, in a full page advertisement published in the *New York Times*, October 2, 2001.

Ally with Drug Cartels and the Russian Mafia

"We need to be really focused, really serious, and just a little bit crazy...terrorists and their supporters need to know that from here forward we will do whatever it takes...it takes a home-grown network to destroy a home-grown network...

"Actually, we would enlist the drug cartels. They have the three attributes we need: they know how to operate as a covert network and how to root out a competing network, such as Mr. bin Laden's. They can be bought and know how to buy others.

"And they understand that when we say we want someone 'dead or alive' we mean 'dead or dead.'

"The Cali cartel doesn't operate in Afghanistan. But the Russian mafia sure does, as do various Afghan factions, drug rings...Something tells me Mr. Putin, the Russian president and former K.G.B. spymaster, has the phone number of the guy in the Russian mafia who knows the guy in the Afghan cartels who knows the guy who...knows where Mr. bin Laden is hiding.

"It is going to be that kind of war...an underground network you fight with moles and exterminators....right now is the season of hunting down people..."

— Thomas Friedman, *New York Times* columnist, winner of the National Book Award and the Pulitzer Prize. *New York Times,* September 28, 2001.

The Twin Tower Game of 21

"The appearance of the Sentinel from '2001' at the beginning of the year 2001 and the century it symbolizes (the 21st), marks the symbolic end of the preparatory-processing phase intended to program us into accepting the appearance of the devil himself as our presiding Overlord...The process...culminates in a hermetic game of hazard or 'chance,' 21..This principle corresponds to...the 2001 gateway to the '21' epoch." *Secret Societies and Psychological Warfare 2001*, published July 2001, pp. 15-16.

The attack on the World Trade Center is represented in the Rider-Waite Tarot cards by the number 16 Tower card, and the attack on the five-sided Pentagon by the Tarot's number five of Pentacles. Sixteen plus five equals twenty-one.

The Rider-Waite Tarot deck was first published in 1910 by Rider and Co. in Great Britain. It was designed by the English Freemason Arthur Edward Waite (1857-1943). Waite was the author of *The Holy Kabbalah: A Mystical Interpretation*; *A New Encyclopedia of Freemasonry*, and *The Secret Tradition in Freemasonry: An Analysis of the Inter-Relation Between the Craft and the High Grades*. Waite was one of the founders of the Order of the Golden Dawn.

The number 16 assigned to the Tower card symbolizes the so-called *sectio aurea* ("Golden Section"), Golden Ratio or Golden Number, known as *Phi* (after the 21st letter in the Greek alphabet).

Since the early Greeks, a ratio of length to width of approximately 1.6 has been considered the most aesthetically pleasing in the construction of monumental architecture. Fibonacci numbers are also anchored by 1.6. The ratio of successive Fibonacci numbers gets continuously closer to this "Golden Ratio of Phi." No matter what two numerical values are used, if Fibonacci terms are employed to continue the series, the ratio of the two terms will always be the Golden Ratio of 1.6 etc.

The same is true for the Lucas numbers: 1, 3, 4, 7, 11, 18, 29, 49 etc. The Lucas sequence is made in the same manner as Fibonacci numbers. One obtains each number by adding together the two previous (1 + 3 = 4; 3+ 4 = 7 etc.). If we take pairs of Lucas numbers and divide the higher by the lower we get the same first two 1 6 numbers every time: 18/11 = 1.6363.

29/18 = 1.6111.   47/29 = 1.6206, ever more progressively approaching the Golden Mean (1.6180339887).

In other words, all of these mathematical roads lead to the basic building block of 1.6, which the Kabbalist Waite represented as 16 in his depiction of the downfall of the Grand Architect's construction, i.e. the fall of the Tower of Babel and all subsequent Babels.

All that goes up must eventually come down, but in most cases the fall is the slow crumbling of decay. Whereas, what is built with god-like conceit—the occult "Edifice Complex"—will fall catastrophically. If Freemasons know this, then why do they continue to propitiate their "Grand Architect" and their rivalry with God? We would answer, conceit does not necessarily imply ignorance. The greatest deviltry is performed fully conscious of the consequences. Truth or consequences = the 33rd degree.

The downfall of the tower in the inferno of September 11 (9/11) is the 911 emergency call to the psyche of the Group Mind, unleashing imprisoned energy. A burst of illuminated consciousness was released on 9/11. Properly channeled and directed, this Group Mind energy is harnessed to produce conditions for the imposition of an even more enormous and conceited tower. Every successive Babel is more towering than the previous one, thus does the imposing empire of the Grand Architect "build bigger" from out of the ruins of the old.

The only thing not destroyed in the towering inferno is the principle that built it, symbolized by the number 11, which stays the same even when written upside down. This principle is further elaborated in alchemical imagery by the salamander, the legendary creature that paradoxically thrives in fire.

At the other end of the equation is the five-sided Pentagon, representing both the cosmic force of the five-pointed "blazing star" which, according to Scottish Rite Supreme Commander Albert Pike symbolizes for the Freemasons the "dog star" Sirius, and which was personified in Egypt as *Set-An* (Satan); as well as by the door through which *Set-an*'s power manifests on earth, in the form of the exploitation of the feminine principle of "wounded but undying Nature," under the occult veil of Isis: she who bleeds and is not injured; she who bleeds and does not die. *The divine menstruant is represented numerically by the mean number of days in the menstrual cycle, five.*

The union of the exploding phallic tower (16) and the wounded but functioning pentagon (5) comprises an equation totaling 21, e.g. the point in the flow of time where the process manifests—the 2(00)1 gateway to the 21st century epoch—the age appointed for the corporeal manifestation of the Overlord in "masonic progression": from twenty years ago in 2001, to 2021, where the Overlord walks among us only partially concealed under a flimsy and threadbare cloak which is becoming progressively more transparent, and whose civic acceptance is prophesied to be virtually universal.

According to Gordon Moog of the United Supreme Grand Chapter of Mark and Royal Arch Masons, "The symbolism of Passing the Veils is that enlightenment which comes from Masonic progression...the entire object of alchemic art 'is the uncovering of the inner faculty of insight and wisdom and the removal of the veils intervening between the mind, and dividing it from its hidden Divine root'...the lifting of each veil is accomplished by giving a password..."

This magnum opus represents a departure from the incremental processing of the masses which has hitherto, with a few spectacular exceptions, been the Cryptocracy's modus operandi. Recently it became the process of conditioning through climax, where timing is key. It was necessary to initiate an anti-climax, a planetary false alarm in the form of the Y2K panic, which hundreds of millions of people were duped into believing:

"In relation to the end of one millennium and the beginning of the new one, we see the familiar outline of anti-climax and climax. A legion of false prophets and con-men, who wore an anti-Establishment mantle, but whose views were trumpeted by the Establishment, predicted financial collapse in 1999 and the 'end of civilization as we know it' in 2000, and these soothsayers raised both the physiological and psychological adrenaline of the masses, in some cases to fever pitch in what became an anti-climax of the apocalypse.

"...But the Cryptocracy had rather clearly, through the medium of its anointed prophets, such as Arthur C. Clarke, signaled to initiates and those percipients whose alertness is sufficient to qualify them as self-initiates, that 2001 would serve as the climax entry point for the epoch of human alchemy..." [8]

The miscued *goyim,* with their charlatan Nostradamus, were paralyzed as they passively spectated at the end of 1999 and the dawn of 2000, looking for discernment concerning the future of nature. The 2001 advertising slogan of the giant, Frankenfood agri-business, ADM (Archer-Daniels Midland) gives an initiate's hint at the deterministic contours of the Merlinesque "inevitability" game that is being played. Their corporate motto is, "ADM: The Nature of the Future."

---

[8] Hoffman, *Secret Societies and Psychological Warfare*, p. 13.

Writing in April 2001 (and published in the July edition of *Secret Societies and Psychological Warfare*), we analyzed the making of the atomic bomb from the point of view of occult ceremony. We further cited the propagation of the theory of evolution in fashioning the Cryptocracy's degraded "New Man." In the aftermath of the attacks on the World Trade Center and the Pentagon, Evolutionism's high-priest, Harvard Prof. Stephen Jay Gould, used atomic terminology to refer to the ruins of the Trade Center as "ground zero" and to make reference to "the largest human structure ever destroyed in a catastrophic moment." (*New York Times*, September 26, 2001).

Prof. Gould's arcane "ground zero" cue, (which is now the standard term for the devastated Trade Center site), leads us to a key dictum of atomic physics, the point at which Merlin meets Einstein, "Time relations among events are assumed to be first constituted by the specific physical relations obtaining between them."

This dictum is Camelot arcana restated in scientific jargon, thereby making it more palatable to the post-modern mentality that would scoff at Merlin but embrace Einstein. The underlying principle is the same, however: "...to orient us to the space-time conjunction necessary to the maintenance of the once-and-future inevitability of the Cryptocracy's Camelot allegory." [9]

Gould's imagery recalls that other "largest human structure ever destroyed in a catastrophic moment," the Tower of Babel. Perhaps he was covertly signaling that those who built the World Trade Center were involved in idolatry, because the edifice was another Babel, the "largest human structure ever destroyed in a catastrophic moment" (since Babel).

One peers at the ground zero made at the World Trade Center and glimpses the ruins of a modern Babel, summoning Biblical eschatology. The apocalyptic age, the 21 hazard era, came not in the snare of 1999/2000 as focused for the *goyim* by the Establishment and its useful idiots, but in Year One of the final millennium, at the 21st century gateway which is the 2(00)1 space (time) odyssey to the greatest battlefield of all, the cosmic war between alien scale and human scale, between the anti-Christ reign of number and the Holy Spirit realm of poetic serendipity.

---

[9] Ibid, p. 16.

All this was *consciously* lost on our yahoo friends and neighbors who were deep into a predictable, first-stage pattern of a formulaic spasm of "patriotic" war-fever and self-righteous drivel post-September 11, 2001, through the early stages of the Afghanistan and Iraq invasions. We qualify their perception with the word "consciously" because, as in the aftermath of the Cryptocracy's last great climax in the management of masonic progression—the JFK assassination—there is a sub-rosa, shadow side to the flag-waving persona propelled out of the smoldering ruins of the Twin Towers' "double day" of 11 September, which planted seeds of doubt and wonder deep in the subconscious of Americans.

Of course 21st century Americans are not 1950s Americans; they have been run through the mill that is the psychedelic funhouse ritual rollercoaster, ever since that other "double day" on the calendar of America mystica, the 22nd of November, 1963. In whose wake:

"...the American people were forced to confront a scary alternative reality, the reality of a shadow government over which they had neither control or knowledge. The shepherding process was thus accelerated with a vengeance. Avant-garde advertising, music, politics and news would hereafter depict (especially in the electronic media)— sometimes fleetingly, sometimes openly—a "shadow side" of reality, an underground, amoral 'funhouse' current associated with extreme sex, extreme violence and extreme speed. The static images of the suit-and-tie talking heads of Establishment religion, government, politics and business were subtly shown to be subordinate to the Shadow State, which the American people were gradually getting a bigger glimpse of, out of the corner of their collective eye. The interesting function of this phenomenon is that it simultaneously produces both terror and adulation and undercuts any offensive against it among percipients, which does not possess the same jump-cut speed and funhouse ambiance." [10]

The same freeze-thaw cryonic process is gnawing into the official fabric of the events of September 11. In the subterranean layers of the psyche of even the most convinced Bush-booster and Fed-fan was a corner-of-the eye glimpse of the twin at work. An ancient tradition of occult governance

---

[10] Ibid, p. 86.

holds that the actual ruler does not show himself until his power becomes absolute. Instead, such a ruler's invisible, omniscient presence pervades the land and all consciousness like a shadow.

This sense of hidden rulers behind the figurehead presidents and prime ministers has bored deep into the consciousness of the American people. The attack on the New York Towers and the District of Columbia Pentagon, constitute an electrifying, lightning-like revelation that always accompanies the disruption of mundane routine when overturned by sudden chaos and explosive realignment.

In the presence of this overthrow, the reaction in the percipient is a burst of momentary, X-ray like perception—illuminating what was hidden by glimpsing it in a flash of insight—such as was experienced at Ground Zero at the site/sight of the first atomic incineration.

The shocking perception is subsequently suppressed and denied through the chatter of innumerable talking-head spin doctors, who impose approved "solutions" and expert "explanations."

Hence, slowly and inexorably, excruciating tension builds between the public world of the suit-and-tie solvers-and-explainers with their phonograph-record parroting of the restricted official line — and the Sirius B-side of the record, with its shadows and spectres which hint at the dark truth about the Towering Inferno and the wounded Pentagon and for that matter, the wounded head of John Fitzgerald Kennedy.

A population torn between these two extremes may be said to mirror the psychiatric state termed "bipolar."

Since 2001 these insights have been leaked to the masses by the Establishment itself, in bits and pieces. The frigid 2001 Officialspeak which assailed us from every televiewer has been thawed. Truths about the attacks have flooded the public consciousness, long after effective counteraction has been rendered inoperable; thereby doubling the god-like awe in which the hidden rulers are held, until such time as their power is finally absolute. At that point in their game, the Overlord, "Black Jack," is set to assume public, universal, physical manifestation.

An unspoken, indeed, dare-not-be-spoken, insight was propelled in the psychic pressure cooker ignited on September 11, 2001: the impression that a hidden force was behind the

Pentagon and Trade Center Towers' "special operation," a force much bigger and more powerful than "Arab terrorists." This force was hypnotically suggested not so much by the actual person of the double bin Laden (Osama and Usama), but by the imagery which bin Laden's icon invoked, that of the turbaned seer from the East, whose crystal ball and oracular powers are foreshadowed rather than stated.

This was the trance state induced in the masses, who, in keeping with Revelation-of-the-Method elements outlined in *Secret Societies and Psychological Warfare*, experience certain dream-like, hypnotic cues dropped by the media and the government, suggesting that in special operations of this type it is necessary that they should be deceived by their media and their government; indeed that it is necessary that high officials of the United States government lie to the American people:

"Special operations by their nature are cloaked in secrecy and deception making it impossible to know whether officials who discuss them obliquely are being completely candid." ("Bush Assures Hot Pursuit," *New York Times,* September 29, 2001, p. B4).

The bipolar made visible:

"Last week Secretary of Defense Donald Rumsfeld held a news conference in which he quoted Winston Churchill, 'In wartime truth is so precious that she should always be attended by a bodyguard of lies.' The Pentagon later issued a clarification that Rumsfeld did not mean to imply the government would lie. Yet that seems to be exactly what Rumsfeld was saying." (*Los Angeles Times,* October 11, 2001).

Rumsfeld did not mean to imply the government would lie. Yet that seems to be exactly what Rumsfeld was saying.

In addition to lying to us "for national security reasons," we have also been informed that the special operation, the "game of 21" and that which emanates from it in concentric rings, entail psychological warfare: "...the United States is planning extensive psychological operations..." (*New York Times,* October 3, 2001, p. B4). "The Pentagon also has begun deploying forces to mount psychological operations, or 'psy-ops'..." (*Wall Street Journal,* October 4, 2001, p. 1).

Where, in any of these reports, was there any assurance that the American people were not themselves targets of these operations? On the contrary, the fleeting allusions to the necessity of deception, psychological warfare and psy-ops would seem to hint that no one will be exempt in the mind games dragnet, least of all the taxpayers who fund it.

Psychological warfare operations were launched after September 11 to pre-empt revolt against continued U.S. collusion with the Israelis, and more seriously, revolt arising from inquiry into U.S. government involvement in the attacks.

Hints were dropped, ostensibly about bin Laden, but in fact concerning "our" own elite. For example, "The White House told the media to be careful of broadcasting videos of bin Laden or his lieutenants, saying they could contain coded messages..." (Associated Press, October 11, 2001). Yet when campaigners against Hollywood and Madison Avenue manipulation attempted to document the existence of coded messages and subliminals in Establishment videos and advertising, they were dismissed as paranoid cranks.

George W. Bush's own staffers were caught inserting subliminals into Bush advertisements during the presidential campaign. The American-based Cryptocracy regularly uses seemingly run-of-the-mill news conferences, book illustrations, audio recordings and films to send coded messages. The technique is as old as cryptography, as venerable as the 16th century painting, "Shepherds of Arcadia" by Nicolas Poussin, or of the Victorian artist Walter Sickert, who incorporated clues to the identity of the masonic Jack the Ripper killer in his "Camden Town" paintings.

Detecting the Great Game

Andrea Mitchell of NBC News reported on national television on September 19, 2001 that certain financiers had advance knowledge of the catastrophe and profited from the fall of airline, insurance and brokerage stocks through the purchase of "put options." Mitchell was a bit more authoritative than your average media dork, in that she was at that time the spouse of Federal Reserve Bank Chairman Alan Greenspan.

On September 10, thousands of put options on American Airlines were purchased on the Chicago exchange, worth over $4 million after September 11. Numerous put options were also placed on United Airlines stock in the week before September 11. Morgan Stanley Dean Witter & Co., which occupied 22 floors of the World Trade Center, had over 2,000 of its put options bought in the three trading days before 9/11. This compares with an average of only two dozen contracts per day in the first week of September. This deal too represents millions for the investors involved. A similar pattern was observed with Merrill Lynch & Co. stock, as well as insurance stocks. The identity of the investors has, as of this writing, not been divulged.

The firm that was used to place the put options on United Airlines was, until recently, managed by the man who served as the number three executive of the CIA, A.B. "Buzzy" Krongard, the former chairman of the A.B. Brown investment bank. A.B. Brown was acquired by Banker's Trust in 1997. As part of the merger, Krongard became Vice Chairman of Banker's Trust-AB Brown. In 1998 Krongard joined the CIA, and advanced rapidly to a position as special counsel to CIA Director George *Tenet*.

In addition to the money web in the respectable corporate world of high finance, there is the "evil twin" which spins a web of symbiosis in a mocking, carnival milieu. Ringling Brothers and Barnum and Bailey Circus traveled in two separate units, the Red Circus and the Blue Circus. The U.S. military's psychodrama teams are divided into the Red team and the Blue teams. The *Wall Street Journal* reported: "Mind Games...U.S. Military 'Red Teams' Adopt Enemy Identities..." (October 2, 2001 p. 1). The *Journal* stated that during these "mind games" the U.S. Military's Red team kills its own people, including women and children, then "seeds the landscape with the bodies...when the first reporters and CNN cameramen arrive... (they) announce..." that the enemy did it. (October 2, 2001 p. A12, column 2).

We asked a question in the immediate aftermath of September 11: how many of the System's top luminaries disappeared in the collapse of the World Trade Center, which was home to the New York offices of the FBI, the CIA, the Secret Service and the ATF? How many members of the elite survived the Pentagon crash, an attack which gave wide berth to Secretary of Defense Donald Rumsfeld's offices and the nerve centers of the Pentagon? (The "airliner" [or missile] struck a relatively thinly staffed portion of the Pentagon that had been undergoing renovation).

This writer has only been able to identify two of the System's top functionaries among the victims: the wife of U.S. Solicitor General Ted Olsen, who supposedly died on Flight 77, and

John O'Neill, retired FBI commander who was the intelligence chief in charge of Trade Tower security from his 23rd floor command post.

O'Neill had previously ran the 1993 World Trade Center bombing "investigation." However, like FBI commander William Sullivan who was shot to death by U.S. intelligence because he knew too much about the JFK assassination, O'Neill may have been allowed to perish because he knew a good deal more about FBI culpability in the 1993 bombing than was healthy:

"One of the largest acts of domestic terrorism in U.S. history was the 1993 bombing of the World Trade Center in New York. As it turned out, the FBI was fully aware of the bomb plot before the attack took place. The Muslim group involved had been infiltrated by Emad Salem, a former Egyptian intelligence agent who was hired by the FBI and ultimately paid $1 million. The FBI even provided the Egyptian with a timer for the bomb, prompting the *Chicago Tribune* to publish a report headlined: 'FBI Tipster Said He Built NY Bomb" (*Chicago Tribune*, December 15, 1993).

The Establishment quickly mocked and then dismissed as an "urban legend" the report that Israelis were tipped in advance of the attack on the Trade Center in Manhattan. The account was derided as coming from the "Arab rumor mill." The September 16, 2001 edition of the *Jerusalem Post* reported: "The Foreign Ministry in Jerusalem has so far received the names of 4,000 Israelis believed to have been in the areas of the World Trade Center and the Pentagon...Army Radio reported."

But no 4,000 Israelis have been reported missing by the American media. Did thousands of Judaic persons save themselves due to an advance warning, in part from an Israeli electronic message service? As reported by the Hebrew language newspaper *Ha'aretz*, in a story headlined, "Odigo says workers were warned of attack," we read:

"Odigo, the instant messaging service, says that two of its workers received messages two hours before the Twin Towers attack on September 11 predicting the attack would happen, and the company has been cooperating with Israeli and American law enforcement, including the FBI, in trying to find the original sender of the message predicting the attack...Odigo (is a) well-known Israeli instant messaging application." (*Ha'aretz,* October 1, 2001).

There have also been accounts ("urban rumors") of a group of Israelis videotaping the Trade Tower attacks as they happened. That report is also from *Ha'aretz* newspaper: "5 Israelis detained for 'puzzling behavior': "Five Israelis who had worked for a moving company based in New Jersey are being held in U.S. prisons for what the Federal Bureau of Investigation has described as 'puzzling behavior' following the terror attack on the World Trade Center in New York last Tuesday.

"The five are expected to be deported...The families of the five, who asked that their names not be released, said that their sons had been...kept in solitary confinement...The mother of one of the young men explained the chain of events as she understands it to *Ha'aretz*: she said that the five had worked for the company, which is owned by an Israeli, for between two months and two years.

"They had been arrested some four hours after the attack on the Twin Towers while filming the smoking skyline from the roof of their company's building...The (Israeli) Foreign Ministry said in response that it had been informed by the consulate in New York that the FBI had arrested the five for 'puzzling behavior.' They are said to have had been caught videotaping the disaster and shouting in what was interpreted as cries of joy and mockery." (*Ha'aretz*, September 17, 2001).

The possibility that these Israelis filmed the first impact, and were taken into custody by the FBI after an allegedly outraged witness caused the incident to be made public, fits a pattern.

Absent from the World Trade Center on September 11 was the Federal Reserve's New York President, William McDonough, who was in Switzerland at the time. Missing from Washington, D.C. on September 11 was Alan Greenspan who was also in Switzerland. Federal Reserve Governors Laurence Meyer (in China at the time); Edward Gramlich (visiting in Arizona) and Edward Kelley, who was "on vacation" at an undisclosed location, also missed the attack on New York and Washington D.C.

There are certain telltale indicators when a crime is an inside job. One of these is the failure of law enforcement to interview accessible witnesses who may have had contact with either the victims or the perpetrators. Ted Kaczynski, the "Unabomber," had been under FBI surveillance for years. We surmise that from its early stages the FBI was inside the Unabomber scenario. That is why, when a man matching descriptions of a radical environmentalist, turned up in Kaczynski's adopted hometown of Lincoln, Montana a few days after the arrest of Kaczynski, publicly espousing support for Kaczynski, the FBI did not bother to question or investigate the man. *Why would they? The FBI knew that Kaczynski's only accomplices were other government agents. There was no need to conduct an authentic investigation.*

Our investigation unearthed similar evidence of macabre indifference in the case of 9/11. We have spoken with a relative of a passenger on a flight departing Newark airport just after the hijacked United Flight 93 airliner departed for San Francisco. The passenger, a California executive in the publishing field, took time to look over the passengers on the doomed airliner bound for the earlier flight to California, to see if there anyone he knew. This eyewitness was not contacted by the FBI. His jet took off after the hijacked airliner, from a nearby gate. The FBI, while making a great show of "interviewing thousands" and following "tens of thousands of leads," didn't bother making contact with a prime witness, and others like him.

The year 2000 edition of *Criminal Acts Against Aviation*, published by the Federal Aviation Administration (FAA), cited bin Laden as a "significant threat to civil aviation, particularly to U.S. civil aviation." The warning was ignored by U.S. Law Enforcement. National Public Radio's Morning Edition reported on September 29, 2001 that the FBI knew before 9/11 that bin Laden-connected associates were training as pilots in the U.S. The U.S. spends $40 billion a year on the eleven intelligence agencies that comprise its huge secret police network; that's a total of $400 billion in the past ten years. Yet, the Bush Administration says it was taken by surprise.

On September 11 the "Arlington Road" script was implemented, as in the Oklahoma City ruse, where the patsy McVeigh was apprehended the day of the crime by means of self-incriminating license plates.

The Cryptocracy left no room for doubt as to who was to blame for the Trade Center and Pentagon attacks. *Within 10 minutes* of the second tower being hit, CNN declared Osama bin Laden had done it. Cell phones which were apparently impervious to interception only that morning, were suddenly yielding congratulatory phone calls to bin Laden's associates that afternoon.

By September 12 the U.S. government and media somehow had managed to obtain incriminating Arab-language flight manuals, Last Wills and Testaments of the hijackers, and copies of the *Quran* which turned up in the perpetrators' vehicles, or in luggage conveniently abandoned at Boston's Logan airport.

And what of the tale of quickly finding a passport bearing an alleged suicide bomber's real identity, in the vast World Trade Center rubble, before it had barely been sifted?

As in the Oklahoma City dramaturgy, self-incriminating "evidence" was swiftly and conveniently "discovered" in order to imprint the Group Mind with a lasting "first impression," while evidence of official involvement was made to disappear, such as where were the American military's air defense fighter jets after the first tower was attacked?

Placing the High Stakes Black Jack Wager

Those who engineer the reign of dead matter over humanity are virtuoso risk-takers. Placing the high stakes Black Jack wager is part of their DNA. On Monday, June 5, in the year 2006, on page A19 of the *New York Times*, the "newspaper of record" read by millions, the Cryptocracy inserted the following advertisement in the form of a news report for a highly disruptive, indeed revolutionary counter-narrative of the 9/11 terror attacks. [11] In an article that comprised nearly one-third of the page, the *Times* reported:

"Such was the coming-out for the movement known as '9/11 Truth,' a society of skeptics and scientists who believe the government was complicit in the terrorist attacks.

"In colleges and chat rooms, this band of disbelievers has been trying for years to prove that 9/11 was an inside job."

The article asked:

"...how the building at World Trade Center 7" (which wasn't hit by an aircraft) "collapsed like a ton of bricks."

---

[11] nytimes.com/2006/06/05/us/05conspiracy.html
The article that appeared in the print edition of the paper was titled, "For 9/11 Conspiracy Buffs, A Chance to Compare Notes." The same article online has a different headline, "500 Conspiracy Buffs Meet to Seek the Truth of 9/11." No imputation of wrong-doing or conspiracy is alleged concerning the author of the 2006 *New York Times* report.

The *New York Times* article of 2006 goes on to draw attention to incendiary facts that have been hotly denied by the *Times* and other legacy media ever since:

"...the military command that monitors aircraft 'stood down' on the day of the attacks" and "the towers did not collapse because of burning fuel and weakened steel but because of a 'controlled demolition' caused by pre-set bombs."

The *Times* went to far as to publicize a dissenting technical "report written by Steven E. Jones, a professor of physics at Brigham Young University (BYU) and the movement's expert in the matter of (building) collapse."

The "newspaper of record" even provided the correct Internet URL (which was an active link online in 2006), containing Dr. Jones' rigorous scientific critique of the official engineering analysis of the collapse of the Twin Towers that had been issued by the National Institute of Standards and Technology: physics.byu.edu/research/energy/htm7.html

(The link was removed some years later by BYU).

As of this writing, other than the assassination of the President of the United States in daylight in masonic Dealey Plaza, no spectacular crime has so stimulated the collective psyche of the American people as that which occurred on September 11, 2001. Consequently, it was a perilous Revelation of the Method gamble in 2006 for the Cryptocracy to point to the Internet location of the painstaking and meticulous critique by Prof. Steven E. Jones, a credentialed academic, of the 9/11 tale as told by the government and an overwhelming majority of the corporate media.

Here is a matter of life and death: establishing that the towers were brought down by explosives as part of a controlled demolition and not as a result of the impact of the two jet aircraft striking the "Twin Towers." Unraveling the official tale, and proceeding to apprehend and prosecute the actual planners, perpetrators and concealers of the terror attacks, would represent a solar high wind of cleansing power blown through America.

Consider this: less than six years after the September 11 attacks, on June 5, 2006 readers of the *New York Times* were handed a key to the puzzle palace. What did they do with it?

Next to nothing.

There was no great groundswell of sustained activism. After receiving this revelation, the millions of percipients continued their drowsy ramble deep into The Process, as the Black Jack players had gambled on them doing, cognizant that an astonishing revelation that does not produce a mighty movement arising in reaction to the alarming public manifestation of high crimes and misprisions, instills deeper hypnosis, paralysis, demoralization, misdirection and confusion in the target audience.

Howard Dean: Bush Knew

Memory refresh: the 2006 Revelation of the Method by the *New York Times* was preceded in 2003 by another.

Former Vermont Governor "Howard Dean, whose penchant for off-the-cuff comments has proved both a strength and political liability, is facing a new flap over suggestions that President Bush had advance knowledge of the September 11 terrorist attacks...

"Dean suggested Bush 'is suppressing evidence' that could aid the Kean Commission in its reconstruction of events leading to the terrorist attacks. Leaders of the commission — which is headed by former New Jersey Gov. Thomas H. Kean — have complained that the Bush administration has been too slow to provide access to key documents, and has intimidated witnesses by insisting that CIA and FBI observers attend sensitive interviews. The president has declined to turn over highly classified intelligence reports to the panel, despite threats of a subpoena (*Los Angeles Times*, December 9, 2003).

Diane Rehm: "Why do you think he (Bush) is suppressing that (September 11) report?"

Howard Dean: "I don't know. There are many theories about it. The most interesting theory that I"ve heard so far — which is nothing more than a theory, it can't be proved — is that he was warned ahead of time by the Saudis. Now who knows what the real situation is?" [12]

"Bush called it an 'absurd insinuation' to raise questions, as (Howard) Dean did recently, about whether the president had advance knowledge of the September 11 attacks." (Associated Press, December 15, 2003).

This statement by Mr. Dean, who at the time was former Vice-President Al Gore's anointed presidential candidate, and

---

[12] Transcript of remarks broadcast on the "Diane Rehm Show," NPR (National Public Radio), December 1, 2003.

the insipid response from Bush, might signify that a bold gamble by the Establishment was afoot to leak the fact that the Bush administration was implicated in the 9/11 attacks.

The Fabulous Doublecross of His Satanic Majesty

A familiar pattern in the Revelation of the Method is to leak bits and pieces of evidence of criminal conspiracy and then ensure that the perpetrator gives vague answers, or talks around the subject, as George W. Bush did. The goal of the Revelation is to desensitize Americans to the fact of Bush's complicity in 9/11 by exposing them to an intermittent, occasionally dramatic, but mostly low-level buzz. By this conditioning process, awareness of Bush's connivance gradually becomes absorbed into the din of The Process, morphing into the sub-strata of the digital-psychedelic funhouse.

The slowly dawning revelation of Bush's treason becomes not a basis for indictment and prosecution, but a sideshow for the game zone's sarcastic management simulator, a macabre, yet perversely sexy rumor-mill that burnishes Bush's potency and aura, and plays on people's jaded sense of awe in the presence of a "Satanic Majesty" who commands such power that he can successfully mount a fabulous doublecross and still thrive.

The crimes of the Cryptocracy are leaked by the Cryptocracy itself, in part to trivialize them by embedding them within our high-speed electronic freakshow clown culture. 9/11 has become one such phenomenon and President George W. Bush's involvement in the conspiracy has morphed into a fetish of power, accompanied by the subconscious sense that, "If he did allow 9/11 to happen, he did so for our own good."

Consider the Pearl Harbor con. One of the first to penetrate that charade was John Toland in his 1982 book. *Infamy*. The *New York Times* passed sentence on the truth that Toland (and many others) uncovered, with this clever wordplay: "Toland said he had turned up evidence to conclude that Roosevelt had known in advance of Japan's impending attack but failed to inform the naval command in the Pacific in the hope of rousing America from its isolationism. This view put him (Toland) at odds with a series of official federal investigations and historians who said Roosevelt *may have made errors in judgment but neither knew about nor encouraged the attack.*" *(New York Times* January 7, 2004, emphasis supplied).

Get the picture? 1. The Establishment instructs us to believe that Toland is wrong because he is "at odds" with an official consensus. 2. As damage control, the Establishment paradoxically concedes that something about the official line is flawed, but that this flaw consists only in "errors in judgment," not a criminal conspiracy.

In a similar vein, who today believes that, as William N. Grimstad phrased it, "one lone assassin and one very talented rifle bullet" were responsible for the assassination of President Kennedy? Yet the surviving conspirators were never brought to justice. The Cryptocracy has seen to it that while a JFK assassination conspiracy is broadly acknowledged, the issue has become so muddled that Americans have a dizzying sense that "everybody killed Kennedy" — the anti-Castro exiles as well as the pro-Castro Communists; the CIA as well as the KGB; the Mafia and the Birchers.

In these crimes, the role of the Society-of-the-Spectacle's Videodrome is a crucial factor in neutralizing the hunt for perpetrators, by incorporating chatter about a government conspiracy into the infotainment machine. One doesn't seriously call for detectives and prosecutors inside a carnival funhouse. Instead, one marvels in "shock and awe" at the perverse wonder of the spectacle.

The Twin Tower Game of 21 shapes us as part of the continuing process of human alchemy into devolved species, the vaunted "new man" of the early decades of the 21st century, who has since been coagulated into the contemporary laboratory phase of the suppression of nature, wherein recognition of the organic differences between humans possessed of XX chromosomes and those with XY, is proscribed hate speech. Very little of this process would have been possible had the murder pageants, ceremonial bombings and towering infernos been thoroughly and freely investigated, prosecuted and otherwise challenged by intrepid women and men holding positions of power and authority in journalism, law enforcement, the judiciary and the church.

But the wimp factor in the churches is off the meter. The fraud factor in the salons of intellect and the groves of academe is beyond calculation. We are admonished to love thy American special forces golem, to fall down before them in abject quivering idolatry, or fear, as the occasion demands.

With each case of the successful conduct of their

spectacular public crimes, our not-so-hidden masters have been emboldened to proceed to the next stage of their civic diabolism. These thinly-veiled rites possess an inner dynamic which sweeps us along with the power of a psychic tide, in an explosion of communal conditioning which was given an incomparable boost from its 2001 launch pad. From the vantage of 2021, "Childhood's End" can no longer be said to be "hurtling toward us." *It's here.*

Freeze/Thaw: Reagan, Rumsfeld and Saddam

In this third decade of the 21st century Howard Dean is not so very infamous for asking in December of 2003 if "Bush knew." His query has merely smoldered. Mr. Dean gained brief infamy again with his observation that the world was no safer after Saddam Hussein had been captured in Iraq, than before. Which brings us to the other Revelation in the Method-that-is-their-Madness — the freeze/thaw process.

Prior to the American invasion of Iraq, the mountain of facts concerning Ronald Reagan and Donald Rumsfeld's alliance with Saddam Hussein were frozen solid. These facts almost never turned up as questions for Bush in any pre-Iraq-invasion presidential news conference of which we are aware. After the much-coveted Iraq invasion and occupation had been accomplished and the Zionists and "Christian" Zionists got what they wanted, the facts were thawed and headlines in Establishment newspapers blared, "Rumsfeld Made Iraq Overture in '84 Despite Chemical Raids" *(New Times,* December 23, 2003), and "Rumsfeld's '84 Visit was to Reassure Iraqis" *(Seattle Times* via *Washington Post,* December 19, 2003).

Too late! The hurly burlys done. This knowledge, publicized by the corporate media more than nine months after the invasion of Iraq had been accomplished, was at that point mostly ceremonial. It was deep frozen before the U.S. invasion of Iraq, then thawed by time-release after the war was launched. It functions as a kind of nose-thumbing at the peasants, "So Saddam used to be our ally. So what? It's none of your damn business, little man. Your business is to bleed and be taxed and stand in awe of the splendor of our five-pointed and six-pointed astral system."

Information that could have prevented the invasion is used after the invasion to "shock and awe" the minds of Americans.

The whispered reaction of the peasantry to the thawed facts is one of grudging admiration, "Wow, what a bunch of crooks, but hey, crooks *rule!*"

This psy-war component of American foreign policy is overlooked by the Left, which continues to ascribe the maintenance of support for Bush to antique propaganda methods pioneered by Fascist and Communist parties ninety years ago. The Establishment dismisses the reality of the government's psy-war with psychiatric jargon, [13] while a stew of competing conspiracy notions, often generated by the System itself to distract and confuse, proliferate.

As Moshe Goldstein noted, "Hussein's ouster by the U.S. was an afterthought following three decades of collusion." The CIA backed Saddam's Baath party coup in 1969. Reagan hosted Iraqi official Tariq Aziz at the White House. In 1982, the Senate Foreign Relations Committee acknowledged a U.S. alliance with Saddam, who received assistance from CIA director William Casey and Assistant Secretary of State Richard Murphy. $1 billion was overtly conveyed to Saddam through the Department of Agriculture's Commodity Credit Corporation. Covertly, Reagan funneled $4 billion to Saddam through the Atlanta branch of the Italian bank, Banca Nazionale del Lavoro. Under the auspices of the US-Iraq Business Forum, sponsored by the Reagan administration, corporate America, in particular Honeywell, Bechtel, Exxon, General Motors and Westinghouse, profited handsomely from trading with Saddam.

The Israelis had directed their American serfs to use Saddam against the Islamic Republic of Iran. Saddam was encouraged to go to war and invade Iran, resulting in eight years of war and one million casualties on the Iranian side. American media executives who praised Franklin Roosevelt and Harry Truman for insisting on "unconditional surrender" from Germany and Japan, continually lambasted Iran for making the same demand of the Iraqi invaders. Saddam's reward for devastating a fellow Muslim nation on behalf of the Israeli-American bloc was supposed to have been Kuwait.

---

[13] Fifty-six years after its publication in 1965, Columbia University Prof. Richard Hofstadter's *The Paranoid Style in American Politics* continues to serve as the Establishment's manual for diagnosing the mental illness of anyone to the Right of Bob Dole who proposes that the U.S. government engages in criminal conspiracies involving mind control and assassinations.

Moshe Goldstein reports, "It was actually U.S. diplomacy under George Bush Sr.'s presidency that gave Hussein the perception of a green light for his 1990 (Kuwait) aggression."

From the transcript of U.S. Ambassador April Glaspie's remarks to Saddam while he had his troops massed on the Kuwait border, a few days before he invaded Kuwait:

"We have no opinion on your Arab-Arab conflicts, such as your dispute with Kuwait. Secretary (of State James) Baker has directed me to emphasize the instruction, first given to Iraq in the 1960's, that the Kuwait issue is not associated with America."

Of course, Saddam did not receive Kuwait as his recompense for making war on Iran on behalf of the agenda of President George H.W. Bush. He was sucker-baited into the attempt. Saddam was a prize chump in George W. Bush's war depicting him as the fiendish enemy of the American Way; a foe brought to justice by Donald Rumsfeld and the Neocon ideological heirs of Ronald Reagan. Actually, Saddam was part of the post-JFK American Way: the doublecross and plausible denial in the freeze stage—and bragging rights and Revelation of the Method during the thaw.

By every metric of spiritual and psychological disturbance— deep depression, anxiety, despair, childlessness, divorce, drug addiction, alcoholism and suicide—Americans are a radically unhappy people, despite often concealing their condition behind a skillfully maintained persona of a satisfied, if occasionally beleaguered life. Maintaining that facade is a burden that creates more psychic fault-lines. Many tens of millions of Americans harbor a collective death wish which stokes the revival, and consequent psychic energy, of the 3500 year-old Pharaonic death cult.

Let us, therefore, spare ourselves reciting rigamarole about of this or that "occult superpower behind the mysteries of history" as if it were news to the public. This is the 21st century, five hundred years into the western occult and its intensified application of The Process. The future has, in a sense, already occurred, and at present our stage of the alchemical program is post-history, in which there are no mysteries except the ones we conceal from ourselves, lest we break the bonds of the enchantment. We can see hell on the horizon, and we do little or nothing to forestall it; in fact, many of our actions serve to facilitate or even welcome it.

We have an inkling that many "random lone nut serial killings" are in fact ceremonial murders performed as propitiation and conditioning. We have a troubling, lingering sense that many hundreds of perfectly "respectable, moderate" government officials, police, media editors and politicians are co-conspirators in the terror psychodrama. Yet, we play along. We drift along, rudderless, leaderless.

If Satan himself were to land in a starship on the lawn of the White House, Americans would be electrified back to life for several weeks, after which their life force would slowly return to its 30-watt steady state, and the search would be resumed for the Next Big Thrill necessary to again jolt our minds and bodies into momentarily approximating the consciousness of the fully human beings of the past.

There's no place to hide from our responsibility and this book will not provide cover where none is possible.

Some are perhaps reading this text to obtain an amnesiac's thrill: How close does Hoffman come to revealing the ultimate secret? How can anyone forget that some readers and reviewers said we performed that service in our 2001 volume? This 2021 work is not complicit in the masturbation of that vision.

Fertility Then and Now

The application of the blows by the one sex to the other, especially by young men to young women, suggests that the beating is or was originally intended above all to stimulate the reproductive powers of the men or women who received it; and the pains taken to ensure that the branches with which the strokes are given should have budded or blossomed out just before their services are wanted speak strongly in favour of the view that in these customs we have a deliberate attempt to transfuse a store of vital energy from the vegetable to the animal world.

James Frazer, *The Golden Bough: A Study in Magic and Religion* (Macmillan, 1935), volume 6, p. 272

Our 2001 writing was given a bit of stick by some for being "too Christian" and "obsessed with abortion." The groovy pagans wanted to be certain that their conférés understood that in recommending some of our cognition, they were putting obligatory distance between their elevated pagan consciousness and our occasional digression into "pathetic religious fundamentalism."

Pagan? Really? There are pagans in the West these days? Are we on the same page? Are we alluding to the pre-Christian Saxons, Danes and Druids, to the European vegetation folk with their pregnant goddess and her consort, the Green Man — those key elements comprising the vast majority of the paganism of western history?

That paganism is long dead and drowned, fathoms deep. It consisted of a giant and perpetual working, both magical and practical, for invoking and maintaining the inextricable link between the fertility of the people and the land.

The sterile, fetus-fearing and fetus-loathing wraiths haunting the contemporary milieu with their tattoos and anemic imitations of pre-industrial tribal people, are a shabby simulation of historic pagan humanity.

At what level of the sub-cellar of their consciousness do they grasp this truth and yet continue to act a part in the spirit-decaying charade?

It is not difficult to obtain the knowledge that the western paganism of history was a relentless and sometimes frenetic summoning of life in the womb of the woman, and the fertility of the land.

With the exception of an extraordinarily malevolent society such as the Pharaonic Egyptian, only a tiny fraction of the pagans of western history were outside the fertility paradigm and devoted to the deities of thanatos. Yet today western paganism is almost entirely thanatos.

Here we digress to anticipate an objection from the "white magic" pagans who will say they enthusiastically bless fertility and all life on earth.

By way of reply, we ask how many children do the women of your white magic pagan community average? We will bet dollars to doughnuts that the answer is an average of either zero, one or two.

Those tragic numbers are not reproductive. "White magic" pagans cannot reproduce themselves averaging zero, one or two births per woman.

Therefore, we regret to say, they are a death cult indulging in familiar self-deceiving rhetoric about "our love of fertility."

"Little Egypt"

As noted, Pharaonic Egypt was a death cult, and lo and behold we discover that swaths of the American south and midwest, from Memphis, Tennessee to Cairo, Illinois and points in-between, came to be known in the nineteenth century as "Little Egypt," with the Mississippi River reconfigured as the Nile. Much has been made of the innovations in electricity and other scientific advancements presented at the World's Columbian Exposition in Chicago in 1893. We wonder however, whether the midway's most transformative attraction was an apparatus of technology.

Rather, it may have been *"The Streets of Cairo" exhibit, featuring what was, for an audience in 1893, a provocatively erotic performance by a belly dancer named "Little Egypt,"* a charmer who created one heck of a sensation in the emerging American society-of-the-spectacle. Within two years, sheet music was published nationally titled, "The Streets of Cairo." It's alternate title was "The Snake Charmer Song." Care to hazard a guess as to who was being charmed by the snake?

Americans mesmerized by "Little Egypt" were eventually catered to at carnival sideshows throughout the land, where sex acts of varying degrees of lechery, from mild to raunchy, which were typically outlawed in local municipalities, sailed past the censors and were performed outside city limits in "hootchy-kootchy" tents, which for ninety years or so were a sordid tradition making the rounds of *America mystica*, until the mainstreamed deluge of topless and bottomless bars beginning in the 1960s, as well as pornography on videocassettes and later the Internet, made them largely superfluous. And by the way, "Hootch" is a synonym for homemade whiskey, while "Kootchy" is an old slang term for the vagina. [14]

On a mass scale, sex without procreation qualifies as a death cult—a society in which the fertility of the land, the crops and the men and woman of procreative age are no longer the priority.

We are in the stage of the *post*-death cult, where the "progressive environmentalists" of the white race proclaim that

---

[14] For more on "Little Egypt" see pages 147-154 herein.

to have children is an irresponsible and reckless action. When masked as environmentalism, this white people's dogma is not particularly controversial, even though it is an unmistakable manifestation of the 4th century A.D. Manichean Elect, who, as John Marshall has written, believed that "begetting children helped to trap souls in matter and fostered the spread of the 'Kingdom of Darkness."

No, we don't seek to burn Manicheans at the stake. No authentic follower of Jesus Christ ever perpetrated any such abomination. It is more likely that those of us who raise alarms concerning infertility will experience a soft "burning" at the hands of the white environmentalists (i.e. reputation shredded, canceled online, canceled financial transactions and employment, and subject possibly to confinement in re-education facilities).

Feeding the people iatrogenic toxins (pharmaceutical drugs), certain vaccines and that which is alleged to be "food," viz. SAD (Standard American Diet), has succeeded in lowering the ability of men and women to conceive children, think independently, and work effectively. Does anyone imagine that the string-pullers behind these sterility-inducing processes are the friends of a positive life on planet earth?

If we continue to cede our agency to a process of flummery and pretense operated by ingenious conspirators whose sorcerous mystique and ceremonial psychodrama have gained for its simulation of reality a general acceptance by the public, then we will witness the light of humanity extinguished, at least in this age; Doomsday being the most extreme manifestation of the thrill-seekers' quest for a terminal, cortex-crunching adrenalin rush.

In the face of the gossamer-winged illusion that sustains the flimsy occult magnum opus, we assert that we need not be prisoners of a scripted inevitablism.

This time of ours can be the Stage of the Life-Culture. Dead matter need not reign. Amnesia can be dispelled, and indifference overcome. Divine Creation can be loved again, fertility revived and the future restored, *if human beings so choose.*

I

PARALLEL LATITUDES

Twilight Language

An Interview

Interviewer: How did you come to know James Shelby Downard and how did he come to be known to a national audience?

Hoffman: Fortean scholar and visionary Bill Grimstad introduced me to Mr. Downard. I met and traveled with him a few times in the Tampa-St. Petersburg Florida area in the mid-1970s. I spoke and corresponded with Shelby (as his friends called him), for the rest of his life. In support of my work, Mr. Downard would send checks in amounts ranging from $300 to $500, between five and eight times a year on average, during most of the time I knew him.

His breakthrough came when our friend, writer-publisher Adam Parfrey, informed us about a book he was planning to publish, *Apocalyspe Culture*. We believed it would be an opportunity for Mr. Downard so we submitted to Adam's anthology the manuscript of *King-Kill/33*, which Shelby wrote and I copy-edited and enlarged at his request.

Interviewer: Parfrey published it only under Downard's byline.

Hoffman: Yes, he did, but it didn't really matter at the time. *Apocalyspe Culture* was a publishing phenomenon and Mr. Downard and his message entered the public consciousness of a mass audience from then onward, largely thanks to Adam's vision and promotional acumen.

Interviewer: Parfrey was quite taken with Downard.

Hoffman: Very much so. He traveled from California to Shelby's final home in Memphis, Tennessee for a visit.

Interviewer: What did Parfrey regard as so special in Downard?

Hoffman: I think he viewed Mr. Downard as a watchman-bard who perceived the higher elements of an overlooked reality which society had reduced to materialistic dross and Cartesian science. Mr. Downard pointed us to a tale that was being imparted above—and paradoxically inside—the deepest recesses of our heads, most significantly in the first atomic bomb blast and the John F. Kennedy assassination, which he described, respectively, as the Creation and Destruction of Primordial Matter, and the Killing of the King. No one outside the Cryptocracy had that vision of those events before Shelby. He discerned a narrative, the Rosicrucian *Ludibrium* constructed to speak to our subconscious, weaving one of the most powerful of mental attractants: a compelling story. Words like "hair-raising" and "spine-tingling" are pathetically inadequate to describe this narrative manipulation and programming.

Adam observed, "In Downard's writings, the products of his subconscious bubble to the surface and catalyze painstaking research. The collision of the poetic against the logical works especially well in the field of conspiracy; it remains the freshest approach to a field of inquiry…"

Interviewer: Is there a particular example that comes to mind of this tale Downard wove from current events?

Hoffman: There are many. I'll cite the first atomic bomb explosion which he viewed as the culmination of many centuries of occult planning and heavily invested with symbolism, beginning with what he termed, "mystical toponomy." He didn't believe in accidents when it came to events at this level, so for him the siting was deliberate and novelistic: at the end of the most lethal section of the Camino Real, which wound from Mexico City to Santa Fe, the ninety-mile "stretch between Las Cruces and Socorro called *Jornada del Muerto* or Journey of the Dead…Drive east of Truth or Consequences to Engle, get out of your car…Imagine 400 years ago, traveling step by step (on)…the Journey of the Dead." [1]

At the end of that peregrination we arrive at the atom bomb's "Trinity Site." Coincidence? There, besides the bomb, we encounter the medieval alchemical homunculus bottle which the U.S. government dubbed, "Jumbo." The tower from which it was suspended near ground zero vanished, apart from two steel

---

[1] volcano.und.nodak.edu/vwdocs/volc_images/north_america/new_mexico/jornada.html

footings set in concrete. According to the official government website of the White Sands Missile Range: "As confidence in the plutonium bomb design grew, it was decided not to use Jumbo. Instead, it was placed under a steel tower about 800 yards from ground zero. The blast destroyed the tower, but Jumbo survived intact."

As you can see the government website states, "Jumbo survived intact." A very remarkable occurrence not much remarked upon, or scrutinized. An imbecilic oversight if ever there was.

According to Shelby Downard, a homunculus — a mannikin — was perhaps placed inside Jumbo and it was thought by some that the radiation had managed to animate it.

That's not what he himself believed. It was what he said the "sorcerers" (his term) involved with the Creation and Destruction of Primordial Matter believed, and attempted to achieve. Whether they did or did not is an open question.

Shelby recognized the enactment of a possibly delusional but nonetheless long-sought-after alchemical objective, which had been incorporated into earth's first nuclear preparations at the highest levels of what was a top secret government project, and this during wartime. He paid attention to extraordinary anomalies like that when no one outside the secret society did.

Mr. Downard felt that that first atom blast had altered reality, far beyond the contours of the nostalgic observation that, "The world will never be the same again," but rather in the fact that when the world saw the "sun" rise in the morning *from the west* for the first time in recorded history, our reality was forever altered.

The experience of the eyewitnesses in the western desert regions—and there were many thousands of them—they were struck to their core by this shattering experience and some even equated the seemingly miraculous sight with the Second Coming.

In July 2005, during the observances for the sixtieth anniversary of the atomic detonation, the Associated Press reported: "Emmett Hatch's grandmother ordered him to drop to his knees and pray July 16, 1945, shortly after the world's first atomic blast. She was awake at 5:29:45 Mountain War Time that morning in Portales to make breakfast and saw the explosion from more than 220 miles away. 'She thought it was the coming of the Lord, because the sun rose in the west that day,' said Hatch, who was 8 years old at the time."

Sixty years later Mr. Hatch was present at the restricted "Trinity Site," marked by an obelisk inscribed, "Where the World's First Nuclear Device Was Exploded on July 16, 1945."

Interviewer: Aren't obelisks and monoliths associated with the advancement of human evolution, as per Kubrick's "2001"?

Hoffman: The monolith is more of a sentinel, don't you think? One wonders whether it bears some kind of witness, or acts as some type of catalyst for human *devolution*, as opposed to the cover story about evolution.

Interviewer: A third event that galvanized Downard was the Apollo Moon Flight.

Hoffman: Not just Downard. Mr. Grimstad viewed the fate of the Eagle landing module, fired directly into the sun after it docked with the Columbia, as perhaps an enactment of the mystical union of the sun and the moon, which is another storied alchemical objective. He also insinuated that the impact of man leaving his boot tracks and space junk on the moon would have negative consequences, and we now know the astronauts left their feces there too.

The Zuni Indians predicted sterility for the white race due to this violation of the moon, which has been seen in legend as a guardian of fertility on earth. Call it a fairy tale if you like, but the Zuni observation has a certain verisimilitude in light of the fact that after we landed on the moon, the population of the white race sank, with statistics showing vastly higher rates of contraception and abortion. The prophecy, if you want to call it that, has been fulfilled.

Interviewer: The Chinese are sending rockets to the moon and mining the surface and setting off detonations. Will they follow the demographic fate of the whites for their sins?

Hoffman: I don't know. What I do know is that the slow transformation of these formerly pristine celestial objects into a degraded junkyard and slag heap, probably does not bode well for the human race. To a galactic observer it might offer a rather poor testimony to our nature.

Interviewer: And you account for this with the doctrine of Original Sin?

Hoffman: The idea of Original Sin is viewed as very uncool and nerd-like. Call me a fundamentalist or whatever name you wish, but hell on earth is always built when our fallen human nature is denied, and then recruited to build heaven on earth. This Thelemic project is a huckster's call.

Here's a quote from Francois Rabelais describing the "philosophical paradise" of the Abbey of Thelema, "There was but one clause in their Rule: *Do what thou wilt*, because people who are free, well bred, well taught and conversant with honorable company have by nature an instinct—a goad—which always pricks them toward virtuous acts and withdraws them from vice."

Rabelais is repeating, not inventing, Satan's original gnosis. The specially selected and chosen inner elite, are "oppressed and enslaved by base subordination and constraint." The laws of God and nature are condemned as bondage because they interfere with the freedom of this higher class of godlings, all of whom have been "educated so nobly...vying laudably with each other to do what is pleasing to any one of them."

Rabelais exhibited two of the signs of occult initiation, or at least, involvement. The first is blasphemy. He was an ordained priest, a monk and a sinister character. Jesus on the cross cries out, "I thirst." The disgustingly drunken priest in Rabelais' *Gargantua* mouths the same words, in obvious mockery.

The second is the *prisca theologia*, the universalist doctrine that all religions come from a single wisdom tradition, a belief that is impossible for any believer in the literal truth of the Bible. In his *Pantagruel,* Rabelais, the Thelemic prophet, makes a pitch for this religious syncretism, reconciling Plato and Pythagoras with the Gospel and St. Paul in the Third and Fourth Books of *Pantagruel,* on the road to the reign of human brain power, disguised with environmental virtue-signaling, and palaver about "luhv."

Interviewer: And these currents are all headed where?

Hoffman: To the *Jornada del muerto* on the 33rd degree latitude line, and to Dealey Plaza on the 32nd degree latitude line, in what John Dee termed in 1577, "the perfect art of navigation," which leads to the discovery of an exploding mushroom cloud and an exploding head. Signs *nostra aetate*.

Fertility cults are supposed to green the earth. This however, is a blackening, perpetrated by those who "know what is best for us," the high-minded Thelemic disciples of the enemy of the human race.

Interviewer: Who do you identify as that enemy?

Hoffman: Do the math.

Interviewer: Come on.

Hoffman: Gustav Kuhn, a psychologist at Durham University stated, "Magicians seem to be able to carry out secret actions in front of their audience without being spotted. I'm interested in why people don't perceive those actions."

By controlling attention and expectation through suggestion, and exploiting our implanted preconceptions, we are led to participate in our own deception.

We are at the weird stage now where we *do* spot the secret actions of the magicians, after which we take an active civic part in the sorcery of fooling ourselves. We are the audience at a voyeuristic magic act that consists in the secret of spectating at our own death, the highest thrill the Big Top's magicians have to offer. Freedom, redemption, transcendence? They're nowhere to be found in this particular theater.

Interviewer: The Theater of the Revelation of the Method.

Hoffman: That's it. You did the math.

Interviewer: Revelation is supposed to be filled with light, but light's absent in this one.

Hoffman: "From those flames
No light, but rather darkness visible
Served only to discover sights of woe..."

Interviewer: That's from *Paradise Lost*. Milton.

Hoffman: Yes, paradise lost.

Interviewer: What is "Twilight Language"?

Hoffman: Let's see, do I start with a "jack ruby," or sheep dipping?

Where to begin when there isn't a beginning. Measurement has no place here.

There is going to be difficulty among the masses and even conspiracy students and investigators concerning the language which speaks in ways that are non-linear to most minds.

Twilight language is a form of communication that eludes most people's conscious perception, though it is of course perceived by the subconscious. In the 21 century that dichotomy is much less the case, because the initiation of the masses into the civic magic that increasingly appears undisguised has brought the revelation of Twilight Language to the frontiers of the waking mind.

A yarn is being spun and "charmed" conjunctions and interstices are formed, partly from invocation and partly from "surfing" a magnetic attraction that seems to organize anomalies around certain "words of power" and potent symbols. That there is incredulity in the face of this is the least surprising dimension of the phenomenon.

The two extremes which distort our perception are total denial of twilight language on the one hand, and a total immersion in trivial aspects of a case that ends up muddying the key elements of pattern detection. There are researchers who pick a grab bag of symbol books, videos and name references and throw them into a cauldron that they call Twilight Language and what comes of it? A laundry list of increasingly tedious, trivial or contrived links of words. Without enlightened pattern detection such an approach is part of the obfuscation, not the clarification.

We ourselves can generate the phenomena. We can begin to see coincidences everywhere. There has to be a selection so we remain mindful of how *our perception itself becomes part of the process of invocation.*

Interviewer: What do you mean by "trivial aspects" and selection?

Hoffman Deciding what is important and what is effluvia; what qualifies as Twilight Language but is actually a kind of arcane litter, sometimes placed in the field of vision to distract and sometimes invoked by the percipient/investigator himself because he can't detect the pattern, he can't grok what is insubstantial, what is a false lead, even if it does reflect occult dimensions. As in any language, one encounters jibberish and some sleuths are misled into believing it has significance.

We should be keenly aware that not everything in the symbolic stream is of profound remarkability. Discerning the difference between the actual communication being conveyed by Twilight Language—between that and signal noise—is the difference between a higher state of consciousness and a form of debilitation that can mimic the classic symptoms of mental illness.

Some of these investigators who don't possess the antenna, intuition, ears to hear or eyes to see — call it what you will— serve the Cryptocracy by failing to distinguish between the medium and the message. The strangeness of the communication has shocked and awed them to such an extent that their discernment has fallen by the wayside.

A stated goal of the 1960s and '70s psychedelic revolution was, "Ingest those plants and mushrooms and open the doors of perception." But the yin of that process is that those doors can swing too far in the other direction, and we get the equivalent of a kind of data rot, Twilight Language glossolalia or diarrhea. It harkens to a superstitious state of mind that we described in *Secret Societies and Psychological Warfare* at the dawn of the conversion of the pagan peoples of Europe to Christianity (in cases where that conversion was not forced by state actors like Charlemagne who executed tens of thousands of civilians who happened to be pagans).

In the early centuries of its existence, the Christian path was a clean break from minds so immersed in Twilight Language that their every step was fraught with peril, or significant meaning, which was paralyzing their ability to live, and had to be mediated by a ritual of propitiating the gods with a whole series of superstitious gestures and words. It became a type of madness for which the remedy was the simplicity of the Christian Gospel with its warning that the wicked flee where no one is pursuing them.

Interviewer: What are the internal mechanics or dynamics of Twilight Language?

Hoffman: A dynamic yes, mechanics no, because we're in the realm of art. There is no cuneiform tablet for Twilight Language. It functions more like poetry than physics, giving narrative propulsion to the Cryptocracy's screenplays.

Interviewer: It has no basis in neurology then?

Hoffman: Of course it does, just as, if we observed the brain moved by a speech by Hamlet or the entrance of his father's ghost, we would see neural pathways responding. Does the Twilight Language stimulate neuro-chemical pathways? I would answer in the affirmative.

Interviewer: What chemicals?

Hoffman: The chemicals most closely related to behaviors associated with the evocation of sex and violence: catecholamine and gamma-aminobutyric acid.

The way Twilight Language has cachet now is based partly on the rise of the invisible world. Cotton Mather, the New England witch-hunter wrote a book, *Wonders of the Invisible World,* which is the subject of much mirth now. We feel very superior to this "poor fool" Mather and his "ridiculous invisible world." Yet we inhabit a world of invisibles beginning with nuclear physics and the atom; a universe we can't see. The "Big Bang exactly 13.8 billion years ago" we are told, is invisible, but it has, we are told, been confirmed by "gravitational waves" — "ripples in space-time" founded on "quantum fluctuations." Here is a whole invisible cosmos in which we invest our belief; we accept it as true because today's priests, who are too sly to call themselves priests, and instead are termed "scientists," declare it to be so. There is even a 20th century religion that adopted the word for itself, "Scientology." The name gives people the ability to be religious while imagining they are scientific; the perfect modern conceit, courtesy of LaFayette Ron Hubbard.

Faith in an invisible world renders us more attuned to Twilight Language and what we have is a much higher sensitivity to magically activated words, what the Pharaonic Egyptians knew as "words of power," acting as a means for imprinting a prefabricated reality—a sibilant whisper of a counterfeit universe—into the mind, as part of a process where people volunteer to have their brains wired to the data hive.

Interviewer: You're saying that in our video age of Internet, TV and movies we're less visual?

Hoffman: We're less literate and therefore more susceptible to the processing of our perceived reality through signs, bytes and slogans. Twilight Language sometimes consists in slogans pregnant with archetypal imprinting, giving narrative propulsion to the pattern theatre that the Cryptocracy weaves with its ritual murders and other types of spectacular crimes.

When I say less visual I mean we are lacking in the type of memory that is jogged by the visual. Mnemonic is a $50 word that simply denotes any device employed as an aid in remembering something. This device can be visual or literary. In the latter case, one can recall the names of the colors of the rainbow by remembering the acronym ROY G. BIV, which is a mnemonic for recalling the names of the colors red, orange, yellow, green, blue, indigo (black) and violet. Twilight Language sometimes consists of talismanic mnemonics — it summons a mnemonic which the collective subconscious "memorized" long ago, which in turn triggers the thing memorized. For example, "Wicker" is a mnemonic for mind-bending — and for ritual murder.

Interviewer: I don't remember committing the word "Wicker" to memory in connection with serial killings or ceremonies.

Hoffman: True, but you're overlooking a shared subconscious of the human race which Dr. Jung termed "archetypes"— manipulation of those Jungian archetypes, the dreaming mind—the subconscious—by means of Twilight Language, can result in the magical organization of the imagination, and by magical I don't mean enlightening or illuminating, but occluding—narrowing the aperture of our perception, the better to herd us in the direction the Cryptocracy wants us to go. Recall the lines from Christopher Nolan and David S. Goyer's "Batman Begins" movie:

"What's 'scarecrow'?"

"Patients suffering from delusional episodes often focus their paranoia on an external tormentor, usually conforming to Jungian archetypes. In this case, a scarecrow."

A scarecrow can be many things: a harmless, man-sized rag doll who frightens away birds and children on the basis of an illusion, or a lethal predator dressed like a scarecrow as part of a disguise or, in "Batman Begins," a drug-induced hallucination so terrifying it "drives men mad" and renders them powerless.

Interviewer: And "Wicker," being part of the Twilight Language, is part of our unconscious?

Hoffman: Not *unconscious*. It's part of our dreaming or *subconscious* mind. When summoned into the field of the conscious mind and linked to some of the ceremonies and rites which the police and the news media term serial murders or lone nut killings, it becomes a means for processing our minds and spirits.

Interviewer: Can you give an example of the visual that we've lost?

Hoffman: Marshal McLuhan mentioned the "Stations of the Cross" in the Catholic Church. Each "station" has a carved or painted depiction of one scene from Christ's suffering and death. The believer stands beneath each station while consulting a booklet with a prayer related to the particular scene. This is a process of auto-initiation into Christ's suffering for humanity's sins. The viewer uses the mnemonic of the art work at each station to imprint Christ's passion on the viewer's mind.

Interviewer: Why wouldn't television and cinema fulfill this function?

Hoffman: They don't. They're not memory theaters. TV and movies are predigested. They comprise the Videodrome and they're lacking the interior mental architecture. The Videodrome is external. The memory theatre is internal, mnemonic. The mnemonic process is not intrinsic to cinema and television.

The architecture of the mnemonic has been stripped away by the Videodrome and a pre-packaged hallucination is presented in its stead. It's called entertainment. It's even termed escapism. What does it mean to escape reality? It is to go mad. A series of moving *pictures* deceive our mind into seeing motion. This is far removed from the mnemonic.

Interviewer: How do you define a person's self-devised memory theatre?

Hoffman: Let me read you the words of the founder of the Jesuits, Ignatius of Loyola, from his *Spiritual Exercises*, "In contemplation of Christ Our Lord, who is visible, the composition will be to see with the eyes of the imagination the corporeal place where the thing I want to contemplate is found." This is the capacity for interiority which The Machine —call it computers, call it the Alien, the eldritch gods or Skynet — destroys.

Twilight Language moves the interior world into the exterior. It is virtually synonymous with the dreaming mind because of its archetypal cues and content. The subconscious, which is the supreme memory theater above all, is by Twilight Language propelled outside, into the external world, to explosive effect; analogous to atomic physics, which begins in a microcosmic, nearly invisible world and is forced to manifest in the outer world as a mushroom cloud; the mushroom being a symbol of higher consciousness.

Interviewer: Higher consciousness is considered benevolent.

Hoffman: My question would be, from where is this "higher" consciousness derived, from the presence of life or the presence of imminent death?

Interviewer: From death, but it is still a higher consciousness.

Hoffman: Often it's a consciousness tainted by death. It is "higher" than the bovine level of consumerism, by comparison. But there is a consciousness infinitely higher.

Interviewer: What about the idea that Twilight Language is just a code?

Hoffman: A puzzle? Yes, it can be as seemingly as prosaic as that — the "hidden in plain sight" clue. When I was a child I thought that the name of the woman who mercifully wiped the bloody and sweating face of Jesus on his way to Golgotha, was actually named "Veronica." It was only years later that I learned that her name was eponymous and assigned by posterity — "*vera icon*" viz. "true image." If "Veronica" was the name of a suspect in the vandalism of Michelangelo's statue of David or Moses, or some other prominent art work, my interest in the case would increase. If there were other symbolic names and numbers attached to this hypothetical vandalism then I would be interested to see if a story behind the story was being conveyed, a ritual, related in the language we call Twilight by our latest Doctor Syntax.

Interviewer: You say mathematics has nothing to do with twilight language.

Hoffman: No, I do not. What I say is that it is not mathematical. Would you say that mathematics is a determining factor in Shakespeare's plays? Let's not mystify Twilight Language. It's a play; a drama; a script. It sometimes contains allusions to numbers and that world. Truth or Consequences, New Mexico is located on the 33rd degree line of north parallel latitude and so is the Trinity Site, where the creation and destruction of matter first occurred. Let's distinguish Twilight Language from the priestcraft of scientism; from the mystification that lends an aura of higher expertise to expressions of mathematical formulae when applied to this psychodrama. People think if it's mathematics it can't be delusional. It took one of the leading mathematicians of the Victorian age to prick a hole in that inflated balloon.

In Peter Hunt's fine book about Lewis Carroll's "Alice in Wonderland," he directs our attention to the ostensible nonsense that Alice spouts when she mangles her times tables: "Let me see: four times five is twelve, and four times six is thirteen, and four times seven is – oh dear! I shall never get to twenty at that rate!"

We laugh at Alice's goofy mathematical incompetence because *we think we know*. After all, it's mathematics and math adheres to fact-based rules. But Carroll is showing us we don't know, because we're only skimming the surface and we're fixed in a mathematical reality that we regard as the only one possible. We should discourage that mentality when undertaking the study of Twilight Language.

Interviewer: What are you saying? That Wonderland math is accurate? That four times five equals twelve, is correct?

Hoffman: I'm not saying it. Lewis Carroll said it, as Peter Hunt revealed. Alice is actually following a logical progression: 4×5 is indeed 12 in a number sequence using base 18, and 4×6 is 13, using base 21. [2]

Mathematical concepts of number, space and time are not limited to Cartesian boundaries. On planet earth, space and time are mediated by the green witch. England's "scientific" occultists established the prime meridian and the measurement of "mean time" at Greenwich. Think about that word's etymology: Green wic, Grenewych, Greenwitch.

If by mathematics you mean that ingenious act which Oxford Math Professor Charles Lutwidge Dodgson (Lewis Carroll) put in his Alice books, then it has a part to play in ciphering and deciphering esoteric communication and signaling. It seems that Lewis Carroll, mathematician though he was, knew this better than most. Logic consists of the White Queen's observation, "The rule is, jam tomorrow and jam yesterday—but never jam *today*." This is the Mad Hatter's "tea time," wherein Effect precedes Cause. Alice says, "I see nobody on the road," to which the King replies, "I only wish I had such eyes! To be able to see Nobody! And at that distance!"

Anything can happen in Wonderland but *it could only have happened the way it did.* Robinson Duckworth, the Oxford undergraduate who rowed the boat on the river Isis, while Carroll told the story to ten-year-old Alice Pleasance Liddell, testified that Carroll did so extemporaneously, "off the top of

---

[2] The progression only becomes erroneous in attempting to reach 20. Cf. Hunt, *The Making of Lewis Carroll's Alice and the Invention of Wonderland* (Oxford University, 2020).

his head," as if he were channeling it from somewhere; or should I say from erewhon.

Where we are warning people away from "science" or more properly, "scientism," is in the field of measurement. How does one measure anything with the yardstick of art? Using that rod to take the measure of Twilight Language is subjective. It's that inherent subjectivity that protects the objectivity of our study. "No phenomenon is a phenomenon until it is an observed phenomenon."

Interviewer: That sounds trite. What's it supposed to signify?

Hoffman: The person self-described as a scientist thinks his observations of the phenomenon must be correct because they are rooted in what he has been taught is an unalterable reality. Quantum physics teaches that when we take a measurement of something, say, for example, the position of a photon, it takes the form of what we are expecting to see. Whereas prior to our measurement, the quantum state of the photon existed as a wavefunction state vector, containing several observations of the quantum state. These are known as superpositions. Each observation in superposition can contradict the other, for instance, observing one photon to be in different locations simultaneously. In the process known as WavePacket Reduction (WPR), when a measurement of the phenomenon occurs, then only one of the anomalous observations which previously existed, is visible; the rest have vanished. We're where Heisenberg was nearly a 100 years ago, the "Uncertainty Principle" consisting of conjugate variables like time, energy, momentum and position that can't all be known simultaneously, and therefore they act as a buffer against man playing god. The nature of the subatomic universe prevents us from knowing everything.

Interviewer: Many scientists would say that what prevents man from playing god is established rules and stable properties, like those set by Albert Einstein concerning the speed of light being the highest possible speed.

Hoffman: On the contrary, those fixed rules pin God down, like a lepidopterist pins a butterfly to a display board. Look at the physics of non-locality by which quantum computers operate: entangled particles are connected to one another from across the cosmos, no matter how distant. Changes in one are conveyed to the other instantly, in other words, at a rate vastly exceeding the speed of light. In Einstein's "reality" they're far away. In superluminal reality they're unified.

Interviewer: So the science of physics is itself subject to art?

Hoffman: It might be best to think of another name for the words "science" and "physics" in that they are so heavily freighted with an allure of infallible determinancy that renders them more theology than evidentiary method. A truth-seeker would want to deflate this priesthood and its vanity, which is particularly evident in the medical profession and one reason why it's so catastrophic to permit these "deities" to dictate public policy.

Interviewer: Other than the Green Witch/Greenwich aspect to time, do you acknowledge a scientific basis to understanding time and even time travel?

Hoffman: Chemistry and physics can help us to have a better understanding of time. If you ponder the anomalies of absolute zero (or as close to that point as science has been able to approach), you observe that it is defined not by what it is, but by what it is not. Whereas, theoretically there is no limit to heat, in the absence of heat, the coldest possible temperature is only -459° F. At this absolute zero (zero Kelvin), the rate of entropy is zero, expressed as:

$$\Delta S \geq 0$$

Delta S (entropy) will reach zero at 0 Kelvin.

Entropy is defined as the degree of chaos, decay or randomness, from the Greek word for transformation (τροπή). So what does this have to do with time? Well, according to the Second Law of Thermodynamics heat passes only one way: from hot to cold. The process is irreversible. It cannot pass backward, from cold to hot. By this means we distinguish time as the difference between this chemical "before" and "after." Our experience of the passage of time — the past, the future and this present moment — is not an illusion. It is a chemical process.

Interviewer: Aren't you contradicting your own statements about "the inherent trickiness of the material universe"? Some quantum physicists have said there is no past or present, only now.

Hoffman: I'm not going to be ruled by a decontextualized platitude designed for mass consumption, which is what you're repeating. Quantum mechanics in its genius and luminescence, when reduced to the common denominator, can begin to resemble jargon and psycho-babble, which science has no model capable of resolving.

Interviewer: The resolution being in the poetic universe beyond numbers and chemicals.

Hoffman: Matter exhibits many anomalies as absolute zero is approached, including bilocation of elements and other quirks and tears in the script of the Cartesian-Enlightenment deists who ruled "science" (and all that hubris that affixed the word science to their arch materialist secular religions, as for example Marx and Lenin's "scientific socialism"), up until the coming of twentieth century quantum physics, when Albert Einstein's EPR theory was defeated by evidence of the quantum entanglement of particles at vast distances, as we've already mentioned, which proceeded from *the rise of phenomena into existence when measured*, the theory being that the role of the observer is critical to the manifestation of the observation. Here we encounter recondite considerations like wave function collapse.

Some of these mysteries are so arcane they border on parody and even comedy, in the Fortean sense of Charles Fort's hunch that there's a principle that defies every other principle, thereby checkmating the pompous inevitabilist prophecy, rooted in Kabbalah, of a level of omniscient human brain power soon to be obtained and possessed by a class of all-knowing grandees, to whom we will shall owe submission. To maintain that narrative, there can't be too much awareness of the cosmic monkey wrench that, according to Fortean epistemology, is tossed into the machinery of human absolutism and control. Consciousness of that process shatters the glamor and the self-advertised mastery of the Wizards of Tech.

Every significant step taken toward limitless autarchic human and machine control precipitates a loss of control at another level, which is often nearly invisible, even to the would-be Overlords. They will never reach their goal.

In *Through the Looking Glass,* as Alice spots scented rushes and leans from the boat to pick them, she says, "The prettiest are always further." And she says it with a sigh.

Interviewer: How does your art or poetic sense account for reality when mathematicians can't?

Hoffman: Samuel Goldwyn of the MGM [3] (Metro-Goldwyn-Mayer) movie studio said, "Authenticity is everything. When you can fake that, you've got it made."

Interviewer: Words fail me.

Hoffman: You'll recover.

Interviewer: We're in the early decades of the 21st century, where does that put us on your clock of destiny? Are we approaching midnight?

Hoffman: We're past midnight. We're going over to the other side.

Interviewer: What other side?

Hoffman: We're are beginning to live amid the exteriorization of the *tulpa*.

Interviewer: Where other people's thought forms materialize in physical reality?

Hoffman: In what is called material reality. The Cryptocracy is far along in its success story. Immanentizing the

---

[3] MGM = 33. The letter m is the thirteenth letter in the alphabet. The letter g is the seventh. 13+7+13 = 33.

eschaton and giving the appearance of the making manifest of the *tulpa* in our midst, is part of it.

Interviewer: What about the monkey wrench?

Hoffman: It's at work, sabotaging the best laid plans of the sorcerers, but it typically doesn't get up to the plate until the ninth inning. The Red Sea was always going to part for the Israelites but not for a long time. Daniel was put out of the den of lions at the last possible moment.

Until then — until the rescue of the predestined — bondage and hypnotic Twilight Language are the order of the day. Consequently, it can be rightly said, yes, it is very late.

Interviewer: If this were true wouldn't it be a huge wakeup call?

Hoffman: Only if it was brought on suddenly and our familiar props were removed. But the opposite obtains. It has come about slowly, although with gradually increasing speed of late. And the props are in place, giving a sense of the ordinary even as the extraordinary manifests before us. One way the props are maintained is based in the fact that we are the first people in recorded history to live in an age in which we can peer through a window and watch the ghosts of more than a century ago moving about. We do this through the old "silent" movies, some of which are now well over a century old. Imagine people in 1910 or 1914 able to watch films of Napoleon fighting the Battle of Austerlitz, or George Washington on his plantation amid his toiling black slaves; or Jane Austen working at her writing desk. If motion pictures of the early 19th century had manifested on film in the early 20th century, much of the world in 1921 would have still looked like 1821, because the people of 1921 would have grown up with those images of clothing and appearances, as we have in our time.

In terms of something readily noticeable, like fashion, we observe that people looked and dressed very differently in 1921 from 1821.

We've grown up with silent movie images and this translates into the somewhat remarkable fact that many people in 2021 dress somewhat similar to the people in 1921: suits, ties, dresses. In 100 years in terms of fashion and visual arrangements of cities and spaces, we haven't moved that far away from 1921. Motion picture technology has made a century-old vision part of our post-modern vision. In the midst of the huge disconnect we are experiencing in the cauldron of the alchemist's "gay science," the moral, cultural, racial, sexual and technological revolution we've experienced, we're nonetheless continuing to inhabit a mise-en-scène from the early 20th century, which is reassuring. It gives a sense of stability and continuity—being comfortably anchored in spite of the revolutionary changes. This is important to the success of The Process, as Arthur C. Clarke showed in *Childhood's End*, his novel of humanity conditioned to accept Satan in their midst without protest.

Interviewer: Most people don't immerse themselves in silent movies.

Hoffman: Most Americans have seen snippets of silent movies and most Americans have been exposed to, or are familiar at least somewhat, with the Gary Cooper/Clark Gable/Betty Davis/Barbara Stanwyck Americana of the 1930s, the film noir of the 1940s, the "I Love Lucy" of the "Fabulous '50s," and Andy Griffith's Mayberry from the pre-Vietnam 60s — many of these images are still very much present in the psyche of a considerable portion of the American population.

Interviewer: You think this helps to reassure them?

Hoffman: Hypnotically, yes. But as you know, it's a false assurance. Almost all of the actors they are watching in those shows are ghosts; they're long dead. The sets are demolished; where filming was done outdoors in Los Angeles the orange groves are now shopping malls — the quaint neighborhoods razed to make way for 20 or 30 story condominium towers.

We live inside a theatre. We've seen so many "photoplays" and television shows that we all have more than a little of the ham actor in us, the would-be celebrity. Pre-modern children in America were naturally shy. Most of them observed the world in periods of silence. If strangers addressed them or you stuck a camera or a microphone in front of them they would become bashful, mute, though alert and observant. This has been the endearing quality of childhood innocence. But now in our time, many young children who are in front of a camera or a microphone are almost immediately acting and emoting as if auditioning for a part. It's a by-product of spectacular society, where celebrity and exhibitionism are viewed as positive, even when they're negative.

Interviewer: Explain.

Hoffman: Look at Arnold Schwarzenegger the actor. He groped women on the set of his movies. As governor he lied and deceived and favored the corporations. When nurses went on strike for lower patient ratios so they could provide better patient care and quality of life, Schwarzenegger called them "lobbyists for a special interest group." When his trophy Kennedy wife was away for a few hours he took sexual advantage of the family's Mexican maid. This guy seems to be thoroughly rotten, at least in the period to which I'm referring, but he's nonetheless likable old "Arnold, the Guvenator." When someone is famous for being famous, which is an empty and farcical "achievement," then the values being celebrated are eye candy and voyeurism. In spectacular society one can have obviously wicked, corrupt popes, presidents and movie "stars" and the masses will still suck up to them. It's a Hitlerian attraction in a society trained to hiss at Hitler, but the Hitler mechanism—magnetism, charisma—is at the center of America's celebrity culture. If America actually were anti-Hitler it would be anti-celebrity. It would honor and lionize its farmers and carpenters and the mothers and fathers who raise three or five or ten children and give them a decent upbringing. But it's only a paper moon, our society at present; a story board; a stage design.

Years ago I would have followed up this description with the words "Behind that scene exists..." but we're devolving past that direction. Now I would say, "in the midst of" or "in front of this scene," where the *tulpa* appears among us. It's extraordinary — as if a very ugly, hairy red devil was walking around naked in Mayberry, with a filthy tail, billy goat eyes and horns, genitalia exposed, fire coming out of its mouth, and Barney's still looking for the whisky still patronized by Otis; Aunt Bea is continuing to cook her fried chicken, and Opie is being wisely counseled by his father. This devil walks up and down Main Street exposing himself to girls and boys, enslaves the mayor, disrupts the endocrine system of the people, induces abortions in women and almost nothing is said or done about it by the "good people" of rural, small town America. The *tulpa* has materialized out of the interior realm into the exterior. The *tulpa* is here, yet for most of us it is invisible, even though, paradoxically, we *can* see it.

Interviewer: You're saying America is aborting its babies, exposing its kids to porn, permitting the destruction of the innocent—

Hoffman: What I'm pointing to is an *unprecedented* level of perversity, the *union* of opposites, which in very ancient Asian culture was always seen as a harbinger of death, because to maintain—rather than erase opposites and polarities, such as very masculine men and feminine women who are powerfully attracted to one another—it is that magnetic attraction in Nature that gives rise to human life through procreation. To seek to obliterate those natural magnetic polarities, or to homogenize them, is to long for mass death.

In our post-modern death cult, in unprecedented ways, androgyny—the erasure of opposites, the denial of chromosomal reality—prevails under a utopian banner of peace, love, tolerance and a better way of life for all. Yet where opposites converge, there is much death and this is a slaughter house that we are not encouraged to discern, lest it register in our consciousness and awaken us.

According to China's own Health Department statistics, more than 300 million babies, mostly female, have been killed in their mother's wombs in China since 1971. How many western newspaper and cable TV editorials or Hollywood movies have been produced concerning that unimaginable Communist government holocaust? Alas, relatively little or nothing. 300 million missing babies? Yawn.

Republicans in the U.S. are being intimidated by claims from abortion-favoring feminists that "the Republicans are engaged in a war on women." 300 million mostly girl babies have been destroyed in China and it is the anti-abortion Republicans who are "at war with women"? The fact that this claim has any play at all is indicative of mass insanity of "the emperor has no clothes" variety. In 1821 the humanity of black people was denied and their enslavement asserted as a "right."

In 2021 the humanity of unborn human beings is denied and their murder through abortion is asserted as a "right." We're expected to believe that the massive violence of the dehumanized children in the womb has absolutely zero connection to the massive violence and dehumanization of people outside the womb.

We are being led by priests disguised as scientists into a scientism/futurism where the human brain with all of its startling potential for egoism, commands the peasants. Tom O'Hare observed plaintively, "If this year (2021) has taught me anything, it is that people are egregiously prone to be obedient to baseless government pronouncements echoed by many in a mindless and obedient media. That is one of the saddest outcomes of the this (COVID19) pandemic." Dr. Anthony Fauci personified the hateur of a government tyrant who imposes despotism under the banner of medical science.

Stanford University "neuroscientist"/psychiatrist Karl Deisseroth, M.D., PhD. speaks of "sitting and talking to a person whose reality is different from yours — to be face to face with the effects of bipolar disorder, exuberance, charisma...crushing — it can't be reasoned with...as if there's a conceptual cancer in the brain. He saw patient after patient suffering terribly, with no cure in sight."

"Conceptual cancer." That's how this high priest describes people who think differently from him. Allegedly, Dr. Deisseroth seeks to heal the human soul through bioengineering. After all, he went to Harvard and he runs a lab at Stanford, so he knows best. it has been claimed that he seeks to combine the manipulation of light with the manipulation of genes to work a "cure." When one hears jargon like that one sees how utterly primitive it is, despite the fact that it is brought to us in the habiliments of university science, accompanied by command words such as "neuroscience, bioengineering" and "optogenetics." The trigger words formerly were "scientific Socialism," "Better living through chemistry," the "peaceful atom," "Freudian analysis," "Dianetics," and then "Scientology." In the '40s, '50s and '60s these were the futuristic-sounding signs.

One fad, optogenetics, is a technique that allows the high priests to turn our brain cells on and off with a combination of genetic manipulation and pulses of light. This is supposedly being conducted by Dr. Deisseroth, who allegedly confessed to the *New York Times* that he's applied to his patients the favorite device of the psychiatric priesthood now that lobotomy is out of favor: "I've administered electroconvulsive therapy" (electroshock). Perhaps he sincerely thinks he is genuinely helping humanity. Perhaps his intentions are not malicious. I can't know his motives.

But imagine if Dr. Deisseroth had the stubborn and strong-willed, "different drummer" Henry David Thoreau appear before him as a patient, what he would make of this celibate loner with a preference for living in a hut in the woods? Many people thought Thoreau "couldn't be reasoned with." He must have been afflicted with "conceptual cancer." In the 1960s and '70s we termed such people dissidents and freethinkers, but since then the Machine has ascended above the split-wood-not-atoms crowd. Digitalization has taken command.

Interviewer: What does that signify?

Hoffman: It signifies what John Dee dreamed in the Elizabethan Age, the *hegemony of dead matter*. April 21, 2014 the *New York Times* celebrated "brain control in a flash of light." Not one word was printed about the possibility of the misuse of this research. The corporate media are seduced by these egotistical "scientists" possessed of the same mentality that brought us "better living through chemistry, nuclear power too cheap to meter," pharmaceutical drugs in place of nature's herbal medicine cabinet, and the Frankenfood of GMO corn and cloned salmon. We are supposed to defer to the "wisdom" of these big brains, who are affronted and almost shocked by the existence of dissidents who don't get immunized, don't have their babies in hospitals and think the New Testament is a better guide for healing demonic possession, fear and depression than a scientist who can barely believe he is actually "sitting and talking to a person whose reality is different from yours."

The scientific dictatorship is here. Skynet is here. We're voting for these trends with our apathy, in part because we have been taught, through hypnotic induction, that the new world which science, robots and humanoids will forge on behalf of Skynet, will be incredibly thrilling and adventurous; common sense, age old wisdom and prudence be damned.

Interviewer: Some would say you are exaggerating.

Hoffman: It is not an exaggeration to take note of the fact that all life on this planet, from the simplest cell to humans themselves, are all based on the same genetic code, made up of four DNA nucleotides, designated as A, C, G and T. What the Dr. Frankensteins are doing in our time is creating organisms that do not exist in God's creation on earth. These "synthetic niologists" are creating new nucleotides and thereby creating alien organisms — entities with a genetic code of more than four DNA bases.

Interviewer: Which, I take it, means that these are alien life forms, which is what you accuse John Dee of working toward and which Lovecraft predicted was an invasion force about to incarnate through demonic means.

Hoffman: True, but to use the word "demonic" closes the modern mind to the human agents at work — the scientists in serenely shining and peaceful, gleaming, state-of-the-art multi-million dollar laboratories where you'd like your own son or daughter to work, after he or she obtains his or her doctorate from Stanford and does their post-doc at Johns Hopkins. These scientists have pleasant demeanors, are seemingly rational, highly intelligent and idealistic people seeking to "make a contribution to society and the future."

Interviewer: You're poking fun at this.

Hoffman: I'm evoking the banality of evil, and how people's expectations of that evil prevent them from seeing it. They imagine a diabolic operation as being conducted in a foul, dirty place by an obvious madman and his hunch-backed helper. In contrast with that image we have attractive, successful, high-achievers, the envy of many who wish they could rise as high as these god-playing scientists have done. Hannah Arendt saw that Adolf Eichmann was not outwardly a monster, but a bland bureaucrat and that the evil he perpetrated was committed while he was a member of a respected, elite governmental organization. Doing evil was his respectable job.

As we said in the booklet, *King-Kill/33*, the eternal pagan psychodrama is escalated under these modern conditions.

Sorcery is not what 21st century post-modernists can accept as real; yet in the sub-cellar of their mind, they know it is.

Interviewer: Then it's all over, no hope for humanity?

Hoffman: When you have people enamored of thrills such as sex without children, and the pursuit of their greatest thrill of all, to get as close to death as one can without actually dying, then the prospects are poor in the face of that sort of bestial animalism.

Interviewer: You call it primitive and animal-like but your opponents would say it is visionary and progressive.

Hoffman: It's simian stuff; crude, debased materialism running amok on this planet more than ever in recorded history. Animals are stuck in the carnal although actually that's an insult to my dog, who has a more generous and expansive side to him than many of these master manipulator Brahmins who imagine that their tinkering at one or two degrees in the Cosmic Complexity (for which they have no respect), serves as a god-like rival to the Supreme Being, or may even constitute a surpassing feat of self-initiated godhood.

There is no end to the extremes of delusion to which demonic pride is subject. We are warned of it in the Greek, Roman and Norse myths and in the Book of Revelation. But "The One Ring" that Tolkein warned us about, has us in its power; the same "Ring" that was used to make the "Lord of the Rings" movies in yet another post-modernist act of double-minded negation of the principle being hailed.

The Society of the Spectacle: no matter how sterile and empty it is at its core, it will manage to attract the flies to the spider by the magnificence of the technical, VR, 3-D illusions which is the spider's bait; eye candy for the puffed-up scientoids who, with their personal computers, can access the Oracle of Delphi (the Internet and "Google"), ask it any question and come away satisfied, at least temporarily, with being wired to the data hive. This is how this tethered Group Mind's hive-like energy is harnessed and farmed.

Interviewer: Virtual reality technology is in use and the hallucination is heightened. Real life can be simulated inside a cubicle: sex, exhilarating adventure, travel, space exploration.

Hoffman: State-of-the-art, mass induced hallucination mainly for fun, for "entertainment purposes" of course. So who can object? Just as human embryo manipulation, cloning and genetic modification are sold to us as compassionate medical techniques —to heal the deaf, dumb, and blind; the diabetic, cancerous and heart diseased. Who can object? Even though these same "humanitarians" are exterminating Down syndrome children through abortion. Is there anything more neo-Nazi than that?

Along with VR "reality" there is hologram "reality" that appear in one's living room, not on a wall or on wide screen plasma or 4K television. John Wayne will fight the "Redskins" directly in front of you. The reputed homicidal gas chambers of Auschwitz-Birkenau will pour their toxic Zyklon B onto the dying bodies of Judaic persons who will seem to be writhing and gasping for breath on your carpet.

There is no apparent limit to the degree to which the Spectacle will invade the world because there is no clearly demarcated limit on the ambitions of the technology propelling it. Unsupervised infants and young children walk into highway traffic thinking it's a game, drink lye mistaking it for sugar, hop in a car that is idling and try to drive it. Older and wiser folk restrain their offspring's destructive infantile urges until their children can become adults and obtain enough experience of the technology, learning what is appropriate and what is not.

Infantile scientists however, are unrestrained by our infantile media. The philosophical maxim of the brave new world is—if it is technically or scientifically feasible, then go ahead with it—to hell with the possible unforeseen consequences.

GMO technology is just a few decades old. No one truly knows the possible long term effects, because it has been rushed into use based on the profit motive, and the assurance of the kiddies called scientists who have a string of alphabet letters after their surnames. They decree it to be "safe." How can they know, when only time will tell?

Frances Yates was one of the first historians of science to reveal the sorcery behind "science," how it is being directed by practitioners of ritual magic, how it is not objective, is not based on the best and most open-ended type of measurement, how it has been constrained and pointed in one direction: *the perfection of a supposedly imperfect universe through the intervention of human brain power.*

Who is doing the covert directing? Let's just say that it is a force that is unimaginably hostile to the human person and Creation itself. As the coils and folds of illusion pile ever higher and thicker, it will be that much more difficult to trace the designs of this force.

Interviewer: But the fact that you are revealing this could alert and awaken humanity.

Hoffman: Maybe. I can certainly visualize it happening. For it to happen a *dis*enchanting process of massive proportions has to occur so that people would choose life over death, and acclimate themselves to the poetic joys of a non-modified natural world, while disconnecting from their previous addiction to digitally-generated illusion.

It would be a test of character and it would require that someone like this writer, though not necessarily me personally, would become adequately well-known to the masses of planet earth, or the West, for a start, to disenchant a population in thrall to The Process. Frankly, it would be a tall order and take a miracle of God's grace, and then at the very least, many hundreds of thousands of people inclined to cooperate with that grace would have to do so.

Interviewer: And if we don't do so?

Hoffman: If we don't, then the Twilight Language hallucination will continue to occupy both mental and, increasingly, actual physical space in our material world and all of the negatives we have been discussing will accelerate.

Interviewer: What would that entail?

Hoffman: It depends on how the situation devolves, and what the script decrees. We could see blood-smoking pyramids where Main Street once was, with people's hearts ripped out of their chests atop the pyramid's capstone, while other folks go about their business at the Aztec shopping mall. They would be physically and mentally sick, enervated and disoriented without knowing it, while being told they were the beneficiaries of advanced science, and immortality-research aimed at working to keep them alive forever. And similar nonsense.

Even now the life is draining out of people. I was born in the 1950s and I can remember how lively people were then, even in the midst of their cigarettes and beer.

Genuine eroticism, not the canned kind applied like a volt of electricity to a cadaver through pornography, or the easy availability of "recreational" sex, but huge, magnetic attraction between men and women with even some of the wildest and most intractable women possessing a certain nurturing kindness, because the vast majority of them had never had an abortion, and the men had not yet begun to develop the "Playboy" mentality that would give rise to a culture-wide selfishness toward women. I could say much more about those times. I'll just say here that the vitality of women and the virility of men was something we could grok, and we can grok the substantial lessening of those qualities since then.

Interviewer: Rather than being something special, this sounds to me like the traditional nostalgic lament of every generation about their own imagined and self-dramatized idyllic past, which they think they experienced as children or adolescents.

Hoffman: You could be right. Thackeray, in his novel *The Newcomes* writes of a time "when the sun used to shine brighter than it appears to do in this latter half of the 19th century; when the zest of life was keener."

The fact that the lost lament for a better time may be a recurring aspect of human nature doesn't necessarily cancel the likelihood of the universe being changed or disturbed by a signal event, such as the first explosion of the atomic bomb in 1945, the first day in the recorded history of the world when the sun appeared to dawn twice in one morning. The atomic sun manifested in the darkness. "The sun at midnight" was one of the deepest mysteries of ancient Egypt, available to everyone at death, and in the deepest mystery of *America mystica*, to those living three thousand years later, in 1945.

After that event could the world ever be the same? Was the sky as blue, the soil as verdant? Scientism-trolls would respond that, according to their instruments of measurement, yes, the sky is just as blue, the soil just as fertile. Yet, what are their primitive instruments compared with the vibrations received by a fine-tuned human being?

Interviewer: The war, as you see it, is between the world of numbers and the world of poetry.

Hoffman: Edgar A. Poe championed ratiocination, a form of reasoning which factors the limits of the empire of mathematics. In "The Purloined Letter," Auguste Dupin, Poe's master sleuth, points to the limits of number-calculations: "Mathematical axioms are *not* axioms of general truth."

James Shelby Downard intuited that the woman playing The Great Whore role in mid-20th century secret society rites in America, spontaneously experienced orgasms in places that were vortexes of power. No mathematics sees that.

By poetic intuition one may discern that magnetism in and between humans is dangerously low now, indicative of pathology; of species attack.

Interviewer: Franz Anton Mesmer, the pioneering hypnotist spoke of "magnetism" and his system allegedly operated by means of it.

Hoffman: Officially the Establishment dismissed Mesmer as a quack. Unofficially it was acknowledged that this invisible magnetism was real.

Interviewer: How so?

Hoffman: Torsten Enßlin is a theoretical astrophysicist at the Max Planck Institute for Astrophysics in Garching, Germany. He states that magnetism "is a little bit like a living organism, because magnetic fields tap into every free energy source they can hold onto and grow. They can spread and affect other areas with their presence, where they grow as well."

Interviewer: Science, until recently excluded this phenomenon from its system of measurement.

Hoffman: In the sense that Mesmer dramatized it, his theatrical presentation of this magnetic reality, yes, that's true. But as early as 1845 the devout Christian genius Michael Faraday detected it by measuring the polarization of light waves at different frequencies. He discovered that a magnetic field rotates the polarization direction of light passing through it. The Faraday Rotation is determined by the power of a magnetic field and the frequency of the light.

Mesmer taught that magnetism permeated the universe. How did he know and teach that fact before Faraday was working? Other than gravity, magnetism is the only known force that determines the structure of the universe. It has the power to do this over immense distances.

Interviewer: If this is strictly a matter of scientific reality why has it become associated with weird spookiness?

Hoffman: Part of it is the mystique of Mesmer's magnetic-based hypnotism and part of it is the nature of the thing itself: it's intangible. Magnetic fields can only be detected when they act on something else. For example, microcosmically, magnetic fields cause charged particles to twist in spirals, which is a mirror image of the macrocosmic reality of the spiral galaxies manifesting on a vast scale.

Interviewer: What's the relationship between magnetism and hypnotism?

Hoffman: Mesmer believed that the human body possessed a magnetic field that could be manipulated to "sympathetically" influence the mind when that field was penetrated.

Interviewer: And the earth has a magnetic field that protects us from the sun's rays.

Hoffman: It partially shields us from periodic bombardment by charged solar particles that comprise the "solar wind."

Interviewer: Didn't Mesmer claim he could detect the strength of a human being's magnetic field?

Hoffman: He at least insinuated that he could and it's probably safe to say he believed he could.

Interviewer: Isn't that impossible?

Hoffman: One should hesitate to use that word because even today so little is known about magnetism by the scientific yardstick. Knowing the nature of the universe is not possible without knowing the nature of magnetic fields which control the density and distribution of cosmic rays in the interstellar realm. This is mostly a mystery to physicists and astrophysicists, at least in terms of what the public is told. Science in the public realm can't answer fundamental questions, such as how the magnetic fields of planets, stars and galaxies are maintained. Scientists continue to depend on the 176-year-old Faraday Rotation for what knowledge they have obtained of the field component of magnetism. Their futuristic quest is to measure Faraday rotation against what's termed the "Cosmic Microwave Background," produced by magnetic fields.

Before quantum physics, before the discovery of what Einstein and others derided as *spukhafte Fernwirkung* ("spooky action at a distance"), Mesmer's alleged ability to turn his human mechanism into a means of detecting and employing magnetism would have been laughed out of contention.

Interviewer: And now, not so much?

Hoffman: Not now, not until we can answer this question: what's the relationship, if any, between magnetic fields and hypnotic control of the human mind?

Interview: Is this question a pursuit of science?

Hoffman: On the esoteric plane not divulged to the public, I would answer in the affirmative, but in terms of the open scientific study of magnetism it seems to me that scientists are almost solely preoccupied with the macrocosmic; with the connection between detecting magnetic fields in space and correlating those measurements with the development of the structure of the universe. But what if the human body is a microcosm of the universe? In that instance there would be parallel fields available for more localized study. It appears that Mesmer engaged in those studies.

Interviewer: And the Cryptocracy has built upon his work? He was an occultist, right?

Hoffman: A member of a secret society? Reputed to be a Freemason. His educational career, both at Ingoldstadt University and in the medical school at the University of Vienna, was supervised by the Jesuits, and both institutions of course were of the Church of Rome. He was a polymath. He taught Mozart to play the glass harmonica, the strangest western musical instrument with which I'm familiar, other than the Theremin. Mesmer himself played an improved version which rotated on a spindle, this particular updated gizmo having been invented by the Freemason Ben Franklin. Mesmer used the glass harmonica during his employment of magnets and hypnosis. In his book *Mémoire su la découverte du magnétisme animal* published in 1799, he wrote in number sixteen of his twenty-seven propositions: "It is communicated, propagated and intensified by sound."

Dr. Mesmer stated that magnetism suffused the universe in "tides," which is pretty much the astrophysical description now, two hundred years after Mesmer.

James Shelby Downard spoke of human magnetic fields in mesmeric terms, as "sympathy" and "rapport." He believed this force could be used for good or evil.

I see it as the probable foundation of the control of the Group Mind of masses of people when all of their attention is focused on an object of vision, whether it be a Superbowl football game or the mass murder of Country and Western music fans in the presence of Pharaoh's ritual objects in "Sin City."

The mesmerists employed it to hypnotically control the individual mind. In my view it's also employed to hypnotically control the Group Mind, and as a consequence of the negative use of that control, to gradually condition us into something other than human; into a lower order of being, contemporaneous with the emergence of artificial intelligence (AI) which exerts its own rapport, or what Elon Musk called a weirdness that was likely to be malevolent and that humanity would begin to experience circa 2024.

Interviewer: Hypnosis is induced by inducing a sleeping state and then the hypnotic suggestions are imparted.

Hoffman: Yes, and there are post-hypnotic suggestions as well. It was often said in the early 20th century by people like

Gurdjieff that, "Humanity is asleep." It's a common-enough refrain but people miss the fact that it's something that is subject to the change of era. Has the future already happened? The future we visualize as healthy and prosperous and advanced? Did it occur in the 1890s or the 1920s, and has it been downhill since then, commensurate with the conclusion of the dream of natural, life-enhancing progress? Has the eclipse been initiated and engineered by the Revelation of the Method?

Interviewer: Masses of people intentionally exposed to the making manifest of spiritually and psychologically devastating secrets, 'top secrets,' are very much awake.

Hoffman: Up to a point, but after the trauma of the revelation—in the post-adrenalin shock—the percipient is exhausted and sleep is very much desired. The sleeping state is then induced, together with more hypnotic suggestions concerning what constitutes reality. By this method the power and believability of false constructs of reality are exponentially increased as a result of the cycle of unveiling alarming, formerly clandestine facts on the one hand, followed by a sleep which does not refresh on the other.

When I specify sleep, I mean a state of sleep that is occurring during apparent wakefulness. It's repetitive shock therapy for the purpose of psychic driving: Revelation of the Method followed by somnambulism and hypnotic direction...Revelation of the Method followed by....homunculus, Jumbo, the mushroom cloud, king-kill in Dealey Plaza; taking *prima materia* back to *prima terra* and jettisoning the landing craft into the sun; twilight language serial murders, Son of Sam and Wicked King Wicker, the Oklahoma City bombing, the 9/11 terror attacks; the attacks in Columbine and Aurora Colorado and Las Vegas, Nevada, accompanied by synchronized clues, and jokes on the victims planted in Hollywood movies and other corporate media.

If there is any "pandemic" today it is the schizophrenia brought about by this bipolar excursion into a madness wherein the kind, benevolent, virtue-signaling leaders we are taught to admire, are revealed in flashes and bursts of illuminating intensity, as monsters of iniquity.

Interviewer: You wrote in *Secret Societies and Psychological Warfare* that this devolutionary process was "powered" by Twilight Language. You added the irony that what you call "bestialization" was accompanied by widespread announcements that humanity is entering a wonderful new level of advancement, selling us on the idea that we are headed toward becoming an ageless super humanity as long as we cooperate with the *zeitgeist*.

Hoffman: A super imbecility is more like it.

Interviewer: Give an example.

Hoffman: The manner in which in the year 2020 the television-watching imbeciles swallowed hook, line and sinker the remarkable fable that a seriously over-hyped flu virus dubbed COVID-19 was grounds for locking down the population of the United States, while we all waited for the "benevolent creative geniuses" in the pharmaceutical industry to sell the government a "cure," in the form of a vaccine.

It only takes a little mental acuity and initiative to learn two words that explain how humanity overcame the plagues of the past ten thousand years prior to the dominion of man-made laboratory drugs: the cultivation of *natural immunity*. How do we develop and strengthen our immunity by natural means?

Since the iatrogenic drug-pushers can't make billions of dollars answering a question like that, which entails the knowledge and use of plant-based medicines and radical lifestyle changes in terms of remineralizing the soil and other health improvements, they direct their moronic TV "news" talking heads to avoid the subject. Consequently, Americans sat stupefied in suspended animation awaiting a miracle at the end of a needle, instead of getting on with life, as the "benighted superstitious peasants" of the past managed to do in the midst of the Spanish Influenza, and other powerful flu outbreaks that occurred periodically throughout the 20th century and which killed hundreds of thousands of people without calling a halt to school, commerce and life outside the home.

By the way, with the introduction of the internal combustion engine and vehicles powered by it, millions of people have been killed in car and truck accidents since the early 20th century, and something like upwards of an average of 40,000 people in America are killed every year, even now. If everyone who traveled in a motorized vehicle wore a NASCAR crash helmet, three-point seat belt and flame retardant suit, those deaths and crippling injuries would be dramatically reduced. Do we see any sustained demands for those reforms on the part of the Establishment media's safety campaigners who virtually shut down this nation to "save lives" during the "COVID-19" epidemic of 2020-21?

Improperly prescribed pharmaceutical drugs kill hundreds of thousands of Americans per annum. Outcry? Reforms?

COVID-19 has been the focus of a selectively indignant media-panic with an agenda of social engineering having little or nothing to do with the health and safety of the people.

Interviewer: The hidden agenda.

Hoffman: This is the Black Jack game. It's not hidden. In the 1930s there was a Saturday afternoon movie serial featuring a Chinese villain, "Ming the Merciless." In 1981 Dean Koontz, writing under the pseudonym Leigh Nichols, published *The Eyes of Darkness*. On p. 353 of the paperback reprint edition printed under his real name, Mr. Koontz writes, "...China's most important and dangerous new biological weapon in a decade. They call the stuff 'Wuhan-400' because it was developed at their RDNA labs outside of the city of Wuhan. Wuhan-400 is a perfect weapon...."

On page 356 we read, "Bollinger knew how fast Wuhan-400 claims its victims, and he just panicked. Flipped out. Apparently, he convinced himself he could run away from the infection. God knows, that's exactly what he tried to do."

Interviewer: Are you saying Kootnz's Wuhan-400 was a type of precursor Twilight Language?

Hoffman: On page 364 it's revealed that the character Danny's "newfound psychic abilities were a result of...his repeated exposure to Wuhan-400."

Interviewer: So this Danny person sees things most of us can't after he contracts the Wuhan-400 virus? Are you suggesting that Koontz's *The Eyes of Darkness* has something to do with COVID-19 and the 21 Gateway?

Hoffman: Divide the number 400 Dean Kootnz identified with Wuhan by the COVID number 19 which Donald Trump identified with Wuhan China, and you have 21. [4]

Interviewer: What does this mean?

Hoffman: It's a haunting. As far back as 1576 Fleming in his *Panopl. Epist.* (228) made a medical reference to being "haunted with a fever," but by 1594 Shakespeare was using the word in terms more familiar to us: "...haunt me in my sleep, to undertake the death of the world." (*Richard III*, Act 1, Scene 2). There is also the medieval connotation of haunting as being habituated to some thing or event.

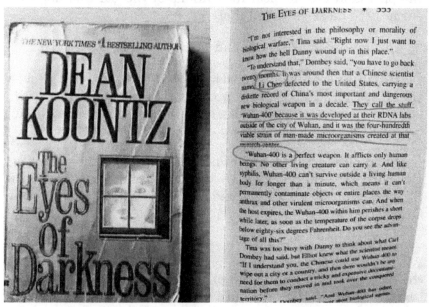

Interviewer: And the significance is what?

Hoffman: Haunting us with the spectre that COVID-19 was staged. Here's another chapter of the psychodrama that shapes the fable being conveyed by those who have traveled to

---

[4] To be specific, exactly 21.0526315789.
Separating the decimal numbers as: 05,263 and 15,789 and then adding them = 21,052.

the subterranean crypt and returned to our world to tell about it. [5]

Interviewer: In other words, a script.

Hoffman: In the argot of dramaturgy, script is shorthand for manuscript. In the twentieth century it denoted a "shooting script" fashioned in the curious craft of writing for cinema, television and video gaming. In the age of electricity, much of what has been used to process a mass audience is from a script, particularly fallible forecasts about the future that are presented as infallibly prescriptive. In the sense we're discussing here however, this haunting and the subsequent memory shaping and encoding—it seems to be a more venerable process—the shadows that dance around the campfire and the musical intonations of the bard as her voice enraptures those gathered there.

Interviewer: We see it and we don't see it.

Hoffman: Our subconscious *groks* it, to use Robert Heinlein's term, and as we proceed through this Time of the Gateway, we are seeing the story emerge into our waking consciousness and even materialize as a physical presence.

Interviewer: Is there an inception point for this scripting? Downard said the plan for the JFK assassination was laid in Shakespeare, New Mexico and the Storyville section of New Orleans.

Hoffman: In the early modern era we see it first in the West in the origin of the Rosicrucians with the publication over the period from 1614 to 1615 of their, at that time, anonymous texts, *Fama Fraternitatis* and *Confessio Fratenitasis*, ostensibly anti-Catholic tracts but actually products of papally-enabled Kabbalistic gnosis.

Interviewer: Which is what?

---

[5] To our knowledge, author Dean Koontz is not and was not involved in any conspiracy or wrong doing relating to his novel, to Wuhan or the pandemic. His book reflects well on his talent and prescience.

Hoffman: The human alchemy of "Magia and Cabala" pioneered by that prodigy of the Church of Rome, Count Pico della Mirandola. The Rosicrucian texts announced the formation of a secret society dedicated to shaping and directing science. The inaugural texts were authored by members of the "Tübingen Circle," a group whose German-Papist-Nominalist forefathers 125 years earlier, had initiated the first concerted intellectual and theological propaganda for ecclesiastical permission for usury.

Interviewer: You claim that the manifestation in the sky of the mushroom cloud by the explosion of the first atomic bomb, at the terminus of the old Mexican road known as the Journey of the Dead Man, on the 33rd degree of north parallel latitude, at the "Trinity Site," in the U.S. state whose nickname is "the Land of the Enchantment" is a direct result of the occult scripting of the Rosicrucian Ludibrium, correct?

Hoffman: It's more than a script, don't you think? It's a haunting tale contrived by an apparition bearing the vanilla names "bureaucrat" and "technocrat."

Interviewer: Which you say is the smokescreen behind which the occultism is hidden because it's so improbable coming from nerdy functionaries like that.

Hoffman: It would not have been improbable in 1615 when the *Fama* and the *Confessio* were presented in terms of the yearning for an advanced science. The Rosicrucian texts were couched in the lofty rhetoric of humanist calls for "reform," in terms of advanced propulsion of the acquisition of *scientia est potentia*, the new age of *scientific power* over nature.

The first edition of the *Confessio,* was published in Latin, together with something called the *Consideratio brevis,* an abstruse alchemical treatise by the enigmatic "Phillippus a Gabella." This person's *Consideratio* was known in English as a "Short Consideration of the More Secret Philosophy." It was a Hermetic explication of the *Monas hieroglyphica* that had been formulated by the English mathematician Dr. John Dee, during the time he served as sorcerer for the regime of Protestant Queen Elizabeth I. We are a bit behind the times in being disinclined to conceive of the mathematics of sorcery at the Trinity Site in 1945.

Interviewer: Why did the elite of the early 17th century see nothing sinister in magic married to mathematics?

Hoffman: One of the strengths of Frances Yates was her study of the difference between how magic in medieval times was perceived, as compared with during the Italian Renaissance. In the Middle Ages magic was almost always viewed as filthy, dark and demonic. By popularizing the concept of an "angelic Catholic" Kabbalah, allegedly representative of God's own branches of divine knowledge, Pico della Mirandola and his Medici network cleaned up the image of sorcery and identified mathematics and the other learned disciplines with it. From that infernal marriage, both Cartesian mechanism and scientism's "repair" (*tikkun olam*) of a supposedly "imperfect Creation" through the intervention of human brain power arose, with fairly disastrous results for Nature and this planet, as witnessed in the Land of Enchantment's spectacular theatrical crucible, 330 years later.

Interviewer: How can the deterministic world of science find common cause with sorcery?

Hoffman: As you know the universe as envisioned by quantum physics is not deterministic, it's indelibly probabilistic. Quantum states reflect our own knowledge of physical reality, rather than being faithful representations of something that exists independently. A case in point are the particles that don't have definite properties until those properties are measured.

Interviewer: And you believe that?

Hoffman: It may or may not be prudent to believe it. It does however beg the question, "Is there a hidden deterministic reality that's not modeled by the mathematics of quantum mechanics?"

Interviewer: How are we missing the whole science and magic connection?

Hoffman: It hasn't been missed by the New Age and hippie movements, beginning in the 1960s, though the knowledge was mutilated and misdirected. There are shelves of books and films devoted to it. The "Tao of Physics" etc.

Interviewer: Not in connection with the atom bomb.

Hoffman: Other than meditation on Oppenheimer's observation from the *Bhagavad Gita* which he allegedly uttered at the detonation, "I am become death, the shatterer of worlds."

Interviewer: I thought we were in the Revelation of the Method era?

Hoffman: We are, but there are paradoxes generated, adumbrated, as expressed in the maxim "hiding less in order to hide more," something which occasionally attends the Revelation but is not reducible to it.

Interviewer: Then it undercuts the Revelation.

Hoffman: Not if, however apparently circuitous the route, it leads to its manifestation.

Interviewer: How?

Hoffman: Hiding less in order to hide more seems to me to be an adjunct of the Revelation of the Method process itself. It's possible that the process doesn't operate in alignment with our expectations, for example that it's almost always going to manifest as a combustive flash. It appears to function in certain circumstances in ways that are analogous to what's known in computer science, in the year 2021 anyway, as iO, short for "indistinguishability Obfuscation." iO enables the creation of "deniable" encryption, wherein the user can plausibly convince a percipient that she was sent an entirely different message from the one actually transmitted. They are given the actual message but they don't recognize it. A method of obfuscating processing, rendering it indistinguishable, involves initiating people into the program without them perceiving the program's internal secrets. That's comparable to homomorphic computer encryption, in which a cloud computer has the ability to compute encrypted data without acquiring its internal dynamics.

Interviewer: Where does the Revelation of the Method come into play in this scenario?

Hoffman: Well, in that case you have RQM, which is relational quantum mechanics, which asserts that the value for one system is always relative to the system it's interacting with. For example, time and space. Time relations among events are constituted by the specific *physical relations* obtaining between them: for instance, the ongoing presence in time of a haunted place. Charged events occurring in a specific place can manifest in perpetuity in future time as a "haunting." To create this perpetuity an action is "charged" through expertly calculated, impeccably executed rituals, sometimes involving the shedding of blood.

Interviewer: How is the expertise to accomplish this gained?

Hoffman: Through what formerly was known as sorcery.

Interviewer: And you think this is what some "serial murders" and "lone nut gunman" type shooting massacres really are, using magical, ceremonial phenomena in space for haunting future time; channeling it in directions where the sorcerers decide it has to go to achieve their supreme objective?

Hoffman: Haunting the future, yes. Another word would be imprinting the future, so that it bears the stamp and image of the sorcerers. Out of that alchemy comes a drastically occluded vision that can't conceive of anything other than what we're told the future will be. And the command ideology has prophesied that humanity will settle for it because they can't see how it can go any other way. Late in the game, when the full Revelation of the Egyptian-thanatos, occult criminality is made manifest, it won't matter. That's Black Jack's wager.

Interviewer: And less of this is hidden by the Revelation of the Method pageantry, so that more can be concealed. That's the "21" Black Jack stage you claim we're in.

Hoffman: Yes, as we're led through the 21 Gateway, certain strategies, tactics and methods of operation remain concealed in the short term, for the purpose of successfully performing, without obstruction, the final revelation, according to what I surmise is a primordial script that gained motive force in the city-of-dark-night that was ancient Egypt, and then fueled by the two-tiered law-givers and secrets-keepers of every eon, and whose ultimate fulfillment is reputedly destined to be "expertly calculated" and "impeccably executed."

Interviewer: For the purpose of?

Hoffman: For the permanent ascendance of the enemy of the human race. There's a persistent legend that Satan can make people stronger, that he wants them to have joy, unlike God who is portrayed as a nay-sayer and killjoy. But actually Satan is the enemy of the human race. His empire consists of abortion and autopsy and the dominion of dead matter.

Interviewer: As a Biblical Christian how do you reconcile this dark future with Scripture?

Hoffman: Because I explore the beliefs and mechanisms of the Cryptocracy, it doesn't follow that I personally believe in their efficacy or fulfillment. When a psychiatrist provides a case study of a psychotic patient's delusions it doesn't signify that he shares those delusions.

The confusion arises in the concept of potency. Unlike an everyday schizophrenic who possesses no more than average personal power or wealth, the psychotics running the occult imperium are potent operators who have convinced large swaths of humanity to buy into their deceptive phantasmagoria. Sociopathic master criminals often possess a considerable capacity to successfully mount swindles and fraud. When this capacity is repeatedly honed, improved and passed down to the heirs of the gnosis by a criminal gang that has utilized these sophisticated techniques of mind control for millennia, the hallucination they project will become a kind of reality for much of humanity.

Interviewer: With quantum physics in mind, don't we have to question what reality is?

Hoffman: The yardstick of quantum physics serves as a check on our arrogance and a reminder that any measurement that falls short of the highest aspiration for truth and the purest curiosity, will be a subjective and corrupted one.

Interviewer: Quantum physics is wrong then in suggesting all of our perceptions about reality are subjective?

Hoffman: We go wrong when we fail to recall that quantum physics itself is a form of measurement. Its quantifications are subject to the same limitations as all other evaluations and computations.

Interviewer: Then we're locked in a cognitive trap set up by an occult reality, with no chance of escape. Trapped by freeze-the-secrets/thaw-the-secrets; and hide-less-to-conceal-more, Revelation of the Method lockdown hypnotic control, dead matter supremacy.

Hoffman: That's the proper belief seeded by Control.

Interviewer: According to you that's our present reality.

Hoffman: That's the present *script*.

Interviewer: It's our reality, in the present!

Hoffman: No. The present "reality" doesn't exhaust the reality that's out of sight and beyond our comprehension.

Interviewer: I'll anticipate you're going to say, "The reality that is Jesus."

Hoffman: I'm saying we should deal in Nature, Creation and the cosmos. A play has been run on us to believe in polytheism, the notion that there are two supreme beings, Jesus and Satan, and that it has yet to be determined who shall win and reign.
The reality is that the person who raises people from the dead and raises Himself from the dead, is in charge of the universe. In Matthew 28:18 it is written that all authority in heaven and earth has been given to Jesus. The impressive sorcerers and occultists that we've been discussing are in fact

pitiful chumps. The dazzling eschatology they've devised with extraordinary virtuosity, the glamor they've employed to induce in us obsequious devotion and shuddering awe, is one act in the infinite theatre of God's inescapable will.

Interviewer: You worked as a hospital orderly in a large psychiatric facility in upstate New York.

Hoffman: Yes, a psychiatric hospital of some fifteen hundred patients with the Twilight Language keyword, "Willard" in its name — Willard State Hospital, a.k.a. Willard Psychiatric Center.

Interviewer: Is there a Twilight Language dictionary? How do you determine what is a key word in this lexicon?

Hoffman: I don't think it's so formal. It's often a matter of intuition and pattern detection. And then too, the phenomenon is shape-shifting. Personally, for me there are a number of ways to try to detect a key word or phrase in this context, most often when it becomes prominently associated with something truly out of the ordinary. The word "wicker" for example, which, as I said earlier, is associated historically with ritual immolation, and etymologically with the bending of reality. Then it crops up in the symbol-laden, serial-killer book, *The Silence of the Lambs*. Furthermore, a member of the Son of Sam serial murder cult signed his letter to New York reporter Jimmy Breslin, "Wicked King Wicker." Wicker is a palimpsest of Twilight Language, a form of communication which bends the ordinary reality of our half-asleep, workaday consciousness and which can be formed and imprinted through selection, repetition and association: selecting a word that's usually already freighted with etymological weirdness, and then repeatedly associating it with, for example, ritual murder, so that it becomes a type of invocation.

Interviewer: Is there a twilight language separate from human intervention?

Hoffman: That's a worthy question and to explore it we should ask another: how does synchronicity arise and order itself? Is it exclusively manipulated by an extra-human agency? If not, what role does human agency play? Using Mesmer as a navigator, is there a kind of Nikola Telsa-like "tower" or "antenna," not necessarily purely physical, that attracts and orders synchronicity? If something like that exists, is it aimed, like a weapon or a means of engineering humanity? If so, how does it operate and who is the operator?

Interviewer: Would you say that the ability to perceive these signals or translate this language is not mental illness?

Hoffman: Wouldn't the ability to detect patterns that actually do have significance as "Twilight Language" be a stepping stone to seeing the operations of the world we inhabit with greater clarity?

Interviewer: Leading to total clarity?

Hoffman: A claim of total clarity overlooks that inherent trickiness of the material universe since The Fall.

Interviewer: Looks like we're back to Original Sin again.

Hoffman: People imagine that seeing the world as cursed by Original Sin is a needlessly prejudicial and negative form of inevitabilism that creates the condition it presumes to diagnose. The "positive thinker" believes that each person creates the world they perceive around them with their own thoughts, which is true, but only up to a point. One cannot become God through one's thoughts. It is only *within* God's Creation and within the time, space and personnel that God has brought into existence, that viewing all of that created phenomena with a positive view of potentiality, makes it resonate on a higher plane of harmony. And then only to a point, because how do you banish the darkness, the accuser, this *satan*, this force that is the opposite of love?

We know two world-champion positive thinkers who have written books and founded successful, transformative businesses founded on positive thoughts and affirmations. They traveled a long way ahead and they continue to go that way, but a few years ago they suffered an enormous setback that nearly destroyed all of their work in a major American metropolis. In the end even they had to concede that they were horribly attacked by The Darkness, due to the fact they were manifesting love to such a degree that the Darkness intervened with very serious consequences for their commercial enterprise, which also happened to be philanthropic.

Yes, good comes out of adversity, but the point is that the force we might wish to denominate as The Opposite of Love, is a function of the distorting process wired into the post-Edenic material universe—a Christian would say it manifested "After the Fall." Like the existence of gravity and magnetism, The Opposite of Love is so fundamentally wired into our world it is outside the process whereby phenomena are called into existence by our positive or negative attention.

Interviewer: I'll return to what you said was loaded with negative connotations and ask you, are you willing to say that another name for the "inherent trickiness of the material universe" is Original Sin?

Hoffman: Yes, but only if it's understood to denote an event that occurred *after* a harmonious primeval relationship with the Creator was sundered. To state that the material universe is inherently tricky from inception, in its very nature, would be to succumb to the error of Platonism—the occult detestation of Creation paradoxically coming up with utopian programs—what Thomas Molnar termed the perennial heresy, the attempt to build a planetary paradise with the concomitant belief that congenitally flawed, postlapsarian human nature can be altered independent of Jesus Christ.

Interviewer: This is bleak. Humans have to huddle in perpetual pessimistic wariness? That's their only path out of the occult?

Hoffman: Where you see pessimism I see a joyful community of brothers and sisters in Christ, having an awareness of human folly and a healthy suspicion of kings, governors, dictators and rulers in general. First, we acknowledge that God is the author of our inalienable human rights. When the Creator is removed from the equation then the Leninist, the Maoist or the neo-Nazi steps in to say that rights are conferred by The Party, and can be legally and ethically withdrawn by The Party. Second, where fallen human nature is acknowledged (which is a supremely anti-occult acknowledgement), flawed human beings will not be entrusted with unrestrained authority.

Interviewer: So all that is good in community and brotherhood is explicitly Christian, and anything outside of it is not? For a collector of Fortean anomalies like you, that's pedestrian.

Watkins Glen

Hoffman: Fortean anomaly? Let's travel to a glen bearing the name of Sherlock Holmes' assistant, Watkins. The date is July 28, 1973. The site is the largest gathering in the history of the United States. 600,000 people in Watkins Glen, New York for the "Summer Jam" rock music festival, featuring The Band, the Grateful Dead and the Allman Brothers, all taking place on the "Psychic Highway"—the 42nd degree of north parallel latitude. Other than cops outside the concert attempting to direct traffic, among those 600,000 people there was no policing and there was no crime reported. There were however dozens of cases of people ill from drug overdoses and two babies were born. A "city" of that size enjoying that level of almost complete freedom from crime, is fairly unique.

Interviewer: It wasn't a Christian gathering.

Hoffman: True. Christians were present, however. There had to have been prayer and supplication in a population of that size.

Interviewer: Still, it's an anomaly. You mention births. No deaths?

Hoffman: One death.

Interviewer: Do you know who?

Hoffman: Yes. His name was Willard.

Interviewer: How did he die?

Hoffman: He burned to death, Icarus-like.

Interviewer: In Watkins Glen? How?

Hoffman: The official story is that he was a 35-year-old sky-diver who parachuted out of an airplane and then caught fire as he flew through the air.

Interviewer: And the unofficial story?

Hoffman: Well there's this labyrinth see, and then there's this Greek son of Daedalus who possessed the secret of it, who's warned not to fly too high. And then there's Willard Smith, age 35, who flew too high over Watkins. Whether he had the secret of the labyrinth I don't know.

I do know that Willard resided in the city of Syracuse in upstate New York. Its namesake is the ancient Greek city of Syracuse; the one-time capital of Greece's Sicilian colony.

Wikipedia and the *New York Times,* two sides of a counterfeit media coin, both report he carried flares that set his "suit" on fire.

Some of his friends and sky-diving students regarded Willard as a "daredevil." At Watkins he carried aloft an artillery simulator, akin to the M-18 smoke grenades that were somewhat notorious for malfunctioning. And this unstable artillery gadget appears to have exploded prematurely while it was on Willard's chest-mounted reserve parachute.

Willard Psychiatric

Interviewer: You believe Willard is a significant Twilight Language name and you worked at the facility that bore that name. Did anything strange happen there?

Hoffman: One could say that when strangeness becomes commonplace it's no longer strange, which is a description of the process of human alchemy.

Interviewer: Yet this alchemical processing renders the majority of people living in modern times evil, which is very strange.

Hoffman: Not evil, but lukewarm, which T.S. Eliot observed was worse than evil. As far back as 1933 he told Paul Elmer More, "Not many people are alive enough to be evil." He said that the number who need to "borrow vitality and can't pay it back is immense."

Willard itself was indeed a place of high strangeness, much like the Willard Hotel in Washington D.C. and the action in Richard Brautigan's book, *Willard and His Bowling Trophies*.

I was born and raised in an upstate New York town on the "psychic highway." Willard was approximately 20 miles south of our family home. When I was a child I heard the word Willard and it gave me the willies. I overheard grown-ups talking, sometimes in whispers, other times in anguished shouts and cries, about someone having to be "sent to Willard," or as a threat, sometimes idle, that a person, "Ought to go to Willard!" When I was about twelve I was walking to my grandparent's house on North Main Street, and I witnessed an altercation in a parking lot behind a residence. I recognized a short man who worked for the city highway department, grappling with his wife as she seemed to be trying to enter a car and I heard him say, "They're going to take you to Willard if you keep this up!" It was a refrain, like a fragment from a song; an ear worm one can't entirely dispel.

It seemed in my youth that people in my town of some 20,000 were either going to Willard or coming out of Willard, or they were patients in Willard. The sound of that name conveyed to me a nervous, jangling feeling, as well as a place of confinement. Then when I was in my early 20s I found myself employed there.

Interviewer: Were you afraid to be there?

Hoffman: I was never afraid there. I was sad at times and at other times joyful, and even elated.

Interviewer: Why weren't you afraid?

Hoffman: Willard was located on what might be called a white or crystal stream. I'm not speaking literally, but in terms of the spirit of the place, the *genius loci*. It was a beautiful location on the shore of Seneca Lake, with magnificent deciduous trees, a fine theatre building that was many decades old at the time. It exuded peace and serenity. In autumn I considered it one of the loveliest places I had ever seen.

Interviewer: No haunted buildings, no feelings of menace?

Hoffman: One building, which had been the original asylum from the 19th century, was alleged by some to be severely haunted. It was vacant save for a few secretarial offices at the front of the building, on the lakeside. I knew an employee who was also a semi-professional thief and he told me of how he would enter the building at night to steal antiques, and as greedy as he was, he had to give up his burglaries because he was too badly frightened on occasion to proceed.

Interviewer: In what way?

Hoffman: With an overwhelming sense of foreboding, which may have led him to hear noises and see lights.

Interviewer: What had happened in that building?

Hoffman: In the 19th century? Misery. People confined, chained, beaten.

Interviewer: Did you ever enter it?

Hoffman: A couple of times in the course of my duties I had to visit the secretarial pool there at the front. I did not feel or notice anything weird or unusual. The building was architecturally distinguished; a kind of solemn Victorian style, but since what frightened the bejeebers out of me in that time (the 1970s), was a garishly lighted, soullessly concrete K-Mart store, that old building seemed benevolent by comparison. The secretaries were women, some of them young, who enlivened the quarters they occupied. I was told that few if any lingered after hours or in the dark, and that none wanted to be alone there, but I don't know how true that is.

Interviewer: Did you have access to the rest of the building?

Hoffman: I could have had access. I had access to almost the entire campus, which was hundreds of acres, including a by-then abandoned farm and orchards. Like most of the employees on the floor, I had the master key that fit the doors of every ward and every room where patients were housed.

Since I was trusted with that key, I could have asked someone to let me in the back part of the old asylum, but I didn't and I can't say why, for certain. I passed it every day and it seemed to have eyes like the House of Usher, but in comparison to the world that patronized K-Mart it just didn't seem sinister to me on the same scale of horror.

I lingered on its lawn and sometimes took my lunch in the shade of its maple trees. I respected it as a fixture of a time and place that had its own context that couldn't and shouldn't be judged by the modern mentality.

Interviewer: What happened to you when you went to K-Mart?

Hoffman: When I went to K-Mart? I felt blinded by its harsh light, that cash register light, the light of commerce without human concord, amid junk for sale, the decent town folk who became ugly in that light. I was uneasy, nervous and even embarrassed when I was in establishments such as K-Mart. I tried to avoid them. I had no luck in places like that. They were more haunting than Willard but not gothically so, not in that classically spooky way we've come to equate with evil.

Interviewer: "Willard" had been a locus of strangeness for you while you were growing up and all of a sudden it became benign?

Hoffman: Sometimes benign, even though death both gradual and violent occurred there, and the stifling of life, the wasting of lives, but also there were lay saints residing there, and by that I mean inmates who were too good, too holy, too kind, to prosper in our society's rat race, and they took refuge at Willard and the extent to which Willard offered them asylum as opposed to treatment, it was a boon.

Interviewer: What role did you play within that context.

Hoffman: I tried to the best of my ability to offer the people confined there what Dorothy Day termed hospitality.

Interviewer: Not treatment?

Hoffman: In the original understanding of an insane asylum, it was a place of refuge and protection for gifted and troubled people who would otherwise be exploited and mistreated by the outside world. In this sense of asylum one offers above all, hospitality.

Interviewer: What was wrong with Willard?

Hoffman The heavy drugging and electro-shock therapy, which were two main forms of what you would call "treatment" when I was employed there. Mental illness becomes iatrogenic —is manufactured—in people by those methods. One woman patient in her 30s had experienced more than a hundred shock "therapies" and was violently insane as a result. She caused the death of a beautiful octogenarian lady patient on the floor above the one on which I worked.

There were some psychodrama sessions that probably did good and there was a young psychologist who had conversations with acute— meaning short-term—care patients, which probably helped them. But the main point of these facilities should be to protect the lay saints from the outside world and protect the world from the possessed. That's what an asylum is and that's what Willard appears to have been.

Interviewer: You had patients who committed suicide, who murdered people.

Hoffman: Yes. One of our patients had had sex with a cow. People took their own lives. A young man who was released into the community on a weekend pass, returned home ten miles down the road and slaughtered his entire family while his father was absent. He killed his mother and his siblings. We had people guilty of infanticide.

We also had poets and pianists and tragic ones who had been there for forty years. Chain-smoking Arthur Rimbauds. Wives of Cornell University professors. Cornell University students. Vietnam veterans with post traumatic stress. A father-son psychiatric team wherein the psychiatrist father had his psychiatrist son committed by court order. Employees who were admitted as patients; all under the aegis of *"Willard."*

Interviewer: Aside from this mayhem was there anything occult going on?

Hoffman: That's a good question because the Cryptocracy in the past spread the legend and possibly believed it, that certain "mentally ill" people "shine" in the sense of levels of psychic ability or potential, and that these people are used or farmed in some way. I was only at Willard for a little over a year and in that time I can't say I observed any Svengali at work in that way, but the potential was always there. James Shelby Downard believed that something like that happened to him when he was committed to Bolivar State Hospital against his will. He felt he was tortured and abused there. That is perhaps why for the rest of his life he had tremendous compassion for marginalized and damned people he considered genuine scapegoats.

Electro-shock therapy is torture. I was ordered to assist at one shock treatment and that was the first and last time that I did so. I told them they could fire me but I would never help electro-shock another patient again.

Interviewer: Well, was Willard a sinister place or not?

Hoffman: For the brief time I was employed it was both a blessing and a curse for the patients, depending on their circumstances. In the nineteenth century it seems to have been a horrorshow, but what hospital for the insane wasn't in that era?

Interviewer: You see the name Willard as part of the Twilight Language.

Hoffman: I see that someone or some thing, whatever it may be—and I don't discount coincidence, I only ask if coincidence itself is somehow governed and arranged—the name Willard has associations with madness and power that may have, or may have had for a time, an imprinting function on the Group Mind.

But in terms of my experience there, it would be wrong to say it was unrelievedly negative or horrible.

Sometimes I would pose as a patient.

Interviewer: What do you mean?

Hoffman: I worked the day shift, Tuesday through Saturday, and Saturday was a comparatively slow day apart from emergency cases the sheriff would drag in shackled. The main event of Saturday was escorting patients to Hadley Hall, which was the large and lovely old theatre, for a movie. I remember watching a movie there with my patients which was the version of "Tom Sawyer" starring Jody Foster and Warren Oates, with a lovely soundtrack by the Sherman brothers.

Many of my older patients and some young ones were dressed in cast-off clothing that would be valuable today as vintage '50s and early '60s fashions, but which were out of place in the mid 1970s. Sometimes I would dress in the same vintage clothing as my patients and instead of remaining inside the theatre after escorting them there, I sat outside with the patients who were nicotine fiends and kept them company while they smoked. I wanted to see how other employees treated them when they assumed they were alone only with patients present. I remember one lady employee arriving after we seated ourselves outside. She began to be quite rude to one of my patients and I told her so. Thinking that I too was a patient she scolded me to sit down and shut up. When I protested her indignities she raised her hand as if to slap me. It was at that point that I reached into my pocket and fished out the master key that only employees possessed. Fixing her startled countenance with a glare, I dangled the key in front of her eyes and said, "That's no way to treat a vulnerable person."

She was shocked. She scurried into the theatre and I like to think that she afforded the afflicted better care after that.

Interviewer: Were you ever worried that by masquerading as a patient you might cross the line and lose your identity?

Hoffman: I wouldn't call it a masquerade. I permitted percipients to fool themselves. I didn't behave like a patient, I vaguely resembled one on certain Saturdays and the assumptions of those who saw me led them to deceiving themselves concerning my identity. But to answer your question, I saw at least as much insanity outside Willard on the part of well-dressed, well-groomed "respectable citizens," as I did inside. Some considerable portion of the patients at Willard were confined there because they were far more sane that those who did the confining, which is an old story.

Interviewer: Of visionaries labeled as insane?

Hoffman: Yes, but let's be careful not to lose sight of how many sluggards pose as visionary artists to provide cover for their sloth, their irresponsibility and lack of the spark of life. They waste their lives and leech off others. In defense of their behavior they say they are misunderstood and persecuted for their art. It's a cliché.

Interviewer: The yin and yang again.

Hoffman: Two sides of the coin of life. A tossed coin which lands balanced on its edge is representative of a higher state of consciousness. It's a feat.
We have yang, compressed, uptight conformists who accuse those who think differently from the herd of being crazy, and we have yin scroungers posing as gifted artists and accusing their critics of wrongly calling them shirkers. These are the antipodes of life, I guess. In *After the Fall,* Samuel Beckett expressed these swings of yin and yang destiny when he wrote, "This dust will not settle in our time, and when it does some great roaring machine will come and whirl it all sky-high again."

Interviewer: Do you consider yourself the prophet of the Revelation of the Method in our time?

Hoffman: My family would die laughing if anyone were to call me a prophet.

Interviewer: Well, it's a fact that months before the September 11 terror attacks you published your prediction that the year 2001 would be momentous, would be the gateway to an extraordinary culmination of occult transformation.

Hoffman: God's grace did that. I was only a vehicle for it. Everyone has the potential.

Interviewer: What about a position as consultant on ritual murders?

Hoffman: I wouldn't turn it down. I fulfilled something akin to that when I was a reporter for the Associated Press. I couldn't refuse now helping to bring the actual murderers of those Country and Western fans in Las Vegas to justice in a court of law. I couldn't say no to that. I would be obliged to assist, and I would try to do it, as best I could.

Interviewer: You've suggested that ordinary life may no longer be very possible for people in the digitalized West.

Hoffman: So much is lost in terms of our humanity as we process ourselves into something less. At this stage in the alchemy we're the ideal hypnotic subjects. That's one reason I spent years among the Old Order Wenger Mennonites, and the Amish. To experience human beings whose lives were not invaded by the command language of television, radio and the Internet. I would take my horse and wagon out at 4 a.m. under the summer stars in Holmes County, Ohio, with my buggy's wooden wheels sheathed in steel, rolling over wooden bridges. That "music" was wonderful. In the early evening after the sunset, from the front yard of the farm where we lived, I watched the fireflies dance over fields of shocked barley in inky darkness, no street lights to intrude on the beatitude.

Geophysically, street lights and city lights have blotted out the trillion star night sky that is still visible on the Hana side of Maui, while mechanized and digitalized noise is a plague that robs us of the ordinary blessings of nature. Here in north Idaho there are defunct gold and silver mines, some of which have been stabilized. To enter one of those mines and experience total silence can heal the heart, mind, body and psyche.

Interviewer: This is where people far from industrial civilization have a blessing.

Getting back to the Biblical prophets and warnings. You do believe we have experienced things like that lately.

Hoffman: Oh, sure. The "Terminator Judgment Day" movies were ominous warnings which put the movie-goers and TV watchers—and those to whom those viewers conveyed the narrative—under obligation when they failed to act on the alarm.

"You were warned" is quite an indictment of those who proceed heedlessly. The autonomous "Skynet defense" put into place to render us digitally safe is itself the digital doom. As noted, years earlier Tolkein said it with regard to the "One

Ring." Which is what makes me laugh about these elite PhD. scientists who are absolute infants when it comes to technology. If they can pick it up they'll mess with it. It doesn't matter what it is, analogous to infants with matches and blowtorches cavorting inside a paper mill, or skateboarding into traffic on the Interstate. Those who suggest the scientists shouldn't be so reckless and heedless, receive the infant's response, "Why not Da-da? I can dood it, so I gonna dood it." That's the romper room "philosophy" of scientism now. Play God *because you can* play God. Blowback be damned.

Skynet is a cinematic symbol of the autonomous AI future and it is about as dystopic as one can imagine, but has it slowed our march toward empowering autonomous robots? Not to my knowledge. People have been granted a vision of the consequences, and they go ahead with it anyway because they seem to be in love with death and catastrophe. The negative karma from oblivious arrogance, when it is rendered moral and permissible because "scientists" are at its head, is incalculable. The death wish on this planet is remarkable. The demand for and insistence upon herd-mentality and extinction has not lessened. The Reign of Dead Matter is arriving on schedule. Our Creator declared, "All those who hate me love death." [6]

Interviewer: How then have some of us managed to still be here and be human?

Hoffman: The grace of God.

Interviewer: What is the most recent serial killer type of event that has galvanized you?

Hoffman: Galvanism was the means by which Frankenstein's monster was revived. I hope I have not been galvanized. To answer your question, as we speak, it is the massacre in Las Vegas that strikes me as laden with anomaly.

Interviewer: Tell us about it.

Hoffman: I intend to, but a few preliminaries are in order.

---

[6] Proverbs 8:36

The Psychic Highway
The 42nd Degree of North Parallel Latitude

"All of these changes were powerfully felt in New York State, where some of the most significant new religious movements of the time had their start. A 'psychic highway' followed..."

Sara M. Pike, *New Age and Neopagan Religions in America* (Columbia University, 2004) p. 43.

Skyline Drive, Bluff Point (Keuka Park) New York
Pre-Columbian: Fifteen acres of mounds and stone circles, including an eight foot monolith. By 1954 the site had been erased.
Nineteenth century witnesses described, "...monuments of stone slabs...still standing in groups of different patterns, some in circles, some in squares and arcs, reminding one of the Stone Henge of England. At the northwest corner was a huge monolith...all about the standing slabs were prostrate ones..."

Jerusalem, New York (approximately five miles west of Bluff Point), 1791:
Founding of the religion of Jemima Wilkinson, the "Publick Universal Friend," the first "transgender, non-binary" leader of a new American creed. The Publick Universal Friend predicted that the fulfillment of some prophecies of the Book of Revelation would begin in April of 1780, forty-two months after "the Friend" had commenced preaching.

Canandaigua, New York, 1826:
Founding of the Anti-Masonic movement which swept the northeastern United States throughout the nineteenth century, after author William Morgan was kidnapped from the Ontario County jail by Freemasons and murdered.
"...William Morgan wrote a book exposing the rituals of Freemasonry. Morgan was kidnapped and (it is presumed) drowned for his perfidy by local Masons. An Anti-Masonic party sprang up overnight; by 1828, Upstate New York was ablaze......a thousand ragged prophets traveled our 'psychic

highway'...We had Anti-Masons and reincarnated Christs and enough necromancers to pester the dead till time's end."
Bill Kauffman, *The American Scholar*, January, 1991

September, 1826: the kidnapping of writer William Morgan by Freemasons, in the Canandaigua, New York jail, on the 42nd degree of north parallel latitude. His assassination would lead to the formation of the largest movement in opposition to secret societies in the history of the United States, headed by former President John Quincy Adams, Lincoln's future Secretary of State William Seward, and U.S. Attorney General William Wirt. [1]

---

[1] Concerning the theft of William Wirt's head by grave robbers cf. *Revisionist History®* no. 101 (Feb-March 2019). In England in 1661 Oliver Cromwell's corpse was punished and the head decapitated by order of King Charles II.

Fayette, [2] **New York,** April 6, 1830:
Founding of the Mormon religion by Joseph Smith, after the putative discovery in 1823 of the "golden plates" at Hill Cumorah (also on the 42nd degree of latitude), from which the the *Book of Mormon* was supposedly derived. (The *Book* was published in March, 1830).

Putney, Vermont, 1844:
On the boundary of the 42nd and 43rd degrees of latitude John Humphrey Noyes established his sexual freedom society, the first successful "free love" commune in American history (enduring 40 years). Eventually the Noyes group moved 200 miles west to Oneida, New York (on the 43rd degree line). Under Noyes' supervision, the "Oneida Community" practiced a "complex marriage" in which, in arrangements regulated by Noyes, hundreds of people engaged in serial heterosexual intercourse without benefit of matrimony.

Seneca Falls, New York, 1848:
The founding of Feminism with the first convention for women's rights in western history. [3]

Hydesville (in what is today Arcadia [4]**) New York,** 1848:
The founding of Spiritualism (mediumistic alleged contact with the dead) by the Fox sisters, which became the fastest growing religion in the mid-nineteenth century continental United States (Hydesville/Arcadia is on the 43rd degree of latitude, but within a few tenths of the 42nd degree line).

"One of the greatest religious movements of the 19th century began in the bedroom of two young girls living in a farmhouse

---

[2] In French *Fayette* denotes "little fairy," as William N. Grimstad pointed out in his inaugural essay on the significance of this entry in the Twilight Language lexicon. Cf. "Fateful Fayette," (*Fortean Times,* no. 25, Spring, 1978).

[3] 1848 was a heady year: the California Gold Rush launched in January, and Karl Marx and Friedrich Engels' *Communist Manifesto* was published in February.

[4] In western lore Arcadia is a pastoral utopia.

in Hydesville, New York." (Karen Abbott, *Smithsonian Magazine*, October 30, 2012). [5]

Auburn, New York, 1859: Home of the peripatetic abolitionist Harriet Tubman's "Underground Railroad" for the organization of the harboring of escaped black slaves.

Notes

Beginning in 1959 the production company behind Rod Serling's "Twilight Zone" television series was named "Cayuga Productions," after his Cayuga Lake retreat in New York, on the Psychic Highway's 42nd degree line. Between Cayuga Lake and Seneca Lake stood Willard State Hospital.

In 1916, the Fox Sisters' cottage was dismantled and moved 150 miles west, to a Spiritualist center on the 42nd degree at Lily Dale, New York, where it was reconstructed. On September 12, 1955, the cottage burned to the ground.

Beginning in 1967 at 1510 Hydesville Road, in the hamlet of Hydesville, on the original site of the cottage, a replica was built upon the intact stone foundation by spiritualist John Drummond, who buried his second wife behind the structure. That building was destroyed by fire in November, 1983. The *Finger Lakes Times* (June 18, 1984) reported that 86-year-old Drummond left the site after the fire, announcing "he had a 'calling' to deliver a message to the Mormons in Salt Lake City, Utah."

Poltergeist and similar Fortean phenomena are sometimes alleged to be associated with pre-pubescent or pubescent girls. After discussing past "rappings" in the replica Fox cottage which he arranged to have constructed, Mr. Drummond related to the *Finger Lakes Times* (October 31, 1983), that there had been no anomalous occurrences at the site in many years, "But perhaps if a young girl—maybe 11 or 15—came in here, they (the rapping) might start again."

In 1852 Ohio's traveling lecturer Joseph Barker was introduced to a medium who supposedly put him in contact

---

[5] Among the hundreds of thousands (or millions of adherents [cf. Braude, p. 26]), were Mary Todd Lincoln, who held seances in the White House; *New York Tribune* publisher Horace Greeley, Arctic explorer Elisha Kent Kane and the abolitionists Sojourner Truth and William Lloyd Garrison. He became a believer in 1854 and remained so for the rest of his life. Cf. Anne Braude, *Radical Spirits* (Boston: Beacon Press, 1989).

with his deceased brother and offered him advice which changed his life. "All this wisdom came through the mediumship of a twelve-year-old girl. As in Rochester (New York), Americans throughout the country found messages from spirits most plausible when delivered through the agency of adolescent girls" (Ibid., Braude, p. 23).

On the indeterminate state between our death and resurrection, the New Testament gives no explicit information. References to spirits of the dead are absent. Many Protestant theologians believe that the dead sleep until resurrection (I Thessalonians 4:16, I Corinthians 15:23; Revelation 20:4). Papal theology teaches an immediate judgment after death, and then heaven, hell or purgatory, preceding the general judgment, post-resurrection.

For further research: Joscelyn Godwin, *Upstate Cauldron* (State University of New York, 2015); Whitney Cross, *The Burned-Over District* (Cornell University, 1982); Glenn C. Altschuler and Jan M. Saltzgaber, *Revivalism, Social Conscience and Community in the Burned-Over District* (Cornell University, 1983), and the aforementioned *New Age and Neopagan Religions in America* by Sara M. Pike.

The Willard Factor

"All I have for you is a gesture in combination with a word: Tenet...We live in a Twilight world..." [1]

Christopher Nolan

Witches are accused of shape-shifting and we may perhaps stand accused of syntagm-shifting.

How much of what we know about command and control mechanisms turns on words? What wisdom teaching is conveyed in the story of Rumplestiltskin? Adam in the Garden of Eden obtains dominion over the earth by naming its inhabitants and constituents. In the beginning was The Word.

The heart of mystery is to confront a person or a force that is unnameable. Such a phenomenon resists our control. In the tale of "Rumplestiltskin" our structural fixation with naming is explored. The queen must sacrifice her infant to an imp should she prove unable to conjure his clandestine name. That she possesses the ability to successfully produce his name is not often the focus of the story. Instead, our attention is directed toward Rumplestiltskin's goblin aspect, which distracts us from the gnomic character of the queen herself. How did she manage to locate and then approach unseen, the secluded wilderness camp of a troll so powerful he accomplishes the alchemical feat of transforming base matter ("straw") into gold? It is by the queen's "wandering" that she catches Rumplestiltskin unawares. She hears him at the precise moment that he happens to shout his secret name. The enigmatic power that allows her to achieve this coup is the sub-rosa dimension of the tale. She is victorious in defeating her enemy because he did not suspect the existence of her power. He did not know the name of that power.

The power of "words over matter" is illustrated by the story transmitted by Mary Baker Eddy's predecessors. A father learns that his daughter has drowned. He collapses, and over the course of several days, takes to his death bed. His attending physician observes somberly that, "He appears to be

---

[1] "Tenet" is a palindrome: a word that is spelled the same way reading backward or forward.

slipping into a coma." Soon news arrives that his daughter has survived after all. On having those words conveyed, the father revives, fully recovered. Words caused his physical mechanism to begin to shut down, and words brought him back to the land of the living. He had been placed "under a spell" when word was sent that his beloved offspring had died. The spell was lifted when word was received that she had in fact survived.

If this process had been deliberately timed and aimed—a life-threatening lie conveyed and later withdrawn—it would be indistinguishable from what we call magic—the sorcery of cursing and healing; as in the spells from the texts of the Egyptians.

In the *words-over-matter* magic of the Egyptian goddess Isis, knowledge of a word of power, described as someone's personal name, is of tremendous importance. In one illustrative story, Isis dispatches a snake to bite the solar deity Re, who begins to die from the venom. She informs Re that if he will reveal the closely guarded secret of his personal name, she will heal him and he shall live. When he does so, she informs him that the snake was not poisonous. Upon hearing those welcome words he quickly recovers.

In this allegory the Egyptians demonstrated the understanding that to possess a hidden name of a powerful being, appreciably enhanced the power of Isis. This account of gaining the secret word was used to demonstrate that Isis was foremost of the gods and goddesses, "ruler in heaven and earth" by virtue of her *words-over-matter* technology.

Pharaonic Egypt is a primeval source of Twilight Language (not to be confused with the directions for decoding Buddhist and Hindu texts that contain layers of multiple meanings, known in Sanskrit as *sāṃdhyābhāṣā;* (cf. Agehānanda Bhāratī [Leopold Fischer], *The Tantric Tradition* [1965]).

Hieroglyphic writing, arising circa 3000 B.C. and first ascribed in legend to Thoth, was not pictorial in its earliest manifestations. With refinement it became a system of signs possessed of symbolism and incantatory properties. By the power of words occult mastery was obtained or revoked, the dead were summoned or consigned to oblivion, and humans were endowed or destroyed. With this language John Dee and others of the magus class, sought to command both humans and nature, and harness disincarnate beings. The language was referred to by various names, "Enochian," or in Dee's parlance, "Angelic," consisting of an alphabet and a phonology. There are parallels between the mandalas of Dee's "hieroglyphic monad" and the Kabbalistic system of *gematria* (number/word equivalents) applied to the texts of the Bible, but these western occult systems obtain the talismanic function of Twilight Language only in a few respects. Twilight Language is not circumscribed by *gematria* or Dee's monad, both of which are artificial constructs that attempt to plot a schematic description of the phenomenon, similar to Cornelius Agrippa's number-symbol tables in his *De Occulta Philosophia*.

The Twilight Language addresses, or "speaks," to the "shadow side," the primordial Jungian archetypes of the subconscious psyche. The time capsule that was and is Pharaonic Egyptian sorcery aimed, by ritual means, at crossing oceans of time to invoke a future in human history in which the immanent would appear in public, in the collective waking hive mind, through ceremonial transcendent processing of the subconscious. It is our opinion that this is the stage in which those living in the early 21st century inhabit.

With Twilight Language there is a long history. This is the case with *Wicker*, the root of which is from East Scandinavian, "to bend," as in the bending of reality.

In his 1637 play "Sad Shepherd" (act 1, scene 5) Ben Jonson wrote, "Hark, hark, hark the foul bird, How she flutters with her wicker wings!"

The associated modern synchronicities are worthy of note. For instance, on December 7, 2011 Michael Carlson wrote concerning the prominent *New York Times* writer Tom Wicker: "...unlike many columnists, he was in most cases a writer who refused to bend reality..."

In the 2016 "The Magicians" television series episode, "The Strangled Heart," magician Richard has a conversation with a magician named Julia Wicker:

Richard: "The reason you treat magic like a drug, is because the people that taught it to you act like drug dealers. They buy it and they sell it, and they fight and they fuck for it. Well, that's not the only way to live."

Julia Wicker: "That's the only way I've ever seen."

Richard: "I'm a very good Magician and I do this. There are good people out there, Julia. People trying to learn about the world and make it a better place. Now, you can be one of those people, you can be a dealer, you can stay here and be nothing.

You get to choose. Look, you think magic is some terrible vice, so bad that you need rehab to get clean, it's not. Magic isn't heroin, Julia. It's a gift."

Julia Wicker: "Oh, god, please. Don't say from God."

Richard: I'm not the guy outside of YMCA yelling at people to repent."

Julia Wicker: "Then what are you, Richard?"

Richard: "Okay, what we call magic is, a set of tools. Leftover from Creation. [*Julia scoffs*]

Richard: "Think about it. The power to bend reality, to make and unmake."

*Julia Wicke*r: "Won't God be pissed we touched His tools without asking?"

Richard: "God—gods, really, they don't do things by accident. The tools were left for us to find."

In the previous examples we can sort the differences between the ancient usage and the use assigned in or close to our time. The assignment itself, if repeated emphatically with sufficient visibility amid a targeted audience, or the masses in general, creates an imprint, or what hypnotists term an induction. Within a certain charged context the word becomes linked to a pattern that has the quality of a meme.

"Willard" is just a word.

How is the charged context created? Through assignment. Why was the word chosen? Maybe because it gives us, in the parlance of American slang, "the willies."

"To have the willies, to be nervous" (*Dialect Notes*, 1896).

"You can now visit Winchester House. But we wouldn't advise it if you suffer from the willies." (*Felton & Fowler's Best, Worst, and Most Unusual*, 1975).

Brand Names

What is certain is that upon the neurological science of word choices and the creation of neologisms depends the multibillion dollar advertising industry. Brand names like Radeon, Raytheon, Teledyne, Nuplazid, Xodol, Xanax, Zantac, Zoloft, IKEA, DARPA, Graphika, Google, Lexus, Etronixx, Exxon, Stuxnet, Kodak and thousands more, are intentional words selected for their phonetic and visual properties and invested with a particular associated meaning. For example, Nuplazid [i.e. new(ly) placid], is the brand name of the generic drug

Pimavanserin tartrate, an "antipsychotic indictated for the treatment of hallucinations and delusions." Nuplazid's parent company bears the name "Acadia." The psycholinguistic function is as follows: *Arcadia*, the ancient utopia, and *Acadia*, belong to the same phoneme.

The utility of certain brand names is obvious. Viagra, proscribed for erectile dysfunction, rhymes with Niagra. Others are not so transparent. The fun/freaky aspect connoted by the brand name "Graphika" suggests a freewheeling graphic design company. However, it's the moniker chosen by a corporation that surveils the Internet for clients such as the U.S. government, including DARPA and the U.S. Senate Select Committee on Intelligence ("Graphika leverages the power of artificial intelligence to create the world's most detailed maps of social media landscapes. We pioneer new analytical methods and tools to help our partners navigate complex online networks"). The clash between the expectation that the Graphika name initially conveys and what it actually denotes, may be intentional. The resulting surprise would be communicated as part of a transmission of a message: Don't assume you know us. Graphika delves below surface appearances and defies first impressions.

A compelling news flash like that is both mildly intimidating as well as intriguing. It relays the impression that one is encountering a potentially highly intelligent, superior organization. It impels us to learn more.

Somehow, whether through intent or sheer coincidence, in modern times the word "Willard" has an association with power, madness and anomalies. Is it a trigger for them?

"Willard" is woven in certain high profile respects, through the religion of Mormonism founded on the occultism of Joseph Smith, one of history's most fervid megalomaniacs.

Before we begin our foray into Willard's eerie dimensions, it is incumbent on us to recall a neglected aspect: the goodness and glory once associated with the name.

One of the most ethical individuals in nineteenth century American history was the reformer Frances Willard (1839-1898), who happened to oppose Mormonism (as she relates in her autobiography, *Glimpses of Fifty Years* [1889, pp. 325-328]). In the Appendix to her book she provides an early Willard family tree:

"Major Simon Willard came from Horsmonden, Kent county, England in 1634, aged thirty-one. The name has been known on English soil for eight hundred years, being five times recorded in the Doomsday Book....Major Willard lived in Lancaster and Groton, Mass. as well as in Concord. Among his immediate descendants are two presidents of Harvard University, also Rev. Samuel Willard, pastor of the Old South Church (he baptized the infant Benjamin Franklin)...and Solomon Willard, of Quincy, Mass. the architect of the Bunker Hill Monument, who refused to accept pay for his services, and of whom Edward Everett said that 'his chief characteristic was that he wanted to do everything for everybody for nothing."

In one era at least of our nation's history, the associations with Willard were mostly positive and no doubt continue to be so for many Americans who bear the name.

Since we're not endeavoring to prove a point, but rather to report a phenomenon, bearing witness to how the name Willard has been employed or incorporated by a putative force, whether intentional, jesting or synchronous, would seem to be a Fortean activity in service to the advancement of human knowledge and consciousness (though Charles Fort would probably object to the missionary tenor of the preceding statement).

"I have more to boast of than ever any man had. I am the only man that has ever been able to keep a whole church together since the days of Adam. A large majority of the whole have stood by me. Neither Paul, John, Peter, nor Jesus ever did it. I boast that no man ever did such a work as I. The followers of Jesus ran away from Him; but the Latter-day Saints never ran away from me...When they can get rid of me, the devil will also go."

— Joseph Smith: founder, prophet, seer and revelator of The Church of Jesus Christ of Latter-Day Saints ("Mormon") Nauvoo, Illinois, May 26, 1844

History of the Church, Vol. 6, chapter 19, pp. 408-409

Conferring the masonic "Third Degree of Master Mason" under the direction of Mormons Willard Richards, Joseph and Hyrum Smith and George Miller. The initiate kneeling at center is naked. [2]

---

[2] Cf. John C. Bennet, *The History of the Saints* (Boston: Leland & Whiting, 1842), p. 273.

The Willard Hotel, Washington D.C.
Founded in 1850

President-elect Abraham Lincoln completed the writing of his First Inaugural address at the Willard, where he lodged from February 24 to March 4, 1861. He left Willard at noon on the 4th to be sworn in as President. Julia Ward Howe wrote the lyrics to "The Battle Hymn of the Republic" at the Willard in November, 1861. In 1963 Martin Luther King penned his "I Have a Dream" speech at the hotel.

In the summer of 2001, Steven Spielberg shot the final scene of the movie, "Minority Report" at the Willard Hotel. Principal filming took place in the "Willard Room" and in the hotel's "Peacock Alley."

Plans for the Federal Reserve Bank were laid at the hotel prior to 1913. In 1916, Willard Hotel was the site of organizing for Woodrow Wilson's League of Nations by Wilson's advisor, Edward M. "Colonel" House, and in Europe by American international banker Willard Straight.

"...the Willard Hotel more justly could be called the center of Washington than either the Capitol or the White House..."

—Nathaniel Hawthorne
(Cf. "Willard Hotel," National Park Service, nps.gov)

WILLARD STATE HOSPITAL.—MAIN BUILDING.

**The Willard Asylum for the Chronic Insane
(later "Willard State Hospital")**

Founded in 1869 in the Finger Lakes region of upstate New York, on the 42nd degree of north parallel latitude, "The geographical centre and Eden of the Empire State."

**Left to right:
Hyrum Willard Marriott; J. Willard Marriott**

J. Willard Marriott, founder of the Marriott hotel chain and the Marriott School of Business, was born in 1900 at Marriott Settlement, Utah, the eldest son and second of eight children of Hyrum Willard Marriott and Ellen Morris. ("My father...had good genes" — Richard Marriott).

At the age of 19, J. Willard Marriott served as a Mormon missionary. In the 1980s Willard Marriott donated at least $1 million to his namesake Willard "Mitt" Romney's political campaign. After his death, enterprises controlled by his family donated more.

Willard "Mitt" Romney

Parley Parker Pratt is the great-great-grandfather of U.S. Senator Willard M. Romney (R-UT), former governor of Massachusetts and the 2012 Republican candidate for President of the United States. Pratt was a confidant of Mormon founder and U.S. Presidential candidate Joseph Smith, who he met in 1830 on the 42nd degree of north parallel latitude at Fayette, New York, birthplace of the Mormon church. Pratt was a founding member of the Quorum of the Twelve Apostles, which would become the governing body of the Mormons after the death of Smith. Pratt was a serial adulterer who had twelve "wives," many of whom were married to other men at the time. He fathered thirty children. Parley Parker Pratt was killed in 1857 by Hector McLean, the estranged husband of Pratt's twelfth "wife," Eleanor McLean.

Joseph Smith had at least thirty-eight mistresses, concubines and wives at the time of his death. As in the case of Senator Romney's ancestor, many of these women were legally married to other men. (cf. George D. Smith, *Nauvoo Polygamy*, 2011, and Todd Compton, *In Sacred Loneliness*, 1997). Smith, a Freemason, was gunned down in 1844 in Carthage, Illinois by a masonic mob, after it was learned that in the nearby city of Nauvoo, Smith had appropriated the secret rituals of the masonic lodge and incorporated them into the rites of his "Church of Latter Day Saints."

Psychiatrist Dr. Willard (at left) outside the entrance to the "Psychopathic Dept."

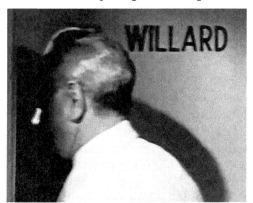

The psychiatrist entering his office

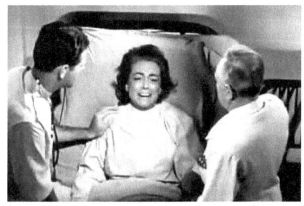

Screen shots from the 1947 movie, "Possessed" starring Joan Crawford as a woman afflicted with insanity and hospitalized in "Doctor Willard's Psychopathic Dept."

Screen shot from the movie, "Sunday Night, Bloody Night"

"Sunday Night, Bloody Night" is an inmates-take-over-the asylum-themed 1972 film (a storyline plotted by Edgar Allan Poe in "The System of Doctor Tarr and Professor Fether"). The plot revolves around an insane asylum established in a mansion located in "East Willard." After several years, the director frees the inmates of Willard asylum. They proceed to massacre the staff and take over the town, filling positions as mayor, sheriff and other government offices. Actors in the cast include John Carradine, Patrick O'Neal and Andy Warhol's erstwhile transgender actor, "Candy Darling."

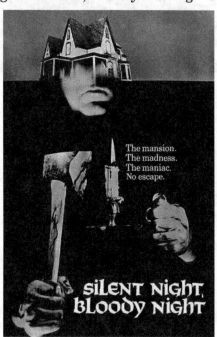

The cover of the 1975 novel,
Willard and His Bowling Trophies: A Perverse Mystery
(Author's collection)

Willard, Utah

Named for Willard Richards, a Freemason and confidant of Joseph Smith and Brigham Young, and an architect (with Smith) of the occult rites of the Mormon religion, derived from masonic ceremony and gnosis. In 1843 Richards married the Longstroth sisters, Nanny, 14, and Sarah, 16. Willard Richards is the co-author of *History of the Church of Jesus Christ of Latter-day Saints* (1858); which is considered by Mormon leaders as an authoritative early chronicle of the religion.

Willard Bliss

"The death of President James Garfield in 1881 was initiated by two bullets fired from a "Bulldog .44" handgun by the mentally ill assassin Charles Guiteau (a former resident of John Humphrey Noyes' Oneida Community), and abetted by Willard Bliss, the physician who didn't believe in the germs and infection that would kill his patient seventy-nine days later. As an exercise in incompetence and careerism, the entire episode qualifies as tragedy."

Willard (1971), 105 minutes

Hollywood film about the eponymous character who is mocked by society and forced from the business founded by his late father. His closest relationships are with the rats that infest his house. When one of the rats is killed, Willard runs amok, slaughtering those he believes are responsible.

Willard (2003), 100 minutes

Hollywood remake of the 1971 movie

TWENTY-EIGHTH ANNUAL REPORT

OF THE

BOARD OF MANAGERS

OF THE

WILLARD STATE HOSPITAL

For the Year 1896.

TRANSMITTED TO THE STATE COMMISSION IN LUNACY.

Subliminals in a TV Commercial that Denies and Mocks Them

The Progressive Insurance television commercial titled "Theory" (probably short for "Conspiracy Theory"), was nationally broadcast in 2017 over the weekend of February 25-26.[3] It appears to mock two conservatively dressed men who are shown in a dark basement analyzing TV commercials for evidence of subliminal messaging. They're portrayed as middle-aged moma's boys, and losers so pathetic in their hair-splitting pedantry that they argue over the meaning of the word "awoken."

The message may or may not be construed as: if you want to be able to get married and move out of your frowzy old mother's basement, don't investigate the possibility of Twilight Language in TV commercials; leave that to the "experts" and thereby become a more attractive, respectable, conforming consumer.

The satire aspect could perhaps be interpreted as intended to distract from the suppressive intent of the commercial.

---

[3] No accusation of wrongdoing is here made in regard to the Progressive Insurance company. Their commercial can be taken at face value as merely harmless satire and nothing more.

In one scene the mother informs her son the sleuth, "They're just commercials."

This 2017 commercial itself contained significant words flashed at high speed at the start of the ad, constituting what might be construed as a subliminal message, though not necessarily a negative or malicious one.

From among the first scenes in the commercial, we see scrambled letters arranged in lines and flashed in less than one second.

In the first line is the word "OZ."

In the second line is, "WORN US...KOOX."

The third line mimics ad agency branding: "AMBUX" (American Money).

The fourth line contains the words "FBI" and "BILE."

Anubis, Overlord of the Cosmic Graveyard

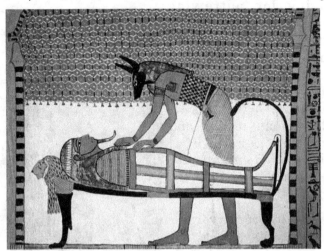

Black Jack commands dead matter

If there is one Egyptian deity who zoomorphically personifies the reign of dead matter, it is the dog-headed one, Anubis, older than Osiris, worshipped throughout the Pharaonic age—he who is the funerary deity presiding over the death-obsessed nation as overlord of the graves in the cemetery that the priests determined lay in the "desert West"—which, for James Shelby Downard and William N. Grimstad brought to mind *our* West—the crucible of the Trinity Site and the Jornada del Muerto; the Black Rock Desert where this writer's ally Jim Keith (author of *Secret and Suppressed*), was fatally injured in a "freak accident" at "Burning Man"; the Nevada that was home to atomic bomb explosions heedless of the "white trash" downwind who suffered the post-detonation consequences; the West of Arthur Manby, who went "headless in Taos;" of Monolith Moab, and of Death Valley, the setting for the final scene of Frank Norris' fateful diorama of the white American future, in *McTeague* (handcuffed to a dead man); and of a town called Truth or Consequences, in "The Land of Enchantment."

American Ground Zero
CARDE GALLAGHER
(1993) Photojournal of the down-winders in Nevada and other Western states, the first nuclear guinea pigs, victims of the American Cold War Holocaust.
360 pages, PB   **AMGZ** $20.00

By the rubrics of sympathetic magic, hungry dogs scavenging for putrefying flesh and bones in early cemeteries was transformed into symbols of the cultivation of the dead in the person of Anubis *imy ut* ("the embalmer"), the jackal-headed mummy magus and autarch of ceremonial autopsies — *Khenty-Imentiu* ("Foremost of the Westerners").

After Howard Carter opened the 3,400-year-old Tut time capsule in 1922, revealing an idol of the jackal-headed one seated upon a shrine of gold leaf and facing west, Anubis' star ascended anew and a mental virus entombed for millennia disgorged its spores in the corridors of our Cynopolis.

He is the unnamed one: Anubis is his title, not his personal name, which is unknown. [4]

According to Carter, to Anubis is ascribed the saying, "I have caused the path to be mistaken."

The *Oxford English Dictionary* states that the word jackal "shows association with the proper name Jack." In English a root of the word jackal is Jack-Call. [5]

Our Egyptian "Jack" is always depicted as being black from the neck upward; thus: Black Jack.

---

[4] Late Egyptian texts name him Inpu or Anpu, the former having an etymological root denoting decomposition. This appears to be a a non-sequitur contrived centuries after the rise of Anubis, in an attempt to solve the baffling mystery of his namelessness. We have no real clue to the name, as opposed to the title, of the jackal deity.

[5] In a prescient text written by D. Pell in 1659 we read, "The lion...will not seek his prey himself, but sends his *Carter(*er) or Jack-call to run about to seek it" (emphasis supplied).

It was he who ritually operated on ("embalmed") the corpse of Osiris himself. [6]

The jackal's counterpart in the heavens is the "dog star" Sirius (Canis major). In Pharaonic Egypt a *five-pointed* star is emblematic of Sirius and associated with Anubis and the menstruant Sothis, whose sanguinary efflux was viewed as tantamount to the annual flooding of the Nile. The average menstrual cycle is five days and the many five-numbered devices, from the Pentagon to the Pentagram, are intended to evoke the power of the menstrual prodigy; viz. the bleeding that does not kill or wound. It is this "miracle" that is the secret of the so-called "Holy Grail," which has mystified researchers for centuries. [7]

In the "astral clock" (calendar) of ancient Egypt, the new year began with the reappearance of Sirius in the eastern sky; the brightest star visible from earth. Sirius was the celestial object of paramount importance in the Pharaonic cosmology. Satan in Pharaonic theology is personified by Set ("Seth"), the god of crime and disease who was ritually invoked by means of Twilight Language, spells and amulets.

According to the myth, Set blinded Horus, the son of Isis and Osiris, in one eye, and was in turn castrated due to his links to sexual violence and "unnatural desire." Set's legendary consort was the Semitic goddess Astarte. We observe his similarity to Anubis in a 20th Dynasty icon (p. 144), which shows Set crowning Ramsses III. In that depiction, Set bears a resemblance to Anubis. In his hand he is shown carrying the tether ("ankh cross") by which animals and slaves were roped.

---

[6] In his corpse work Anubis is assisted by the graveyard goddesses Nephthys ("guardian of the head of Osiris"), and Isis. "Black" in this context is not a racial allusion.

[7] Concerning the awe in which the menstrual period was beheld by the ancients, and as the earliest source of the "Holy Grail" fable, Mary Daly's study in *Gyn/Ecology* (Beacon Press, 1990), is indispensable.

Set, the animal-headed deity at right, crowns Ramsses III (center), together with Horus (left). Circa 1150 B.C.

In the Jack-Call of the 21st century American necropolis, the theology of the Egypt of the Pharaohs is a ubiquitous symbolic and ceremonial legacy.

In 2010 a statue of Anubis, 26 feet tall and weighing ten tons, was erected at the Dallas-Fort Worth airport in Texas. Some would say it served as a tutelary deity.

The media supposed it was a whimsical accompaniment to the touring King Tut exhibit (the statue's "guard" aspect is however, acknowledged in the headline of the article):

"Anubis, that wacky Egyptian god with the head of a jackal and the body of a human, is hanging around Dallas/Fort Worth International Airport.

"Actually, a 26-foot-tall statue of Mr. Anubis, known as the god of the dead or the underworld, was installed Friday at Founders Plaza, at the airport's northwest corner. There he'll stand for a while, watching airplanes take off and land with the other Founders Plaza planewatchers.

"Mr. Anubis, with his back to the airport as he faces north, is there to celebrate the King Tut exhibit at the Dallas Museum of Art." (Terry Maxon, "Anubis Stands Guard at D/FW Airport," *The Dallas Morning News*, December 19, 2008).

It would be more difficult to spin a playful tale about NASA having placed its asteroid exploration vehicle under the patronage of King Osiris ("Osiris-Rex"), for which the craft was named in 2020. Its stated purpose is to bring the origin material (*prima materia*) of our solar system, which NASA believes may be present on the asteroid "Bennu," to earth (*prima terra*). [8]

Don't hold your breath waiting for a NASA spacecraft to be named King Jesus. He who is the "stone" rejected by the builders of our national pagan psychodrama, is nevertheless the cornerstone of Creation (Matthew 21:42).

---

[8] The asteroid pursued by Osiris-Rex is named after the Egyptian avian deity "Benu," a mythical being synonymous with the phoenix of the Greeks: "repeatedly newly arising like the sun." In our book, *The Occult Renaissance Church of Rome* (2017), we study the virulence of the seemingly inescapable Egyptian meme over the past five hundred years of western history.

"Little Egypt"

"American folklore has long been filled with violent heroes: exploits of Memphis badman Stagolee, who shot his friend with a .45 and supposedly took over leadership of hell from the Devil, were still being honored during the 1950s and 1960s in 'toasts,' performed on street corners and passed down from generation to generation..."

Carl Husemoller Nightingale
New York Times, December 5, 1993

Memphis Pyramid, Memphis, Tennessee
Also known as the "Temple of Doom." Constructed in 1991 by the city of Memphis and Shelby County, overlooking the Mississippi River; it is reputedly 2/3 the size of the Great Pyramid of Giza.

Memphis was once the capital city of ancient Egypt and from the beginning of the Third Dynasty a royal burial ground of kings. "...the city of Memphis was founded by Menes, legendary unifier and first king of Egypt..."

Toby A.H. Wilkinson, *Early Dynastic Egypt* [1999], p. 293.

The Mississippi River is likened in the minds of some people to the Nile. "As it (southern Illinois) narrows to a tip, the distance between the two mighty rivers, dwindles from eighty to forty to twenty miles until, at Cairo, you see the Ohio meet the Mississippi. Locals call this the 'land between the rivers,' or 'Little Egypt." [9] (Think of Thebes, Karnak and Cairo, Illinois). In Little Egypt in 1858, Lincoln and Douglas debated the future destiny of the United States.

Cahokia

Circa 1000 A.D., there were between one hundred twenty and two hundred packed earth pyramids covering over 3,200 acres at Cahokia Mounds in southern Illinois, "Ancient America's great metropolis on the Mississippi." At Cahokia, "The large central pyramid...is comparable to or larger than the areas covered by the Pyramid of the Sun at Teotihucan and the Pyramid of Khufu in Egypt.." [10] 22 miles south of Cahokia, natives reported the terrifying depredations of a flying, man-eating "Piasa" creature with an anthropomorphic face. [11]

The Piasa "Bird"

"The first white explorers of the Mississippi River noted strangely pictured rocks at different places along its way. The most striking of these was the one on the bluff at the point where afterward the city of Alton was built. This represented the Piasa or Devil bird...There is a narrow ravine between the city of Alton and the mouth of the Illinois River through which a small stream runs to empty into the Mississippi. This is known as the Piasa. Near the mouth of this stream bluffs of sandstone rise upon which the representation of the Piasa birds were made....they were horrible to see. The legend of the Piasa briefly told is this (as related to P.A. Armstrong in 1827): 'Many thousand moons before the arrival of the paleface, a bird of such dimensions that he could easily carry off a buffalo, lived in the locality of these pictured rocks. At one time the bird tested the flesh of an Indian and ever after, one of the Piasa birds would watch opportunity to dart upon an Indian and bear

---

[9] Linda Lee Ream, *Growing Up in Little Egypt* (2012), p. xi.

[10] Susan M. Alt, *Cahokia's Complexities* (University of Alabama, 2018), p. 21.

[11] *Rebirth of Pan: Hidden Faces of the American Earth Sprit* (Jim Brandon [Grimstad]).

him into one of the caves of the bluffs to devour him. Hundreds of warriors were devoured in this way..." [12]

Drawing of the Piasa by William Lewis, April 3, 1825

The head of the Piasa is that of a bearded man with a fierce visage. The head is surmounted with antlers. Piasa denotes "man eater" in the language of the Illini natives.

Of Louis Joliet and Father Jacques Marquette's voyage on the Mississippi in 1673, historian Francis Parkman writes, "Presently they beheld a sight which reminded them that the devil was still lord paramount of this wilderness. On the flat face of a high rock, were painted in red, black and green a pair of monsters—each 'as large as a calf, with horns like a deer, red eyes, a beard...and a frightful expression of countenance. The face is something like that of a man, the body covered with scales; and the tail so long it passes around the body...' Such is the account which the worthy Jesuit gives...The rock where these figures were painted is immediately above the city of Alton. The tradition of their existence remains, though they are entirely effaced by time. In 1867 when I passed the place, a part of the rock had been quarried away...'

---

[12] Lottie E. Jones, *Decisive Dates in Illinois History* (1904), p. 81.

"St. Cosme who saw it in 1699, said it was even then very faint; and (Prof. John) Russell, who saw it in the 1830s says the Indians had almost entirely destroyed it with their bullets and arrows." [13]

"Prof. John Russell of Jersey County, Illinois visited the bluff in March, 1848...He says, 'My curiosity was principally directed to the examination of a cave connected with the tradition as one of those to which the bird had carried its victims...After long and perilous clambering we reached the entrance, about fifty feet above the river...the shape of the cave was irregular, but so far as I could judge, the bottom would average about twenty by thirty feet. The floor of the cave throughout its whole extent was one mass of human bones." [14]

Another "Little Egypt" Dances — in Dallas

On October 16, 1963 an exotic dancer with the moniker "Little Egypt," commenced a ten day engagement at a private supper club in Dallas, Texas known as the "Gay Life." According to an advertisement in the *Dallas Morning News* of October 19, 1963, Little Egypt was performing at Jack Ruby's Carousel Club during her sojourn in Dallas.[15]

Almost as though he had a seat in that front row at the Carousel Club, Elvis Presley's lyricist Jerry Leiber penned the erotic song, "Little Egypt." [16] Presley performed "Little Egypt" in the 1964 movie "Roustabout."

---

[13] Clark McAdams, "The Archaeology of Illinois," in *Transactions of the Illinois Historical Society* [1907], p. 38

[14] Clara Kern Bayliss, "The Significance of the Piasa," in *Transactions of the Illinois Historical Society* [1908], p. 117.

[15] *Warren Commission Report*, vol. 25, pp. 339-340, exhibit 2356 (1964). Though the dancer's manager, Charles Curtis, admitted that he and Little Egypt knew Jack Ruby personally, he may have been embarrassed by the public notice of her performance at Ruby's "nude entertainment" establishment and subsequently denied that it had occurred. Jack Ruby shot to death Kennedy assassination-patsy Lee Harvey Oswald.

[16] Mr. Lieber, who teamed with composer Mike Stoller, wrote "Little Egypt" in 1961. He also penned the words to "Hound Dog," "Jailhouse Rock," "Love Potion No. 9" and "Kansas City," among other hits. "Love Potion No. 9" concerns an aphrodisiac elixir:

"I told her that I was a flop with chicks
I've been that way since nineteen fifty-six
She looked at my palm and she made a magic sign
She said, 'What you need is love potion no. 9."

Little Egypt (song)
By Jerry Lieber (excerpt)

"I went and bought myself a ticket
And I sat down in the very first row
They pulled the curtain but then
When they turned the spotlight way down low
Little Egypt came out a-struttin'
Wearin' nothin' but a button and a bow
Singin' ying-ying, ying-ying
Ying-ying, ying-ying,
She had a ruby on her tummy
And a diamond big as Texas on her toe
She let her hair down
And she did the hoochie-coochie real slow,
When she did her special number on the zebra skin
I thought she'd stop the show..."

A Little Egypt reference is in "Naked Women and Beer," a ditty by Country and Western royal Hank Williams Jr:

"Naked women and beer
We got it all in here
For your eyes and your ears
They show it all in the clear
Way up north and down south
Whoo, somebody shut my mouth

"Now I ain't sayin' it's right
But I ain't sayin' it's wrong,
But myself I enjoy the sight
Of pretty girls dancing to their songs,

"And it's been like that
Since way back when —

From Little Egypt to the Vegas Strip [17] —
And when the music starts groovin'
And the girls start movin'
Ain't nothin' gonna make them quit..."

Beale / Beall / Baal

At its founding in Memphis, Tennessee in 1841, Beale Avenue (later Beale Street), featured mansions to the east and merchants and music to the west.

In Memphis, Beale was known as "the underworld." During the Roaring 20s, virtuoso musicians gathered on Beale, including Louis Armstrong, Memphis Minnie and many others, "Giving Birth to the Blues."

I've seen the lights of gay Broadway,
Old Market Street down by the Frisco Bay,
I've strolled the Prado, I've gambled on the Bourse
The seven wonders of the world I've seen
And many are the places I have been.
Take my advice, folks and see Beale Street first.
You'll see pretty Browns in beautiful gowns,
You'll see tailor mades and hand me, downs
You'll meet honest men and pick-pockets skilled
You'll find that bus'ness never closes till somebody gets killed.

You'll see Hog-Nose rest'rants and Chitlin' Cafes
You''ll see Jugs that tell of bygone days
And places, once places, now just a sham,
You'll see Golden Balls enough to pave the New Jerusalem.'
You'll see men who rank with the first in the nation
Who come to Beale for inspiration...

(W.C. Handy, 1912)

---

[17] The Luxor Pyramid was constructed on Nevada's Las Vegas Strip in 1993.

In a review of Peter Guralnick's *Sam Phillips: The Man Who Invented Rock 'n' Roll* (2015), August Kleinzahler wrote:

The "short ride along Beale Street turned out to be the most important experience of Phillips's young life...

"The city of Memphis commands a bluff on the eastern shore of the Mississippi. It's a blasted, crime-ridden shell of a city nowadays, and Beale Street a tawdry tourist attraction, but when Phillips arrived it was a thriving trade center...with a population of around 400,000.

"...Eleven years later he opened the Memphis Recording Service in a small space at 706 Union Avenue, and two years later set up an independent record company there called Sun Records...

"If I could find a white man who had the Negro sound and the Negro feel, I could make a billion dollars,' Phillips said in the early 1950s.

"That white man walked into his studio in June 1953, ostensibly to record two songs for his mother but almost certainly with the hope of impressing Phillips and being taken up by Sun...Elvis was 19 at the time, making his living as a truck driver, hanging around Beale Street..."

(*London Review of Books*, February 8, 2018, pages 27-28).

"Far from the glamour of Jacqueline Kennedy Onassis, her eccentric aunt and cousin, former socialites who were both named Edith Beale, lived in squalor in Grey Gardens, a sprawling house in East Hampton, N.Y., along with...the decaying trappings of their earlier lives in high society. Among these trappings, the Beales' heirs say, was an oil painting of the former first lady as a teenager, bequeathed in lieu of a financial inheritance to the elder Ms. Beale by her brother, John Vernou Bouvier III, who was Mrs. Onassis' father and a well-to-do stockbroker known as Black Jack."

(*New York Times*, February 16, 2018 p. A26).

"The Magruder Farm in Darnestown, Md., has a history both famous and infamous. Before being called Magruder Farm, the property had gone by several names, including Springfield, the Maples and Iler Farm...This property can be traced back to Ninian Beall, who acquired thousands of acres, starting in 1750. Beall's son-in-law Hardage Lane inherited part of the land in 1799 and renamed his portion Springfield...

Ross H. Snyder, a lawyer, and his wife, Jennie, bought the farm in 1941 as a summer home before moving there permanently in 1946 with their son and daughter. They renamed it The Maples. In November 1946, their 14-year-old son, Robert, took his father's shotgun and shot his father, mother and sister in the kitchen because he was upset with them. After going to see a movie with a friend, he walked into a Bethesda police station and confessed to killing his parents and sister." (Kathy Orton, *Washington Post*, February 16, 2018) [18]

An anonymous informant said of the former Beall property: "It is beautiful. And historic. But it is also haunted. I'm surprised so many lived there for so long. Maybe the ghosts aren't aggressive, but they are there."

---

[18] "An insanity plea was filed for 14-year-old Robert "Bobby" Snyder who is charged with the shotgun slaying of his foster parents, Mr. and Mrs. Ross H. Snyder, and foster sister, Jane Ann, 32, at their home at 14800 Seneca Rd., Darnestown, Md., on Nov. 23." This writer was unable to discover subsequent news reports concerning the outcome of his prosecution, or the life of Bobby Snyder after 1946.

"The written word is of course a symbol for something...a written word is *an image*...

"Question: What secret did Hassan i Sabbah learn in Egypt that enabled him to control and activate his assassins from a distance?

"Answer: Energy from a virus....And what is a virus?...a pictorial series like Egyptian glyphs *that makes itself real*."

William Seward Burroughs [19]

"Embedded commands are patterns of language that bypass conscious reasoning and speak directly to the subconscious mind."

Neil Shah [20]

---

[19] *The Book of Breeething* (1975). "Beat" author William S. Burroughs (1914-1997), was the grandson and namesake of William Seward Burroughs, the inventor in 1884 of the adding machine. The elder Burroughs was raised and educated on the 42nd degree of latitude in Auburn, New York. Born in 1857, Burroughs Sr. was named for William Seward, Auburn's most illustrious citizen and Lincoln's future Secretary of State. A militant foe of secret societies, in 1830 Seward gained his first elective office (state senator), as the nominee of the Anti-Mason party. He was elected governor of New York in 1839.

[20] Neil Shah, *Introducing Neurolinguistic Programming (NLP): A Practical Guide*, (London: Icon Books, 2011).

FLDR

What are the mechanics of the "union of opposites" — the collusion of certain humans with the ascendance of dead matter? Some sense of it can be gained from observing the utilization of the "FLDR" algorithm, which employs a different game of hazard from the one principally identified with Black Jack:

"A new algorithm, the Fast Loaded Dice Roller (FLDR) has been invented for accelerating the fundamental building blocks of random number generation. FLDR software simulates the roll of dice to produce random integers. The dice can have any number of sides, and they are 'loaded,' or weighted, to make some sides more likely to come up than others. A loaded die can still yield random numbers — as one cannot predict in advance which side will turn up — but the randomness is constrained to meet a preset probability distribution. One might, for instance, use loaded dice to simulate the outcome of a baseball game; while the superior team is more likely to win, on a given day either team could end up on top. Incorporating this kind of uncertainty will help machines make humanlike predictions and better simulate phenomena that rely on probability." [21]

Furthermore, in the language of software developers and hackers there is this jargon: "Jailbreaking is a form of privilege escalation, which is the act of exploiting a bug, design flaw or configuration oversight in an operating system to gain elevated access to resources that are normally protected."

Is breaking out of jail "a privilege"?

Jail-breakers are described as those who "exploit...configuration oversights" that are "normally protected." Are there "configuration oversights" in Twilight Language matrixes which, while "normally protected" can be "exploited" by outlaws ("jailbreakers") in "abnormal" situations and circumstances? If we wanted to talk back to those who embed twilight language in pop culture, would we want to "bug" them" and taunt them with their "design flaws" by calling ourselves the "Jailbreaking Collective"?

---

[21] Cf. Stephen Ornes, *Quanta Magazine,* July 8, 2020, and Steve Nadis, *MIT News* (May 28, 2020).

Shelby was interested in the word "Eureka!" and we have poked around in the provenance and possible symbolic meaning of the phrase, "six degrees of separation;" as well as, "By Jingo!" a fairly common exclamation in the 1950s, but originally a word used by conjurors four hundred years prior. How did it migrate, and why?

Due to the "self-help" mass movement, people are undertaking "affirmations"—a kind of (mostly) benevolent self-hypnosis involving spoken words, beginning with "I am"—"I am beautiful. I am strong. I am becoming stronger. I am becoming more beautiful," and so forth. These practices are based on faith in the power of words.

The same psychology advises awareness of the negative prescriptive power of spoken judgments, such as "My wife is an idiot," "My boss is a jerk" or "My son is a fool," in the belief that stating those words creates a reality in which they become true. Whereas saying aloud, "My wife is brilliant," "My boss is basically good," and "My son is growing in wisdom," creates a reality where those people take on those attributes.

We're not as much interested in discussing the probable truth or falsity of these propositions, as the fact that the population is becoming more aware of and sensitive to, the power of words.

There is also the Rupert Pupkin Effect. He's the Robert DeNiro character in Martin Scorcese's movie, "The King of Comedy." Rupert Pupkin's lack of talent is irrelevant: he succeeds because *he can't process rejection or defeat.*

The self-help psychology movement is sometimes criticized as "magical thinking." It's as if the common folk are being discouraged from doing what elite adepts undertake, after painful initiations.

On the other hand, Jesus was *affirming* a reality when He told the truth about the Pharisees in no uncertain terms. He was admonishing sinners, and his disapprobation was a recognition of the state of their brokenness. Jesus' words didn't create that condition.

Adolf Hitler was schooled in "positive thinking" by his "Thule" handlers in the early 1920s. [22] He ended rather badly though, as the most completely defeated head of a modern state in recent history.

---

[22] Cf. Michael Hoffman, *Adolf Hitler: Enemy of the German People* (2019).

These themes and topics can be analyzed only up to a point, after which intuition takes over to such an extent that subsequent utterances will be classed as whimsy, or at best, informed speculation and conjecture within the "non-fiction" academic sphere.

Is the matter handled best outside that sphere, as literature? Shelby Downard, like Abraham Lincoln and Joseph Sobran, was more than intrigued by Shakespeare's *Macbeth*, [23] and who isn't fascinated by Lewis Carroll's *Alice* books? The list of the authors in this genre is long: Poe, Edward Bulwer-Lytton, Huysmans, Yeats, Lovecraft, [24] Charles Williams, Tolkein, Arthur C. Clarke, Heinlein, Philip K. Dick, William Hjortsberg.

We dare to opine that Fortean phenomenon, taken to its deepest dimension, is *haunted*, and almost always confounds every sleuth on its trail. So it may be that the pursuit of it, the pure "because it's there" George Mallory motivation, more than arriving at a final destination or conclusion—is what we surmise Charles Fort understood in his study of—not so much weird phenomena per se—but its effects on humanity, including in terms of processing and conditioning us toward "induced" beliefs. The investigation of how a phenomenon like Twilight Language processes humanity might be more productive than the study of the pathways and "wiring" of the communications themselves, in that the phenomena often exhibit evanescent qualities.

We propose that contrary to notions of deliberate orienting and positioning, *sometimes* Twilight Language human agents transmit and direct it by "surfing" the mysterious momentum of the language's own magnetism, rather than propelling it by precisely calibrated agency. Art, as much as neuro-linguistic technics, is at work, linked to the invocation and subsequent navigation of coincidence ("synchronicity"), a "science" that is a kind of sorcery (or sorcery that has developed into a science).

---

[23] Mr. Downard's interest centered in part on the identification of President Lyndon B. Johnson with the assassin of King Macbeth in Barbara Garson's "satirical" 1967 play, "Macbird!" starring Stacy Keach. This identification whispered a destabilizing viral message to an American Hive Mind that had been repeatedly reassured by "the authorities" that Lee Harvey Oswald alone was responsible for the death of Camelot's king.

[24] Michel Houellebecq's *H.P. Lovecraft: Against the World, Against Life*, translated from the French by Dorna Khazeni (Orion, 2008), offers unusual insight into the life and vision of the seminal horror author.

To the objection that such a "loose" interpretation opens the exploration of Twilight Language to non-empirical literary realms of imagination and fantasy, we plead guilty.

We would however remind those who object, that a tale crafted by the Tübingen intriguers in the early years of the seventeenth century, scripted the birth of science under occult auspices, a suzerainty which led to the *scientism* that has bedeviled humanity ever since.

Moreover, as a matter of epistemology, we encourage the reader to question the supposition that the alchemical workings of this imaginative "Rosicrucian Ludibrium" are antithetical to avant-garde laboratory science.

If FLDR "randomness...constrained to meet a preset probability distribution...(i)ncorporating this kind of uncertainty (in)...phenomena that rely on probability" — is not a sorcerous summoning of a fantasy script into the material world, then what is?

The Sorcerer's Marathon

April 19, 2011 was the sixteenth anniversary of the catastrophic bombing of the Alfred P. Murrah Federal Building in Oklahoma City, Oklahoma; the eighteenth anniversary of the fiery massacre in Waco, Texas; and the two hundred thirty-sixth anniversary of the American revolutionary battles of Lexington and Concord, Massachusetts.

In "Hour 1" of American Public Radio's "Performance Today" broadcast of April 19, 2011, the concerts featured included "The Sorcerer's Apprentice"; a performance from Marathon, Florida ("right in the middle of the Florida Keys") consisting of the grim, funereal "Élégie" of Gabriel Fauré; yet another elegy—this one performed in Lisbon, Portugal, site of the catastrophic 1755 earthquake and tsunami—and finally, a phoenix ("Firebird") invocation.

In the movie "Red Dragon," centered on Hannibal Lecter and an occult serial killer who slaughters families, the final, attempted massacre takes place in Marathon, Florida, the home of an FBI occult "profiler."

"The Sorcerer's Apprentice" performance was originally broadcast as part of a March 18 Radio France fund-raiser for the March 11 Japanese earthquake/Tsunami victims.

"Performance Today" host Fred Child expressed on the air his feeling that the choice of "Sorcerer's Apprentice" for the benefit of victims of the "most violent earthquake ever recorded" was perhaps "cringe-inducingly inappropriate."

Recall that the Disney movie "Fantasia," scored to a soundtrack of "The Sorcerer's Apprentice," features a magically-induced, drowning whirlpool and out-of-control flood.

A question often asked when seemingly recondite symbolism such as this is pointed out: "Is it coincidence or conspiracy?"

We don't propose an answer in this particular instance, except to say, if it is a communication then it is an excerpt, part of a story; and if it is intelligible to the percipient, then it may be something other than a random or accidental phenomenon.

This doesn't necessarily make it a "conspiracy." It could be what Poe termed a "diddle," but even in that case, macabre japes sometimes tend to induce thought and reflection, after the grin, which Mr. Poe said follows a diddle.

Pike Bites the Dust
Graven Image of Freemasonry's "Supreme Commander" Toppled in Flames

On the eve of Summer Solstice 2020, the graven image of Albert Pike, the chief of nineteenth century Freemasonry and Satanism in America, was toppled and burned in Washington D.C. This could not have happened in decades past. Hallelujah.

On the Internet, we received objections from reactionaries to the preceding jubilation. One man wrote, "The image of Pike's fallen statue *wasn't* toppled by those protesting against Satanism and the NWO (New World Order). It was toppled by brainwashed millennial, Marxist-trained college kids who are leading us into the NWO!"

Another stated, "The rabble who tore it down most likely don't have a clue about the Masonic associations. To them it's just another toppled statue of an oppressive 'dead white male' which needed to be done away with as part of the drive to usher in the revolutionary aims of the Left."

These objections from individuals afflicted with the myopia of Right wing allegiance and partisanship, do not address the point.

The point is the humiliating optics for the masonic Cryptocracy.

Pike was Supreme Commander of the Scottish Rite of Freemasonry, Southern Jurisdiction, the most powerful masonic organization in America, if not on earth. His Satanic magnum opus, *Morals and Dogma*, was an occult catechism embraced by hundreds of thousands of Masons for many decades. In it, Pike detailed the god—or should we say gods—of the Freemasons—the deities of ancient Egypt:

"...the BLAZING STAR...Originally it represented SIRIUS, or the Dog-star, t the forerunner of the inundation of the Nile; the God ANUBIS, companion of ISIS in her search for the body of OSIRIS, her brother and husband. Then it became the image of HORUS, the son of OSIRIS, himself symbolized also by the Sun, the author of the Seasons, and the God of Time; Son of ISIS, who was the universal nature, himself the primitive matter, inexhaustible source of Life, spark of uncreated fire, universal seed of all beings.

"It was HERMES, also, the Master of Learning, whose name in Greek is that of the God Mercury. It became the sacred and potent sign or character of the Magi, the PENTALPHA, and is the significant emblem of Liberty and Freedom, blazing with a steady radiance amid the sweltering elements of good and evil of Revolutions, and promising serene skies and fertile seasons to the nations, after the storms of change and tumult... The Blazing Star in our Lodges, we have already said, represent Sirius, Anubis, or Mercury (Hermes), Guardian and Guide of Souls...by its genial influence dispenses blessings to mankind."

Pike referenced a being who allegedly traveled from a planet in the solar system of Sirius and taught mankind, "the worship of the Gods..." [1]

This entity is known by many names. One is Oannes; another is Satan. Pike taught that Sirius is the "emblem" of the "All-Seeing Eye." [2]

Furthermore, Pike's loathing for black people is indisputable. Writing in his *Memphis Daily Appeal* newspaper, he referred to "the abuse of the privilege of voting by 50,000 ignorant

---

[1] *Morals and Dogma* [1942], p. 376.

[2] Ibid., p. 506.

negroes...Tennessee will not always bear the disgrace of negroism."

In Pike's poem "Ariel," in stanzas 21, 22 and 39 he evinces his vociferous support for the enslavement of black people.

Unlike in times past, on June 19 of the year MMXX, the "Invisible Empire" was unable to keep Albert Pike's icon from being X'ed out—toppling into the dust, in flames. *For a symbol-obsessed cabal that once scaled stratospheric heights in America, this national humiliation was an ominous portent.*

In 70 A.D. Titus the pagan razed the Temple of Jerusalem to the ground. Something similar occurred with Pike's graven image in A.D. 2020 when it was toppled and set afire. Deuteronomy 7:5: "But thus shall you deal with them: you shall...burn their carved images with fire."

Burning was an Old Testament prescription for idols, as testified by Moses, as well as Asa, Josiah and Jehu. Pike's idol, erected by the "Supreme Council" of Freemasons in 1901, stood in a place of honor in our nation's capitol for 119 years and would have probably stood for another 119 years were it left to the reactionary Right wing, which masquerades as upholders of the Word of God while claiming that the Left's iconoclasm is impurely motivated and therefore cannot be salutary in this instance. But it was those anarchists who fulfilled Deuteronomy 7:5 and 12:1-3, as well as Exodus 20:4, 32:20 and 34:13, not armchair "Conservatives" or those in "Holy Orders."

Revolutions devour their own. Pike's Thelemic grandchildren have coiled and bit their erstwhile patriarch, the celebrated secret society avatar of demonic invasion. Twas ever thus. One of Satan's aliases is בַּעַל זְבוּב, in English, Baal-zebub, "The Lord of the Flies."

As noted, there will be a Right-wing reactionary antithesis to the Left-wing revolutionary thesis. The antithesis will be backed by "Conservative" dupes who can't (or won't) see the hidden hand at work in their own circles. We shouldn't be hoodwinked into choosing sides in the phony dialectic process of Left/Right. The Right and the Left are both responsible for the ascendance of the Money Power over humanity.

The fall of the graven image of Pike is an occasion for rejoicing. *May it be a harbinger of the fall of the Cryptocracy itself,* which has ruled our nation by assassination, bribery and the massacre of innocents.

Is it any wonder why many of America's youth are angry, however mistaken and misdirected they may be on many points? They see at least some of the intolerable criminal politics and horrendous financial oppression to which we who have "waxed cold" (Matthew 24:12) accommodate ourselves.

It took a group of Leftists to remove Pike's accursed monument which haunted the capitol for over a hundred years.

In Matthew 24:15-16, referring to the Roman legion that would, in 70 A.D., visit God's justice on the Temple of Jerusalem, Jesus termed that army, "the Abomination of Desolation."

A similar "abomination" exacted justice on the graven image of Albert Pike. It could be that God's hand was in that retributive act as well.

After its downfall, "conservative" President Trump pledged to re-erect the monument to the Satanist. Of all the historical statues that were overthrown by vandals in 2020, restoring Supreme Commander Pike's idol in the capitol of our nation was Mr. Trump's supreme priority.

What a coincidence.

The Moab Monolith

Since the gateway opened on Sept. 11, 2001, every year since has been "charmed." Year MMXX with its "20/20 vision" (as Matthew Bell has perspicaciously termed it), is significant for debuting the "crowned" (corona) COVID19 "peril to our land" national emergency.

2001 had been ushered in on January 1 with the appearance of a "mystery metal monolith" in Magnuson Park in Seattle. In 2020, on November 18, another "mystery metal monolith" was unveiled in southern Utah during our "moment of national peril."

Was the discovery truly accidental or part of a timetable of revelation? What may be its role in processing the Group Mind of the masses?

In 1951 Arthur C. Clarke's short story, "The Sentinel" (also known as "The Sentinel of Eternity") was published.

Clarke wrote of a monolith, an artifact of alien origin, which triggers evolutionary shifts among hominids in target populations. This is the theme of the influential science fiction movie, "2001: A Space Odyssey."

Correspondents have written to say, "Year 2021 seems to coincide with the 26,000 year procession of the equinox and the earth's passage through galactic center."

Chatter about a "26,000 year procession through the galactic center" reminds us of the apocalyptic talk about the thousand-year-old, long count "Mayan Calendar" apocalypse, falsely prophesied for December 21, 2012.

Whatever places us in a psychic pressure cooker is suspect.

Whoever claims the authority to know a 26,000 year procession is imminent, or the Mayan Calendar is about to be certainly fulfilled, is a clairvoyant for the ages.

Consider the mental state of those whose lives are so impoverished they have a psychological need to go from one end-of-the world prognostication to the next, ever more frazzled as they do so.

Imminent End Time expectations are seeded among our more vulnerable people by the agents of paralysis. Their intent is to cause us to intensely psychologically light up for a time, and then burn out permanently.

What is the significance of the attention the Cryptocracy accorded the monolith in Utah in the final months of 2020?

One point of interest is the lack of reporting in 2020 on its predecessor in Seattle in 2001.

Allusions were made to Kubrick's fictional "2001" movie, but not to the monolith that debuted at the start of the new millennium in the park named son of *"Magnus"* (black oxide of manganese produced by blending lead. The resulting manganese, "in color and weight like a lodestone" [magnet], which "from ancient times was used in the manufacture of [a looking] glass").

In 2020, "...The monolith's mysterious appearance amid the rocky desert sparked excitement among the hominids who circled it, intrigued and perplexed.

"But unlike the alien structure made famous by the epic film adaptation of "2001: A Space Odyssey," the metal monolith discovered Wednesday (November 18) by public safety workers in southeastern Utah is quite real.

"The workers were scouring the red-rock region by helicopter for bighorn sheep when a crew member spotted the object, the pilot, Bret Hutchings, told KSL-TV...(it was) the strangest discovery he's made in years of flying over the Utah desert.

"The state Department of Public Safety will not disclose its exact location...

"For now, the monolith is delighting science-fiction fans all over the Internet, who couldn't help but note the uncanny resemblance to the mysterious structure in "2001" that came from aliens and sped up human evolution." [1]

Using satellite imagery, amateur sleuths lost no time finding the Utah site. It was located near Lockhart Basin Road, 17 miles southwest of the city of Moab, on the 38th degree of north parallel latitude. In the days following the monolith's discovery, thousands of people poured into the area.

The timing of the "discovery" is noteworthy—in addition to being in the midst of the COVID19 panic, the "discovery" was announced to the world forty-two days before the 20th anniversary of the 21(200]1]) Gateway.

---

[1] Marisa Iati, "A mysterious metal monolith was found in a remote part of Utah. Um, so who put it there?," *Washington Post,* November 24, 2020.

It was said that the airborne "discoverers" had been on a routine search for "big horn."

Some observers have commented on an alignment between the "phallic" monolith and the "vaginal" crack in the rock formation. From the photograph (below) it appears that the alignment was precise.

As for who erected and installed it, that remains a matter of conjecture and dispute.

Friday, November 27, nearly as soon as it was unveiled before an amazed world, it was reportedly removed by a group which journalist Meaghen Brown of *Outside* magazine (December 23, 2020) said consisted of:

"...four slackliners... Homer Manson, an anonymous companion, Sylvan Christensen and Andy Lewis...in their haste, the group lost the top of the monolith".

Superbow half-time perfomer Andy L. "Sketchy Andy," (also known as "Skandy") Lewis of Moab allegedly took responsibility, along with the others, for tearing down the monolith and posting a video of their operation on a Facebook page.

The video shows the monolith dumped in a wheelbarrow.

Was that an evolutionary or devoluționary move?

The rock star Madonna in a "gold-colored cape and wearing an ancient-Egyptian headdress" while seated on a throne in Indianapolis, the "Crossroads of America," February 5, 2012 during Super Bowl XLVI (46).

The *Chicago Tribune* described Madonna's ritual as an "S&M party in Ancient Egypt."

Andy "Sketchy Andy" Lewis performing with Madonna at the 2012 Super Bowl halftime pageant.

CBS News reported that as of 2012, Madonna's ceremony with Moab's Andy L. Lewis was the most-watched Super Bowl halftime spectacle in history, with 114 million viewers – more than the football game itself (which was viewed by an estimated 111.3 million people).

In 2020 Mr. Lewis was a 34-year-old "talented slackline performer who specializes in high-altitude stunts on a slack tightrope," as well as rituals like the one he enacted for Madonna's 12-minute pagan goddess impersonation during the 2012 Super Bowl pageantry.

The English newspaper *Mirror* published a photo of Lewis naked while he balanced on a high elevation tightrope (not at the Super Bowl). In 2014 Mr. Lewis allegedly pleaded guilty to interfering in an investigation of illegal BASE ("building, antenna, span, earth") jumping at Arches National Park, north of Moab. He was reputedly fined and put on probation.

Sylvan Christensen, also of Moab, told the *New York Times* that he was part of the group that "...removed the Utah Monolith because there are clear precedents for how we share and standardize the use of our public lands, natural wildlife, native plants, fresh water sources, and human impacts upon them.'

"He went on to suggest that the area, especially during a pandemic, was imperiled by the increasing number of visitors —and by the 'Internet sensationalism' surrounding the monolith. 'People arrived by car, by bus, by van, helicopter, planes, trains, motorcycles and E-bikes," he said.

Outside magazine (December 23) however, pointed to the junk that the environmental purists who removed the monolith nonetheless allegedly "regularly erect in the desert" for their own purposes: "Lewis posted a video of the monolith...followed with a lengthy post about the reasons they removed it and the ways in which a monolith is different from the slacklines, climbing bolts, and space nets that he and his friends regularly erect in the desert. (Among other things, the crew has been accused of taking a hypocritical stance on human impacts to the desert.)"

After negotiations between those who razed the monolith and the Federal government, as of this writing what remains of it is in the "custody" of the Bureau of Land Management.

By December, 2020 there were numerous copycat monolith "discoveries" and installations.

Sightings were reported in Romania, on the Isle of Wight, in the Netherlands and Colombia. In the U.S., monoliths appeared in Glenwood Springs, Colorado, atop Pine Mountain in Atascadero, California, and in Joshua Tree National Monument.

A farcical story element manifested in the course of the spectacle. A dwarfish (three-foot) monolith materialized December 3, 2020 in downtown Fayetteville ("Little Fairy") North Carolina.

Referring to "monolith mania," the *New York Post* newspaper reported that on December 8, 2020, "Video obtained by Storyful showed a rowdy crowd—apparently fed-up with the mystifying, multiplying metal objects—toppling one (monolith) that had appeared in a San Diego parking lot on Tuesday.

"...a candy shop in Pittsburgh even commissioned one of the objects—a 10-foot tall, 24-inch wide triangle of plywood covered in sheet metal—to place outside the store...The owner of Grandpa Joe's Candy Shop, Christopher Beers, freely admitted to the gimmick, which he said was a way to remind people to support small businesses."

The monolith which appeared January 1, 2001 in Magnuson Park, Seattle, Washington

> "The monolith stirred worldwide speculation when it appeared in November."

Whether intentionally timed or "just a coincidence," considering its "discovery" a few weeks before the new year in the high western desert, one might venture to say that the concentrated focus on the Moab Monolith ceremonially prepared the American psyche for Black Jack 2021.

II

A SLOW MUSIC

"The actors in the old tragedies, as we read, piped their iambics to a tune, speaking from under a mask, and wearing stilts and a great head-dress. 'Twas thought the dignity of the Tragic Muse required these appurtenances, and that she was not to move except to a measure and cadence. So Queen Medea slew her children to a slow music..."

William Thackeray
The History of Henry Edmond, Esq.

King-Kill/33 Fifty-Eight Years Later [1]

"I think that there were some CIA extremists, fans of 'executive action,' including...James Jesus Angleton, that orchid-growing Anubis of spookitude, who...may even have known in advance that he (President Kennedy) was probably going to die down south."

Nicholson Baker [2]

"Three can keep a secret if two are dead."

Carlos Marcello

Part I: Truth or Consequences

Americans have not yet recovered from the post-traumatic stress brought on by the public slaughter of our President in Dallas — the two major symptoms of which are feeling numb and being afflicted with amnesia. Even in an alternative online magazine like *Salon*, in a long November 2013 article on the JFK assassination, the author did not recall the findings of the U.S. Senate's Church Committee or the investigations and prosecution initiated by New Orleans D.A. Jim Garrison.

What little we do remember about the conspiracy to kill our President leaves us feeling impotent. Thousands of seductive delights and web sites compete for our gaze. The colossal modern machine that has our daily lives ensconced in personal comfort and submerged 24/7 in Internet-TV-movies-video-games-stadium sports and those cathedrals of consumerism called shopping malls, allow us little time for deep reflection, but plenty of attention deficit. The machine grinds on. The rat race beckons. The noise accelerates. *Tempus fugit.*

The Cryptocracy knows this and factors it into its planning for spectacular crimes, from King-Kill/33 to Sandy Hook/13. They know there will be some investigation, some doubt about

---

[1] Portions of this study were first published in the November 2013 issue (no. 69) of *Revisionist History®*.

[2] "Dallas Killers Club," *The Baffler,* July 2014.

the official story and a few heroes who will step forth to risk their lives to pursue the perpetrators. *The Cryptocracy counts on the apathy and amnesia which their ritual crimes hypnotically induce in the population to blunt the effects of what little opposition their unholy enterprise may encounter.*

The Bible tells us that Yahweh commands us to "Be still and know that I am God." Without quiet, without that stillness, we can't know the Lord or His truth as He wants it revealed for the empowerment of His people. We were not destined to be shackled to Satan on the road to the robot-reign of dead matter in a drone-ruled police state. As sons and daughters of Jesus Christ we ought to strive for something higher and better, for ourselves and our posterity.

The *Dallas Morning News*, the *Dallas Times Herald* and the *Fort Worth Star-Telegram* newspapers all photographed three drifters under police escort near the Texas School Book Depository shortly after the assassination. [3] These photographs were transmitted nationwide. The men who were pictured in them became known in the public mind as the "three hobos" or the "three tramps." To this day these pictures are among the most enduring, iconic images of the assassination. Conspiracy sleuths have focused on attempting to discover the identity of the three men and have missed the masonic symbolism of the image itself. It was James Shelby Downard who first linked the photo of the three men in Dallas to the masonic legend of the "Juwes," the "Three Unworthy Craftsmen."

According to media and police accounts, three men were "taken off a boxcar in the Dallas rail yard immediately after President Kennedy was shot," described as drifters, detained as suspects and then released a few days later. Dallas police claimed (falsely) to have lost the records of their arrests as well as their mugshots and fingerprints. "What a coincidence" that of all the suspects in Dallas on November 22 in addition to Oswald, these three were the only ones to get caught in the police dragnet and make a splash in the media. Why was a photograph of three hobos made so prominent?

To answer that question we need to recall that Dealey Plaza was occult sacred space, the site of the first masonic temple in

---

[3] "The railroad yards are across the street from the (Texas School Book) Depository and up behind the grassy knoll and picket fence." James DiEugenio, *Reclaiming Parkland*.

Dallas; then we must travel back in time to Victorian England, to the "Dealey Plaza" of that era, London's "Mitre Square," where the horribly mutilated body of Jack the Ripper victim Catherine Eddowes was discovered. A portion of Eddowes' apron had been torn off, soaked with blood and placed in a passageway in the square. On the wall above the blood-soaked apron a masonic message had been scrawled in chalk: "The Juwes are the men that will not be blamed for nothing."

Only a Freemason or a close student of Freemasonry could have written those code words, which is why Sir Charles Warren, Commissioner of Police and one of the highest Masons in the land, rushed to the scene, forbade the police photographer from photographing the wall, and summarily erased the words. *Juwes* was not a misspelling of the word Jews; nor was it an allusion to Jews. *Juwes* is a masonic reference to mythical "ruffians," the "Three Unworthy Craftsmen"—the apprentice Masons *Ju*bela, *Ju*belo, and *Ju*belum—the *Juwes* of lodge legend who, it was said, had assassinated Hiram Abiff, the architect of King Solomon's Temple, which forms part of the "the basis of masonic ritual."[4]

It might be said that the photo of the latter-day Jubela, Jubelo, and Jubelum in Dallas in the wake of the assassination of John F. Kennedy was the signature of the Brotherhood, and that it conveyed an esoteric signal above the heads of the majority of Americans: "This was our work."

Mr. Downard observed another factor in occult murder conspiracies which he termed *"cryonic"* — a freeze-thaw process in which information about accomplices, perpetrators and planners is frozen during the time when the trail is hot and they can be apprehended, interrogated, tried and punished. Subsequently, as part of a process he called "The Making Manifest of All that is Hidden" and the "Revelation of the Method," the information is incrementally "thawed" many years (or decades) later, when the case is cold, those involved are mostly dead and interest is mostly academic. James Douglass, writing in 2008 in an important book esteemed by Robert F. Kennedy Jr., *JFK and the Unspeakable*, states: "...the conspiracy that most Americans have thought was likely (can) now be seen in detail...we know what happened in Dallas..."

---

[4] Stephen Knight, *Jack the Ripper: The Final Solution* (1977), pp. 177-179.

Agreed. It was known in the late 1960s by District Attorney Jim Garrison in New Orleans, by certain cowed journalists, and by the Kennedy family inner circle, yet it remained frozen stiff, like a cadaver in a cryogenics lab, awaiting resuscitation by future powers. Well, the future is here and what does the knowledge bring us?

Primarily it summons within us the sensation which the Cryptocracy intends to evoke: wonder and awe in the face of so virtuoso a masterpiece of conspiracy which could murder the President of the United States in the street, just after high noon, and evade the consequences for decades.

While the suspected Kennedy assassin Charles Harrelson was alive and accessible within the U.S. Prison system, this writer attempted to interest investigative reporters in interviewing him. We went so far as to meet with his son, actor Woody Harrleson, in California. All Establishment doors were slammed shut and even among conspiracy researchers there was no concerted drive to interview the elder Harrelson while he was alive. But now that he's dead the conspiracy community has new interest in him.

If we are to accept Mr. Downard's prognostication, then the full truth about the Israeli attack on the Navy ship USS Liberty in 1967 which killed 34 American sailors and wounded more than 171, will only become widely known after no possible harm can come to any of those who led the attack or covered it up (beginning with President Lyndon Johnson, according to testimony by Admiral Thomas Moorer, former chairman of the Joint Chiefs of Staff [5]).

The same will be true of the Son of Sam murders in New York, the Oklahoma City bombing, the 9/11 terror attacks, the D.C. sniper in Washington D.C., the Boston Marathon bombings, and so forth. In each case there is enough information available to lead to prosecutions *now*, but two criminal elements stand in the way: the government's mouthpiece media, and the secret society assets who comprise the personnel of the U.S. Attorney's offices, FBI and municipal police agencies.

Mr. Downard discovered the Revelation of the Method to be a powerful tool of the Cryptocracy, among the most formidable mind control devices in the psychological warfare arsenal. He

---

[5] *Houston Chronicle*, January 9, 2004.

was also fascinated by the white rabbit in *Alice in Wonderland*. Alice repeatedly encounters the creature inexplicably. In the early stages of its appearance, it seems as though the rabbit was included for comic relief or as a curiosity. What struck Shelby was the fact that when Alice saw the rabbit rushing off to an important appointment, unknown to her the *creature was actually hurrying to her trial*. To Mr. Downard this represented Truth-or-Consequences manifested by the Revelation of the Method: the people to whom it is revealed are on trial and under obligation to act. Their failure to act is a dereliction of duty; a grave sin of omission. Each additional revelation constitutes another count added to the indictment of the American people—the consequences of our refusal of truths placed in the open that *we do indeed see*. (John 9: 39-41).

In the medieval era rulers couldn't reveal to the people the crimes they were committing against them, without risking blowback in terms of insurrection and national upheaval. This was true in British America and in the days of the Early American Republic, and to a certain, though lesser extent, in the 1960s and early '70s with the massive Vietnam protests and black uprisings (on a scale far beyond the turmoil of 2020).

One of the goals of Idaho's Senator Frank Church and his "Church Committee" in the U.S. Senate in 1975 and 1976 was to compile evidence that the CIA assassinated people. Americans found it hard to believe, and the Agency in that era was compelled to deny it. Now "our" government pursues assassinations openly; with drones and by other means. Here is the Revelation of the Method before our eyes — for instance, in the FBI's barely disguised execution of Ibragim Todashev on May 22, 2013. [6]

Americans are immersed in Spectacle. We may jog five miles every day and work strenuously at our job, but our national profile is that of *spectators spellbound by the sight of our own funeral*. As we stated in *KingKill/33,* the booklet we wrote with Mr. Downard in the 1970s, something died in the American people on November 22 and has continued to die after 9/11 and the other state-sponsored (or condoned) ritual murders. There is only so much that can expire inside of us before we are little more than empty husks, which may explain

---

[6] Cf. "FBI executes a friend of the Boston Bombing suspects who had contested their guilt," *Revisionist History*® no. 67 (June 2013).

the fascination with zombies in American pop culture — the walking dead on the screen being representations of ourselves.

In 1991 a bored librarian at the Dallas Public Library referred to the assassination file log which the library maintained for researchers, as "the Kennedy junk." [7]

Truth or Consequences is a television game show and a town on the 33rd degree line of north parallel latitude, in the "Land of Enchantment" (New Mexico). Truth-or-Consequences is a principle that forms the core of the Revelation of the Method from which the American people are in perpetual flight. We wish to be *amused* and our amusements take the form of seeking to be deceived. *We ardently desire to be enchanted.* James Shelby Downard's vocation was that of a *disenchanter*, an unpopular role. He situated the assassination of John F. Kennedy in terms of Sir James Frazer's study, "The Killing of the Divine King," from *The Golden Bough*. In pre-Christian times this killing was perpetrated for purposes of fertility, to supposedly "green" the land. In Texas in 1963 it was performed on the psychodrama stage in Dealey Plaza, south of the 33rd degree of latitude, where, on the westward portion of that line, the atomic bomb had been exploded at the Trinity Site. Kennedy was immolated on the third fork of a triple convergence of streets adjacent to the Trinity River. For Downard this siting was no coincidence or accident. He was the first to declare it part of a ceremonial immolation consecrated for that very purpose, as precisely as the rituals, gestures and rubrics in the Lodge itself are performed.

Twilight Language Psychodrama

Frazer's volumes furnish numerous precedents for King-Kill/33, but for Shelby the strongest parallel was found in the killing of King Duncan in Shakespeare's play, *Macbeth*. In both killings we observe an elaborate ceremonial work of enchantment, replete with the theatrical elements of staging, choreography, iconography, *dramatis personae* and cryptic language loaded with arcana. Mr. Downard believed that some of the planning for the Kennedy assassination took place in the Storyville district of New Orleans, and Shakespeare, New Mexico. Kennedy's administration was repeatedly identified as

---

[7] Josh Alan Friedman, "Jack Ruby: Dallas' Original J.R.," wfmu.org/LCD/20/ruby.html

Camelot, and the mystical sheen of that Arthurian parable has haunted America's subconscious ever after. Among the circle of his assassins stands his Vice-President, Lyndon Baines Johnson (LBJ), of the Scottish clan of Macbeth by the way of the Baines. [8] Johnson was referred to in the media of the time as a type of the Scottish king-killer Macbeth—under the moniker "Macbird." Kennedy's wife Jacqueline was regarded as a queen of eros and high style and Kennedy has been called the most charming and handsome of all American presidents. On the day of her husband's immolation, the President and the First lady flew aboard the plane dubbed the *Angel* and landed at *Love Field*.

The killer assigned to permanently eliminate the talkative scapegoat Lee Harvey Oswald, was Jack Ruby. In the jeweler's trade a "jack ruby" is a fake. In Gaelic the word Kennedy denotes *éidigh ceann*, "ugly head" which is an apt description of the shattered head of our president on the day in which he had his appointment with destiny. His autopsied "ugly head" is among the most photographed in history. After he was shot, Mrs. Kennedy had tried to retrieve a piece of her husband's head from the trunk of the presidential limousine. Secret Service Agent Clint Hill, who had been stationed on the vehicle *behind* Kennedy's car, testified that the "right rear portion of his (Kennedy's) head was missing." [9]

Before the President left for his death in Dealey Plaza, he was serenaded in a ceremony in Washington D.C. by the Black Watch of Scotland, a military unit descended from government militia who had been allies of England's King George II, and consequently, in the eyes of some people, comprised of traitors to the Highland Scots. In the eighteenth century the Black Watch helped to hunt down remnants of the Highland army. Among the original clans affiliated with them was Clan Munro, which traces its patrimony from among the followers of Malcolm II, who was an ally of *Mac Bethad mac Findlaích* (Macbeth).

---

[8] According to Downard the geneaolgy was Baines-Baine-Beyne-MacBain-MacBean-MacBeth.

[9] Cf. "JFK Autopsy Materials," assassinationresearch.com/v2n2/pittsburgh.pdf "Parkland Hospital Dr. Robert McClelland said that 'probably a third or so, at least, of the brain tissue had been blasted out'...In an interview he gave to the *Journal of the American Medical Association*, Jim Humes said that ⅔ of the right cerebrum was gone." (DiEugenio, op. cit.).

In Freemasonry, Scotland possesses a distinct fascination. The most powerful masonic order in America was named the Scottish Rite. It was headquartered on the 33rd degree line of north parallel latitude in Charleston, South Carolina.

We may be accused of doing rhetorical backflips in order to attempt to make a connection between the killing of Kennedy and a masonic type of ritual. Even if this were true, it would be in preference to the bland obscurantism which the Establishment has employed to conceal a conspiracy most foul. Actually however, we are only seeking to have our people accept the evidence of their own eyes and intuition, rather than the sales pitch of the hucksters of media misdirection. Throughout the late 1960s and the 1970s, a majority of the American people did not accept the lone nut conclusion of the *Warren Report*, and this national dissatisfaction with the fabricated story led men of valor, such as New Orleans District Attorney Jim Garrison and Idaho's Senator Frank Church, to convene official investigations which have contradicted important assertions formerly fixed in stone by Justice Earl Warren and his cabal, led by Allen Dulles, the CIA director President Kennedy had fired.

We have referred to a "haunting." This haunting, in keeping with the Truth or Consequences dictum, can go either way. It can serve as a revival of the American fighting spirit, or it can lead to submission to a death script crafted for the acceleration of our spiritual and mental decline. Joan Mellen subtitled her account of Garrison's prosecution of certain Kennedy assassination conspirators, "The Case that Should Have Changed History." The same can be said for the investigations initiated by the Church Committee in the U.S. Senate, and of its important successor, the House of Representatives' hearings, 1976-1978. They ought to have sparked a rising of the people whereby a second American revolution made a clean sweep of the criminal-occult networks deeply entrenched in the U.S. government and its kept press.

The maxim, "Treason doth ever prosper, for if it prosper none dare call it treason," can be compared with our own observation that evil reigns when evil-doers gain advantage from it. No one was ever punished for slaughtering John F. Kennedy. Under those circumstances, evil continues to reign.

When this writer met with Hollywood actor Woody Harrelson in a San Francisco cafe some years ago, it wasn't to rub shoulders with the rich and famous. It was to convince Woody that this writer should be granted access to Charles Harrelson, his imprisoned father, the Mafia assassin of Judge John Wood, for the sole purpose of getting the elder Harrelson to provide, with his son's blessing, the names of the people who may have directed him to fire an assassin's rifle on November 22 in Dallas, which is our personal opinion of the elder Harrelson's role. Woody Harrelson, who once told the press, "My father was a CIA agent," began to weep when I asked him if his father killed Kennedy. He refused to facilitate my request to visit his incarcerated father. Charles Harrelson died in prison, taking his secrets with him. Woody is more successful than ever.

Let us contemplate an old adage, "Tell me who writes a nation's stories and I care not who writes its laws." The System encouraged the use of the word "Camelot" to describe the Kennedy administration. The System promoted a play about Lyndon Johnson, "Macbird," which cast him in the role of a king-killer. Kennedy was murdered on a site replete with masonic significance and symbolism. Humor us, as we suggest that the plot of this bardic psychodrama has more influence over America than we may imagine; that it is an initiator and signifier of a process of human devolution whereby the earth is prepared for Elizabethan Dr. John Dee's prophecy of the coming Reign of Dead Matter and the subjugation of humanity.

The killing of President Kennedy was hugely demoralizing to the American people. Despite his many transgressions and foibles, he was a standard-bearer for a future vision of peace, prosperity, and health. He was endeavoring to return America to the dimensions of a Jeffersonian Republic rather than a National Security State fueled by a Cryptocracy reaping enormous material prizes from perpetual wars and empire. Fact: after Kennedy died, the National Security State was almost immediately hugely engorged, culminating in 500,000 American troops committed to a southeast Asian backwater. The dimensions of this monstrosity have only grown since then, mestastisizing under Bill Clinton and especially George W. Bush, culminating in the government staging the 9/11 terror attacks and a decade of wars in Afghanistan and Iraq.

Every effort to defeat the dragon runs into a blackened sense of the inevitability of its triumph.

Much of the resistance today is halting and spasmodic. How does this pertain to the prophesied Reign of Dead Matter? A truly demoralized, degenerating being, once human and now barely so, can look in the mirror and see his own dissolution and destruction and be unable to compel himself to do what is necessary to save himself. Hollywood movies that are viewed by millions, such as "Terminator 3: Rise of the Machines," and "Terminator Salvation," feature robot networks that are granted autonomy by the U.S. military. These robots then conquer the world and enslave the remnant of humanity that has not been exterminated. Robots are of course dead matter. These films, whether by serendipity or intent, offer us a Truth or Consequences warning about our future.

The "Dr. Dees" of our time shill for the reign of robots over humanity. Law Professors Kenneth Anderson of the Brookings Institution and Matthew Waxman of the Council on Foreign Relations wrote in the *Wall Street Journal*, eighteen days before the 50th anniversary of the killing of the King of Camelot: "Contrary to what some critics of autonomous weapons claim, there won't be an abrupt shift from human control to machine control in the coming years. Rather, the change will be incremental: detecting, analyzing and firing on targets will become increasingly automated, and the contexts of when such force is used will expand. As the machines become increasingly adept, the role of humans will gradually shift from full command, to partial command...and so on. This evolution is inevitable as sensors, computer analytics and machine learning improve...and as similar technologies in civilian life prove that they (robots) are capable of complex tasks..."

Notice that the Reign of Dead Matter is described as *"inevitable."* These elite law professors revealed that humans will incrementally cede control to militarized robots: "the role of humans will gradually shift from full command, to partial command...and so on." Why the weasel phrase, "so on"? Why the reluctance to state outright, without beating around the bush, that the ruling class intends to grant Artificial Intelligence (AI) complete autonomy over the most advanced lethal weapons and their use? This fact portends the rule of machines over a disarmed or at the least, vastly outgunned humanity. Proceeding further on this continuum of perverse and degenerate futurism, we are being persuaded that it is a fixture of absurdly antiquated notions of personal privacy and quality of life, to expect that the surveillance of our lives by the NSA, and the militarization of local police forces, can or will be halted in subordination to our Constitutional rights.

The futurism projected by the script-writers teaches us that the evils imposed on us are inescapable. An "inevitable" dark future is being designed which commands acceptance through an external visualization implanted in our minds.

It does not have to be. We the living choose the contours of our lives. The future need not be commanded by pulse-pounding, digital phantoms. We can, by the grace of God, turn our nation in any direction in which we will it to proceed. The strength of our hidden masters is entirely illusory. They serve a cosmic loser, the devil.

In a godly society, the perpetrators who killed Kennedy would have been found out, apprehended and, after a fair trial, publicly hanged in Dealey Plaza. Much of the spiritual fog infusing our collective national soul with demonic incentives for a Dead Matter future, would have dissipated as a result.

But the success of the Truth or Consequences gambit in the assassination of a president, the impunity with which it was perpetrated before the eyes of the nation, emboldened the Cryptocracy to further gambits, from the killing of the "Black King of Memphis" (M.L. King), and Robert F. Kennedy in 1968, to the shooting of George Wallace in 1972, and the Oklahoma City, Pentagon and Twin Towers attacks. The police state now coalescing would be dust in the wind without the success of those conspiracies. Our failure to bring to justice the masterminds of these crimes is what ensures that the empire of criminal politics continues. Those who insist that these successes on the part of the Cryptocracy are due solely to the enemy's command of geo-politics, covert operations and brainwashing, and refuse to countenance the Cryptocracy's use of ritual magic for shaping and processing the human psyche, are hopelessly outclassed in this great battle.

Forgive us if we see in the death march from atomic bombs first initiated at the Trinity Site on the 33rd degree, and the Killing of the King near the Trinity River south of the 33rd degree, a pattern. Ancient pagans sacrificed their king in the superstitious belief that his blood fertilized the earth and made crops grow, and children springing to life in greater numbers and vitality.

The King of Camelot was slain for very different reasons. He was sacrificed as part of the *Jornada del muerto,* the long journey to make dead matter the monarch over life. The aircraft named *Angel* delivered the King and Queen of Camelot to *Love Field* where, shortly afterward, the king's head was shattered, and his brains rendered garbage for the street sweeper, after which Ruby was nationally televised blowing the guts out of a scapegoat. Post-assassination, the former First Lady, the survivor of tremendous trauma upon whom we have compassion, descended into a porn theater habitué and a lover of stunted millionaires; ending her life in the arms of a wealthy, obese adulterer, about whom she said, "I admire his success." Her personal *Jornada del muerto* does not differ materially from that of millions of other members of the audience at the immolation of her king.

We do not insist on proving the intentionality behind this alchemical devolution. You are welcome to accept that it is all just a coincidence. Pusillanimity in thrall to a tyrannical master is often the last thing a scoffing slave will notice.

The assassinations of John Fitzgerald Kennedy and Lee Harvey Oswald recount an archetypal scapegoat scenario. Are we prepared to accept the Cryptocracy's monopoly on discernment and interpretation, or can we see and think independently of it?

We are made in the image and likeness of God, and it is by the decisions we make in our personal lives that this battle will be lost or won — in those profiles in courage, as President Kennedy termed them — where, at risk to our personal security and comfort, we refuse the blandishments and bribes of the rich and powerful in order to do what we know to be right.

For the counter-cultural Christian, life is an incandescent protest of the System and of the reprobated majority, who, in their frivolous inconstancy, are beguiled by the world, particularly now, when poll-driven "majorities" determine morality (or its overthrow) by popular vote; as if the implementation of the Ten Commandments could be decided by a plurality of Golden Calf worshippers.

Part II The Conspiracy

"...understanding that moment in Dallas, the seven seconds that broke the back of the American century."

Don DeLillo

"I'm just a patsy!"

Lee Harvey Oswald, November 22, 1963, 7:55 p.m. [10]

"I spoke in Clinton, Louisiana last month, at the oldest working courthouse in the United States, I believe. The judge who introduced me asked the audience how many believed that Lee Harvey Oswald was guilty. Not a single hand went up. That audience knew the Warren Report was nonsensical because it was in East Feliciana Parish, in the hamlets of Clinton and Jackson, that Oswald appeared in the company of Clay Shaw, and a CIA contract pilot named David Ferrie, in the late summer of 1963, three months before the assassination. In the audience were actual witnesses, including the barber who cut Oswald's hair."

— Prof. Joan Mellen, January, 2006 [11]

Richard Case Nagell

Richard Case Nagell, who was profiled in Dick Russell's controversial biography *The Man Who Knew Too Much* (2003), was an Army counterintelligence officer from 1955 to 1959, and a CIA asset under Desmond Fitzgerald, with responsibility for monitoring the KGB. On Sept. 7, 1963, Nagell contacted J. Edgar Hoover warning of the impending assassination of President Kennedy. Fearful of being made part of the

---

[10] After his arrest, Oswald asked for New York attorney John Abt to represent him, or any lawyer who was a member of the ACLU and would believe in his innocence. ACLU members came to the jail on November 22 but were told that Oswald did not seek legal representation. Cf. Douglass, *JFK and the Unspeakable*, p. 365.

[11] Lecture by Joan Mellen at the Ethical Culture Society, New York City, January 24, 2006. joanmellen.net/NYC_2006article.html

assassination conspiracy, on Sept. 20, Nagell walked into a bank in El Paso, Texas with a gun, fired two bullets into the ceiling and then calmly waited for the police to arrest him. He served 54 months in prison and thus removed himself from the assassination and its aftermath. On October 31, 1995 the Assassinations Records Review Board (ARRB) sent a letter to Nagell requesting access to documents in his personal possession concerning President Kennedy's death. On November 1, Nagell was found dead "of natural causes" in the bathroom of his home in Los Angeles.

Rose Cheramie

On November 20 in Eunice, Louisiana, Rose Cheramie, who had a reputation as a drug addict and had worked for strip club proprietor Jack Ruby at his Silver Slipper Lounge and Pink Door club, told Louisiana State Policeman Francis Fruge that two men she met at the Silver Slipper planned to assassinate the president when he came to Dallas. Historian James Douglass in *JFK and the Unspeakable* has identified the men as Sergio Arcacha Smith and Emilio Santa, Cuban exiles who worked for the Central Intelligence Agency. Aracha Smith visited former FBI agent Guy Bannister's office at 544 Camp Street in New Orleans prior to November 22. Bannister was an associate of both Lee Harvey Oswald and Arcacha Smith. The later shared an office with Bannister in New Orleans, at the address Oswald printed on his "Fair Play for Cuba" leaflets which he publicly distributed.

Trooper Fruge subsequently became part of New Orleans District Attorney Jim Garrison's investigative team. "Fruge showed photographs of Cubans provided by Garrison to Hadley Manuel, the manager of the Silver Slipper. Of the two men he had seen with with Rose (Cheramie), Manuel identified Sergio Arcacha Smith...Will Fritz, the Dallas police captain, told Fruge of diagrams of the Dealey Plaza sewer system that had been found in Arcacha's Dallas apartment." [12]

According to James DiEugenio in his book *Reclaiming Parkland*, CIA agent E. Howard Hunt helped Aracha Smith establish the "Cuban Revolutionary Council," an anti-Castro organization. Cheramie was hospitalized November 21, at the East Louisiana State Hospital, where she told hospital staff

---

[12] Mellen, p. 208.

that Kennedy would be killed the next day. How did a lowly exotic dancer with a drug habit possess this information?

On Sept. 4, 1965, less than 22 months after she made her statements, Cheramie's body was discovered at around 3 a.m. on a highway east of Big Sandy, Texas.

She was either the victim of a bullet to the head, or a car that had driven over her head. The ambiguity rests in the fact that her autopsy results have been "lost."

The state of Texas refused District Attorney Garrison's request to have her body exhumed. Among the many omissions of the *Warren Commission Report* of 1964, the elision of the accounts of major witnesses such as Cheramie render the *Report* on par with the heavily compromised *9/11 Commission Report* issued four decades later.

Julia Ann Mercer

At around 11:00 a.m. on November 22, 23-year-old Julia Ann Mercer was driving through Dealey Plaza when she noticed a man with a rifle case exit a truck driven by another man who she would later recognize as Jack Ruby. The man toting the case carried the apparent weapon up the grassy knoll. Ruby remained in the truck. After telling friends about what she saw, she was questioned for hours by the FBI and Dallas police.

On November 23, 1963 she picked Ruby out as the grassy knoll man's driver from photographs of several men supplied to her by the FBI. Fearing for her life, Mercer went into hiding.

Mercer was the wife of a former Illinois Congressman. Her initial eyewitness affidavit was recorded by the Dallas Sheriff's Office on November 22 and can be read at jfkassassination.net/russ/testimony/mercer.htm

When she met with Garrison in January, 1968 he showed Mercer her statement as printed in the Warren Commission Exhibits. Reading them, she shook her head. She told Garrison, "These have all been altered. They have me saying just the opposite of what I really told them." [13]

---

[13] Douglass, pp. 254-257.

Lee Harvey Oswald

Oswald had served as a radar operator for the CIA's secret U-2 spy plane. The best evidence extant points to him as a CIA counter-intelligence asset sent to the Soviet Union as part of "ZR/RIFLE." According to Senator Church's Committee to Study Governmental Operations, the CIA's Richard Bissell developed the ZR/RIFLE assassination team, shielded by "forged and backdated documents" and with contingency plans for "blaming Sovs" (Soviets) for assassinations that became public or were intended to be made public.

CIA assassination scapegoats like Oswald were to have a fraudulent "201" personnel file and appropriate Soviet connections. The Church Senate Committee and the House Select Committee on Assassinations (HSCA) discovered that CIA Counter-Intelligence Chief James Jesus Angleton's department had a 201 file on Oswald from 1960 onward. Former CIA Director Allen Dulles told the Warren Commission on January 27, 1964, that no CIA employee, even under oath, should ever say truthfully if Oswald was in fact a CIA agent. [14]

"...one of (Richard) Helms's most trusted associates, David Phillips, also known as Maurice Bishop, met with Oswald two months before the Kennedy assassination...Sen. Richard Schweiker of Pennsylvania stated, 'Oswald had intelligence connections...the fingerprints of intelligence' were all over him." [15]

Oswald was working for both the FBI and the CIA. Texas Attorney General Waggoner Carr informed J. Lee Rankin, the Warren Commission's general counsel that "Oswald was an undercover agent for the FBI." The FBI agent in New Orleans in 1963, William Walter, testified to the House Select Committee on Assassinations that "Oswald did indeed have 'an informant's status with our office." [16] J. Edgar Hoover ordered all Louisiana FBI agents to refuse to cooperate with District Attorney Jim Garrison. "...we are not becoming involved in any way in Garrison's investigation," Hoover said.[17]

---

[14] Douglass, pp. 65 and 334.

[15] Patrick Nolan, *CIA Rogues* (New York: 2013), p. 43.

[16] Douglass pp. 65 and 334.

[17] Mellen, pp. 232-234.

On October 16, 1963 Oswald gained employment at the Texas Book Depository overlooking Kennedy's November 22 parade route, by means of Ruth Paine, a friend of Oswald's wife, Marina. Paine was introduced to the Oswalds in February, 1963 by CIA contract worker George de Mohrenschildt, who subsequently received $200,000 from the Haitian regime of CIA asset Papa Doc Duvalier, for "geological" work, even though De Mohrenschildt was not a geologist.

On October 23, 1964, J. Edgar Hoover wrote Warren Commission counsel J. Lee Rankin urging him not to release FBI "reports and memoranda dealing with Michael and Ruth Paine and George and Jean de Mohrenschildt." De Mohrenschildt died of a shotgun blast in Florida in 1977.

Michael Paine, Ruth's estranged husband, was the stepson of Arthur Young, inventor of the Bell helicopter. Michael Paine's mother was a friend of Mary Bancroft, the mistress of CIA director Dulles. Ruth Paine's father, William Avery Hyde, received a three year government contract in 1964 with the CIA-connected Agency for International Development. Ruth Paine's sister, Sylvia Hyde Hoke, was an employee of the CIA in Virginia.

On pp. 290-298 and 459-462 of *JFK and the Unspeakable,* James Douglass astutely debunks the official story of Oswald's supposed killing of Police Officer J.D. Tippit, based in part on Douglass' interviews with surviving witnesses who were movie patrons or employees of the Texas Theatre, as well as with journalist and future Dallas Mayor Wes Wise. [18] Mr. Douglass documents that the CIA used an Oswald lookalike for the killing of Tippit. This double was a passenger in a car bearing license plates taken from an automobile registered to Carl Amos Mather, an employee of a Texas communications company that did contract work for the CIA.

Douglass also demonstrates, "the FBI's consistent record in covering up, falsifying and destroying evidence that might incriminate the government in the assassination" (p. 462). This is an assertion he repeatedly substantiates. In the case of both agencies, to paraphrase Douglass, comprehending their

---

[18] Mayor Wise saved the Texas School Book Depository from destruction in the early 1970s. Guy Bannister's *dual* New Orleans headquarters (544 Camp Street/531 LaFayette) with one entrance, was razed in 1973, thereby permitting PBS "Frontline" in 1993 to lie and claim that the two addresses did not lead to the same office, as many witnesses (such as Bill Turner of *Ramparts* magazine) and D.A. Garrison, had always maintained.

involvement does not mean that we can limit the responsibility for the JFK assassination to the Mafia assassins who served the CIA,[19] the CIA itself, the Secret Service (which in addition to its other traitorous acts, spirited the president's corpse out of Parkland Hospital before Dallas coroner Earl Rose could perform an autopsy), and the FBI.

(For more on the Parkland Hospital chicanery cf. *JFK: Conspiracy of Silence* [1992], by the dying president's Parkland surgeon, Dr. Charles Crenshaw).[20]

Oswald was interrogated for twelve hours after the president's death with no tape recording and no stenographer present.

If anyone imagines that tape recording technology was too unreliable or primitive in 1963 to have been part of a major case, they should recall that in that year FBI agents had been surreptitiously recording several hours' worth of Martin Luther King's activities in private residences, with adequate audio fidelity.

Follow the trail of Oswald from the moment he met David Ferrie in the Civil Air Patrol, to the point near the end of his life—the attempted phone call he made to military intelligence officer John Hurt the day after he was arrested in Dallas. Remember that in the Marine Corps Oswald was a lowly radar operator who had been singled out for testing in Russian language proficiency.

Oswald was being trained in the language as part of a future assignment — which a bogus hardship discharge enabled him to do — defect to Russia. He was sent to Russia as a phony defector and returned to the USA being maneuvered across a chess board.

William Pitzer

In November, 1963 Lt. Commander William Pitzer was director of the Audio-Visual Department of the Naval Medical School. He took photos and 16mm movie footage of President Kennedy's cadaver at Bethesda Naval Hospital, including close-ups of his frontal throat wound and rear head wound. He

---

[19] According to retired Army Special Forces (Green Beret) Lt. Col. Daniel Marvin, "...the Mafia provided the CIA's pool of able assassins for hits in the U.S." (Douglass, p. 320).

[20] For a defense of Crenshaw cf. Douglass, pp. 307-311. For one of the most flagrant instances of FBI evidence tampering cf. Douglass, pp. 335-338 and p. 472, and *New York Times*, "FBI Chiefs Linked to Oswald File Loss," Sept. 17, 1975, pp. 1 and 21.

concluded from the photographic evidence that the president had been shot from the front, contradicting the *Warren Report*. Pitzer was shot to death on October 29, 1966, four days before he was scheduled to retire from the military and accept a television broadcasting opportunity that appeared to include broadcast of his Kennedy cadaver film footage, which went missing after his death.

Jack Ruby

According to the Establishment's leading JFK conspiracy denier, Vincent Bugliosi, Jack Ruby "was no more of a mobster than you or I..."

Researcher James DiEugenio documents that Ruby was an associate of Joseph Civello, who was present at the 1957 Apalachin meeting in New York of U.S. mobsters, including Sam Giancana and Vito Geovese. Ruby was also an associate of Lewis McWillie, who resided in Cuba under Fulgencio Batista's regime, where McWillie managed the Tropicana Hotel in Havana, which was co-owned by Mafia boss Santo Trafficante and the mob's financial intellect, Meyer Lansky. Elaine Mynier, McWillie's girlfriend, testified that Ruby "would do anything for McWillie..."

"In the late 1950s...Ruby, a Chicago mob functionary transplanted to Dallas, ran guns to Fidel, so that the Mafia could hedge its bets on the next Cuban government by supporting both the dictator Batista and the insurrectionist Castro. The CIA monitored the shipments...After Castro turned Communist, the CIA and Customs encouraged shipments to anti-Castro forces...in January 1959...Ruby began to supply weapons, now with CIA support, to anti-Castro Cubans...working with another CIA-connected gun-runner, Thomas Eli Davis III." [21]

Even Warren Commission investigators Leon Hubert and Burt Griffin noted in a Commission memo, "The most promising links between Jack Ruby and the assassination of President Kennedy are established through underworld figures and anti-Castro Cubans..." [22]

After Oswald's arrest, in the evening of the assassination of President Kennedy, Ruby infiltrated Dallas District Attorney

---

[21] Douglass, p. 358.

[22] John Armstrong, *Harvey and Lee*, 948.

Henry Wade's press conference, posing as a reporter. Ruby corrected Wade when the D.A. erred in stating that Oswald had been working for the "Free Cuba Committee," which was a Right wing organization.

Ruby interrupted him to state, in front of the assembled reporters, that Oswald had actually worked for the "Fair Play for Cuba Committee," a Left wing organization. Just a few hours after the assassination of the President and a strip club sleazebag was exhibiting more knowledge about the mysterious Lee Harvey Oswald than the Dallas District Attorney.

Dallas police received three different phone calls early Sunday, November 24, the day Oswald was shot, warning that he would be killed. In one call, as reported by Dallas Police Officer Billy Grammer, the caller said, "If you move Oswald the way you are planning, we are going to kill him."

Hence, "In spite of this series of warning calls...the authorities, instead of transferring Oswald secretly...Oswald's police guards once again led him...right into the vicinity of a waiting Ruby...Dallas authorities seemed to have had higher orders. They in effect gave Ruby an easier opportunity to kill Oswald..." [23] Officer Patrick Dean was in charge of Oswald's security detail. The House Select Committee on Assassinations concluded that Patrick Dean was a key figure in Oswald's shooting. Dean refused to speak to the Committee.

When Oswald's murder was televised live, it was perhaps the most shocking event ever shown on American television. Ruby shot Oswald at 11:21 a.m. Ruby was signaled by the blast of a car horn. "The first horn goes off at almost the exact second that Oswald emerges...The second horn goes off about a nanosecond before Ruby plunges forward to shoot Oswald" (DiEugenio). Ruby wrote his epitaph in terms of the horns. In a letter obtained by Bill Diehl of the *St. Louis Post Dispatch*, he wrote that he was gravely ill and about to be hospitalized. He concludes with the words, "If you hear a lot of horn-blowing, it will be for me, they will want my blood."

In 1996 former Deputy Sheriff Al Maddox testified that before he died, Ruby told Maddox that he (Ruby) had been part of a conspiracy to silence Oswald. When he was terminally ill,

---

[23] Douglass, 368. As for who those "Dallas authorities" might be: "Earle Cabell, the mayor of Dallas when Kennedy and Oswald were killed, was the brother of Charles Cabell, Deputy Director of the CIA under Allen Dulles..." (Douglass, pp. 482-483, and Garrison, *On the Trail of the Assassins*, pp. 118-121).

Ruby told Dr. Werner Teuter that he had been "framed to kill Oswald." [24]

After shooting Oswald and while in custody, Ruby asked to speak with Gordon McLendon, a veteran WWII Naval Intelligence officer and manager of "Liberty Radio Network" in Dallas. Fifteen years later, in 1978, McLendon formed a partnership with David Atlee Phillips, former Western Hemisphere chief of the CIA, and Stansfield Turner, CIA director, to rehabilitate the agency's public image.

According to D.A. Jim Garrison: "Ruby...was working for the intelligence community...as a member (associate) of the Mafia, part of which had become subservient to the CIA...he was actively engaged in the assassination. He delivered one of the riflemen to the grassy knoll, as one witness (Julia Ann Mercer) observed; although the government, the FBI, changed her testimony, I subsequently got the true testimony from her...Jack Ruby knew what he had to do to Oswald because he (Ruby) was already a key player in the assassination plot. He had carried out the dangerously visible task of delivering a gunman to the grassy knoll...The CIA could hold Ruby in reserve for the murder of Oswald, in case Oswald was not killed by the Dallas police in the Texas Theater, as turned out to be the case." [25]

Dorothy Kilgallen

Kilgallen was the only reporter to whom Jack Ruby is believed to have confided during a private interview. Her father was James L. Kilgallen, a fearless Catholic journalist for the Hearst newspapers who investigated the Lindbergh baby kidnapping. His daughter was a tough-as-nails reporter for the *New York Journal-American* and a panelist on the nationally televised "What's My Line?" CBS game show. She was known for her keen wit and independence. In 1954 she questioned the official story of the bludgeon slaying of the wife of physician Dr.

---

[24] "Framed" is the right word. Another example: Oswald's alleged right palm print and left fingerprint of his index finger on the bag containing the rifle occurred when the Dallas police showed him the bag and allowed him to handle it. There is also the possibility that the bag in evidence did not match the Texas School Book Depository paper samples and was fabricated to frame Oswald. DiEugenio demonstrates the confused and questionable provenance of the bag.

[25] Douglass, p. 360.

Samuel Sheppard, who was wrongfully convicted of the murder. She has the distinction of being the first nationally prominent reporter to ask questions about a possible Kennedy assassination conspiracy.

One source has stated that when "Kennedy was assassinated...Dorothy was devastated. Ten months before, she had taken her young son Kerry on a tour of the White House...To their surprise, President Kennedy invited them into the Oval Office and was extraordinarily kind."

Miss Kilgallen began asking tough questions of the authorities. She had a valuable contact within the Dallas Police Department who furnished her with a copy of the original police log that chronicled the minute-by-minute activities of the department on the day of the assassination, as shown in radio communications. This allowed her to report that the first reaction of Chief Jesse Curry to the shots in Dealey Plaza was: 'Get a man on top of the overpass and see what happened up there.' Kilgallen noted that Curry lied when he told reporters the next day that he initially thought the shots were fired from the Texas School Book Depository. Dorothy challenged the credibility of Howard Brennan (who supposedly gave police a description of the shooter). She wrote articles about how important witnesses had been intimidated by the Dallas police or FBI." [26]

Kilgallen died at age 52. In a November 9, 1965 obituary, the *New York Times* stated, "In August, 1964, officials of the Warren Commission expressed distress that a Kilgallen column had contained testimony before the commission by Jack L. Ruby, the convicted murderer of President Kennedy's assassin, Lee Harvey Oswald." Asked by the FBI to reveal her source for the testimony, "She stated that regardless of the consequences she will never identify the source to anyone." [27]

"One of the biggest scoops of Kilgallen's career came when she obtained the 102-page transcript of Ruby's testimony to the Warren Commission. Readers were shocked at the hopelessly inept questioning of Ruby by Chief Justice Warren..." [28]

---

[26] Sara Jordan, "Who Killed Dorothy Kilgallen?" *Midwest Today*, (2007).

[27] FBI memo of August 24, 1964, attached to a letter from J. Edgar Hoover to J. Lee Rankin, general counsel for the Warren Commission.

[28] Jordan, op. cit.

In March, 1964, during his trial for killing Oswald, Kilgallen had a private interview with Jack Ruby, whose lawyer, Joe Tonahill, stated, "This interview with her was a very significant point in his (Ruby's) classless life.'

Tonahill affirmed that Ruby 'cooperated with her in every way that he could..." [29]

Kilgallen conducted research in Dallas and New Orleans. She stated, "If it's the last thing I do, I'm going to break this case." [30]

Before her death on November 8, Kilgallen had written in her September 3 newspaper column, "This story (the JFK assassination conspiracy) isn't going to die as long as there's a real reporter alive..."

She perished of acute poisoning from three kinds of fast-acting barbiturates — secobarbital, amobarbital and pentobarbital, combined with alcohol. Kilgallen's friend, Marlin Swing, "laid the blame for Kilgallen's death on Italian-American criminals...."

A sophisticated Stanford University dropout with a reputation as a ladies man, Ron Pataky was an associate of mobster Sam Giancana. Someone had Pataky inveigle his way into Dorothy's life. He wined and dined her over the course of several months, pledging his eternal love and having access to her and her home at all hours. After her mysterious death, Pataky published a grimly sardonic poem, "Never Trust a Stiff at a Typewriter." It reeked of the vitriol which the Chicago mob felt for the reporter who intended to use Ruby's disclosures against the Kennedy assassination conspirators. In the poem, Pataky "asserts there's a way to quench a gossip's stench' that 'never fails.' He notes, 'One cannot write if zippered tight,' and that somebody who's dead can 'sell no tales!" [31]

At the time of her death, Kilgallen was under contract to Random House (headed by her friend and fellow "What's My Line?" panelist Bennett Cerf), for a book to be titled, "Murder One." [32] She was known to possess a folder containing her

---

[29] Jordan, ibid.

[30] Lee Israel, *Kilgallen* (New York: Dell, 1979), 380-381.

[31] Sara Jordan, op. cit.

[32] Sara Jordan: "Fellow 'What's My Line?' panelist and book publisher Bennett Cerf recalled, 'She read me the preface of the book she was finishing for us at Random House, titled 'Murder One."

Kennedy assassination notes and research. "Nothing of what Dorothy gathered, surmised or wrote during her private interview with Jack Ruby...has ever come to light." [33]

Seven days after Dorothy's death: "Dr. James Luke, a New York City medical examiner, said she died from 'acute ethanol and barbiturate intoxication, circumstances undetermined.' That was not a common phrase for his office to use...Even though the circumstances of her death were listed as 'undetermined,' for some reason the police never bothered to try to determine them....

"Since Dr. Luke had gone to the scene the day of Dorothy's death and then did her autopsy, it would have been customary for him to sign her death certificate. But he did not do so. Instead, it was supposedly signed by Dr. Dominick DiMaio. Asked about this, Dr. DiMaio was nonplussed. 'I wasn't stationed in Manhattan (where Kilgallen died),' he asserted. 'I was in Brooklyn. Are you sure I signed it? I don't see how the hell I could have signed it in the first place. You got me. I don't know why. I know nothing about the case. I never handled it."[34]

According to journalist Sara Jordan, Kilgallen's biographer Lee Israel told her, "Ordinarily in the case of a woman's suspicious death, the police would go out and at least ask pro forma questions of the people who were around her the night before. But the New York cops did nothing. I mean nothing." [35]

Bill Hunter, Jim Koethe and Tom Howard

Jack Ruby shared an apartment in Dallas with George Senator. When Senator learned that Oswald had been shot he telephoned an attorney, asking for legal representation for his roommate, *before it was announced that Ruby was the killer.* [36] Within approximately 48 hours of the shooting of Oswald, Senator met with a trio, consisting of attorney Tom Howard, and reporters Jim Koethe of the *Dallas Times Herald* and Bill Hunter of the *Long Beach Press-Telegram*. By March of 1965, eight months before Kilgallen's own demise, all three men

---

[33] Lee Israel, op.cit., pp. 426-427. When the news of her death was made known, viewers of CBS were watching a pre-taped show, "To Tell the Truth," in which Dorothy Kilgallen was a participant.

[34] Jordan, op. cit.

[35] Jordan, ibid.

[36] DiEugenio, op. cit.

would be dead. In April of 1964 Bill Hunter was shot to death by a Long Beach policeman. The cop was convicted of manslaughter and sentenced to three years *probation*. On September 21, 1964, Jim Koethe was found dead in his apartment. The Dallas County coroner ruled that he had died of a broken neck by a blow to the throat. 48-year-old Tom Howard's death in 1965 was attributed to a heart attack.

Jim Garrison

The death of witnesses connected to the Kennedy assassination conspiracy was effective in intimidating other witnesses, including those who New Orleans District Attorney Jim Garrison required to prosecute suspect Clay Shaw. Among those witnesses who, out of fear, would not reveal what they knew to Garrison, were Richard Case Nagell, Alfred Moran, Herbert Wagner, Woodrow Hardy and Vernon Gerdes.[37]

Robert K. Tannenbaum, one of the HSCA lead investigators, located a memo from the office of CIA Director Richard Helms: "It revealed how the CIA had followed, harassed and attempted to intimidate Jim Garrison's witnesses." [38] Joan Mellen's *A Farewell to Justice* documents the staggering level of harassment under which the intractable Garrison labored as he proceeded to prosecute CIA agent Clay Shaw for the murder of the president. Garrison was opposed by J. Edgar Hoover, by the Kennedy family led by Robert F. Kennedy, and even by Texas Governor John Connolly who rejected the magic bullet theory, yet "harbored animosity toward Jim Garrison." For much of the rest of his life Garrison was harassed with false charges of racketeering, homosexual acts, [39] Mafia bribes,

---

[37] Mellen, p. 299.

[38] Mellin, p. 344. The HSCA hearings were valuable for the important raw evidence and testimony they gathered at a time when the assassination trail was relatively "hot." Its formal conclusions however, were nearly as wayward as those of the Warren Commission. Other than acknowledging that a conspiracy to kill the president probably had occurred, the HSCA whitewashed the CIA and the FBI of any culpability.

[39] In 1969 Garrison's supposed homosexual partner was alleged to be Pierre Bezou, the son of Clay Shaw's friend, James Bezou. The elder Bezou "committed suicide" five years later. Coroner Frank Minyard regarded Bezou's cause of death as suspicious.

corruption, and income tax fraud, by government agencies and the CIA's friends in the media. [40]

Garrison prosecuted Shaw, the CIA's Louisiana handler of Lee Harvey Oswald—twice. Once as an accessory to the murder of the president, for which Shaw was acquitted, and a second time for perjury in claiming he had never worked for the CIA and did not know Bannister, Ferrie or Oswald.

The perjury case was assigned to Judge Herbert Christenberry whose wife had written to Shaw, congratulating him on his initial acquittal.

In the autumn of 1969, in the midst of preparations to prosecute Shaw the second time, Garrison stood for reelection as district attorney. New Orleans' two major newspapers endorsed Garrison's opponent, Harry Connick, the lawyer who had been part of Shaw's defense team and whose well-funded mayoral campaign outspent Garrison ten to one. Nonetheless, the people of New Orleans reelected Garrison.

On June 1, 1970, a Justice Department Strike Force opened in the city, the sole purpose of which was to put Garrison behind bars. Garrison's physical health deteriorated and he began to play around with other women, causing his wife Liz to leave him.

On behalf of D.A. Garrison, New Orleans Prosecuting Attorney Irvin Dymond had asked Clay Shaw on the witness stand during his trial for perjury, "Have you ever worked for the Central Intelligence Agency?"

Under oath, Shaw answered, "No, I have not."

On May 28, 1971, Judge Christenberry dismissed all of the perjury charges against Shaw.

As part of the cryonic process, 21 years after Shaw's perjury acquittal, the facts of the documentary record were thawed: the CIA's History Staff surveyed CIA files that had been made available to the HSCA between 1977 and 1979. Among 64 sequestered boxes of documents there was one revealing Clay Shaw to have been a CIA employee. In 1992 the CIA's PROJFILES "CIA Matters" division of its History Staff

---

[40] Bobby Kennedy was perhaps warned privately that support for apprehending the perpetrators of his brother's murder would result in more Kennedy deaths. Bobby was not killed until it appeared that his election as president was likely. The notion that without the power of the presidency, RFK should have pursued his brother's killers, is questionable. Mellen implicates Bobby in a plot to assassinate Castro, which Jim Douglass refutes (cf. Douglass, pp. 250-252).

released the document. The History Staff's Director, J. Kenneth McDonald admits, *"These records do reveal, however, that Clay Shaw was a highly paid CIA contract source until 1956."* Shaw had indeed perjured himself. The CIA's own staff revealed the truth, two years after Garrison was in his grave.

On June 29, 1971, a Federal agent planted an envelope containing a sum of cash in Garrison's drawer. On June 30 Federal agents raided his home in search of the "bribe money." On December 3, 1971 Garrison was indicted in federal court for income tax fraud and conspiracy to obstruct law enforcement. The case went to trial on August 23, 1973; *Judge Christenberry* presiding.

Garrison represented himself and addressed the racially mixed jury for three hours. Garrison's estranged wife and five children sat in the front row of the spectator's section in support of their embattled husband and father. Mellen recounts how, defining the Declaration of Independence as a document designed to protect individuals from government, Garrison requested that the jury stand as a shield, protecting him from the Federal government which had made a systematic effort to frame him. He admitted that he was not without flaws, "It has been nearly 2,000 years since the last perfect man was on earth," but insisted that he was innocent of the charges against him. Don't let the devil triumph, he advised the jury, his voice cracking with emotion. Two black jurors were seen to weep. The jury returned a unanimous verdict of not guilty. The "Federal Organized Crime Strike Force" packed its bags almost as soon as the jury delivered its verdict. It seems the Feds believed there was only one source of organized crime in New Orleans. Local Mafia boss Carlos Marcello's operations were of little interest.

Toward the end of 1973 Garrison was again facing reelection. Never a man with mercenary motives, his court battle had left him broke. He lost by 2200 votes to Harry Connick, who began destroying Garrison's official assassination conspiracy records upon taking office.

Garrison was indicted and tried again in March, 1974 for income tax evasion. This time the jury acquitted him in less than an hour, but his marriage to Liz was now finished and his health was compromised. Nonetheless, ever the fighter, in 1978 Garrison ran for the Louisiana Court of Appeals, Fourth Circuit, with money he obtained by mortgaging his property.

Black civil rights organizations endorsed his opponent, who had a $100,000 campaign chest, compared to Garrison's $40,000. Black voters however, supported Garrison and he became an appeals judge.

Garrison had a flair for writing. He penned an account of his investigation, *On the Trail of the Assassins*. It was published in 1988 and made into the movie, "JFK," filmed in 1990 and distributed in 1991.

Garrison had never been a businessman; he had never been motivated by money. He included his editor and the publisher of his book *On the Trail of the Assassins* on substantially more of the profits he received from selling the movie rights to the book to Oliver Stone, director of 'JFK,' than he was contractually obligated to do so. One of his sons, who by then was an attorney, objected, telling his father that he was being overly generous. "Son," Garrison said, "these people did me a favor. They published my book when no one else would."

Mr. Garrison received approximately $135,000 for "JFK" in movie royalties and a consulting fee. He was apparently owed more, but the movie studio reneged. He was at least able to pay off his mortgage and the delinquent property taxes on his home on Owens Boulevard. He deposited the remainder of the money, about $85,000, in a non-interest bearing account.

When his son advised him to put the funds into an interest-bearing account, Garrison told him that he did not desire to receive usury. [41]

Toward the end of his life he and Liz were remarried. He died of natural causes in 1990, at age 70. His tombstone in Metairie, Louisiana is emblazoned with the words, "Let Justice be done though the heavens fall."

Dallas Police

On November 22 at 10:30 a.m., Sheriff Bill Decker withdrew security from Kennedy's scheduled motorcade, ordering his deputies and detectives pulled from the surrounding area. Dallas Police Chief Jesse Curry issued a similar order to his force. According to William Manchester, Curry told his men to "end supervision of Friday's crowd at Houston and Main," which was a block short of the ambush site. Chief Curry later

---

[41] Mellen, p. 367.

wrote that he was merely carrying out orders issued to him by the Secret Service, which also directed local police motorcycles to ride in the rear and not alongside the president's car.

U.S. Secret Service

The hypnotic mindset of the deniers of a conspiracy to kill the president is on display in virtually any photograph of the president and First Lady in the Dallas motorcade. The president's limousine is shockingly exposed to gunfire (or any other lethal object). Kennedy is riding in the slow-moving limousine, without protection. Examine photos of the motorcade when it traveled through "Bloody Elm Street" in Dealey Plaza: there are no Secret Service men on or around Kennedy's car and there is no motorcycle escort next to it.[42]

The President was a sitting duck. Can the conspiracy deniers truly say that this was a coincidence? An "accident"? Even in 1963, presidential protection was meticulously planned every step of the way. In many previous JFK presidential motorcades Secret Service Agents rode on his limousine and a motorcycle escort flanked it. Where this was not strictly the case, U.S. troops lined the route facing the crowd and Secret Service agents and policemen were stationed atop buildings. None of these precautions were in place in Dallas. *Kennedy's protection had been withdrawn.* Anyone with eyes can see that. It is in plain view. This is an "emperor has no clothes" observation. In Dealey Plaza, the conspiracy to murder him was "hidden" in plain sight. It is a sinister joke on every American.

How do the conspirators attempt to get away with this? By insulting our intelligence with the lie that Kennedy himself ordered his protection removed. In addition to the *Warren Report*, famed Establishment historian William Manchester is one of the earliest sources for the allegation that the president had ordered protection withdrawn from his limousine. In his sanitized best-seller, *The Death of the President,* Manchester wrote, "Kennedy grew weary of seeing bodyguards roosting behind him every time he turned around, and in Tampa on November 18, just four days before his death, he dryly asked

---

[42] Agent Clint Hill briefly mounted the rear of the President's limousine four times in Dallas prior to the assassination and quickly dismounted. He was not on the vehicle when the shots were fired.

Agent Floyd Boring to 'Keep those Ivy League charlatans off the back of the car. Boring wasn't offended. There had been no animosity in the remark..."

One problem with Manchester's claim: Boring was not interviewed for Manchester's book and he denied ever hearing Kennedy make the statement attributed to him. In a recorded interview with Vincent Michael Palamara, Boring stated, "I never told him (Manchester) that." Agent Gerald Blaine was probably Manchester's source for the fake story. He was interviewed by Manchester on May 12, 1965. Not everything about the Kennedy conspiracy is revelation of the method — Manchester's research material and witness notes for his book are "under seal" at Wesleyan University until 2067.

"Official history has claimed that the president was difficult to protect and had even ordered the Secret Service to take certain actions that left JFK wide open for assassination...In fact, JFK was very cooperative and did not interfere with the Secret Service." [43]

In 1992 the former Special Agent in Charge of the White House Secret Service Detail, Gerald A. "Jerry" Behn, a 28-year-veteran, was tape-recorded informing author Palamara, "I don't remember Kennedy ever saying that he didn't want anybody on the back of his car."

Boring, the aforementioned Assistant Special Agent in Charge, a 23-year-veteran, stated to Palamara in a recorded interview on September 22, 1993, "JFK was a very easy-going guy...he didn't interfere with our actions at all."

Assistant Special Agent in Charge Rufus Youngblood: "President Kennedy wasn't a hard ass...he never said anything like that (removing agents from the limo)."

Secret Service Agent Arthur L. Godfrey, when asked if Kennedy ordered the agents not to observe standard security procedures replied, "That's a bunch of baloney; that's not true. He never ordered us to do anything. He was a very nice man..."[44]

Special Agent in Charge Robert I. Bouck told Palamara that having agents on the back of the limousine depended on factors independent of any alleged Presidential "requests."

---

[43] Vincent Michael Palamara, *Survivor's Guilt*, p. 2.

[44] Ibid., p. 24.

James J. Rowley was Chief of the United States Secret Service in 1963. Under questioning by Warren Commission Chief Counsel J. Lee Rankin, Rowley testified that: "No President will tell the Secret Service what they can or cannot do...sometimes it might be as a political man or individual he might think this might not look good in a given situation. But that does not mean per se that he does not want you on there (the rear of the limousine). And I don't think anyone with common sense interprets it as such." [45]

Rowley's predecessor as head of the Secret Service was Urbanus E. Baughman. He wrote, "Now the Chief of the Secret Service is legally empowered to countermand a decision made by anybody in this country if it might endanger the life or limb of the Chief Executive. This means I could veto a decision of the President himself if I decided it would be dangerous not to."[46]

What this testimony reveals is that even if the lie were true, and Kennedy had ordered his security detail to leave him and the passengers in his automobile open to attack, the Secret Service agents in charge would have had to have been traitors and conspirators to have complied with him.

"At least two (Secret Service) agents lied to the Warren Commission. Even worse...they implicitly pinned the blame on the fallen president himself, hinting that Kennedy's recklessness or fatalism— not anything the agents had done in Dallas — ignited a tragic series of events. Kennedy's critics still chant the mantra that the president brought it upon himself. These outright lies and half-truths cannot absolve the Secret Service for losing the life of a president..." [47]

President Kennedy's vulnerability to attack in Dealey Plaza is so clearly an indication of the Cryptocracy's intent to slaughter him that the System has had to marshal a substantial array of "explain-it-away" literature. This includes the *Warren Report,* books by Manchester and Jim Bishop; Gerald Posner's *Case Closed* and Gerald Blaine's *The Kennedy Detail,* which was published in 2010, only after the agents who

---

[45] Palamara, p. 13.

[46] U.E. Baughman, *Secret Service Chief* (Harper and Row, 1963), p. 70. Asked about the behavior of the Secret Service in Dallas, former Chief Baughman told *US News and World Report* (Dec. 23, 1963), "I can't understand why Mrs. Kennedy had to climb over the back of the car, as she did, to get help..."

[47] Philip Melanson, *The Secret Service,* pp. 58-59.

would have contradicted him were dead (cf. Palamara p. 22, for a list of those agents).

Former Secret Service agent Abraham W. Bolden Sr., author of *The Echo from Dealey Plaza*, wrote: "I was dismayed at the continued attempts by former agents to deny culpability in the assassination...I was hoping that the former Kennedy bodyguards would show a modicum of contriteness ... instead of trying to blame Kennedy's assassination on the president himself."

Secret Service Agent Emory P. Roberts was one of three shift leaders on President Kennedy's security detail in Dallas. Roberts was the commander of the Secret Service follow-up car. At Love Field, Kennedy's motorcade was filmed leaving the Dallas airport and this footage has been preserved: "...when viewing slow motion black and white video footage of the Love Field departure, one can see agent Donald J. Lawton jogging at the rear of the limousine on JFK's side only to be recalled by none other than Emory P. Roberts, who rises in his seat in the follow-up car and, using his voice and several hand-gestures, orders Lawton to cease and desist." [48]

After the assassination, Roberts received a political appointment as special assistant to President Lyndon Johnson, while still a member of the Secret Service, in violation of Treasury Department rules (the Service was part of the Treasury until being absorbed by the Department of Homeland Security). Roberts was further promoted to the post of Inspector of the U.S. Secret Service in the Nixon administration.

The U.S. Secret Service appears to have done more than contribute to Kennedy's murder by omission. When suspected shooters were confronted in Dealey Plaza by local policemen and bystanders after the president had been hit, the suspects flashed Secret Service credentials. "The assassins of the president controlled the crime scene from the beginning. When witnesses instinctively stormed the grassy knoll to chase a shooter who was apparently behind the fence at the top, they immediately encountered plainclothesmen identifying themselves as Secret Service agents." [49]

---

[48] Palamara, pp. 8-9.

[49] Douglass, p. 260.

"Dallas Police Officer Joe Marshall Smith was one of the first people to rush up the grassy knoll and behind its stockade fence....he smelled gunsmoke right away. He told the Warren Commission that when he encountered a man in the parking lot behind the fence, 'he showed me that he was a Secret Service agent....He saw me coming with my pistol and right away showed me who he was. The man, this character, produces credentials from his hip pocket which showed him to be the Secret Service. I have seen those credentials before and they satisfied me and the deputy sheriff." [50]

"Besides withdrawing security from Dealey Plaza and the presidential limousine, the Secret Service also planned the turn that slowed Kennedy's limousine to a crawl.[51] That forced slowdown completed the setup for the snipers in waiting. The Secret Service advance man, Winston G. Lawson, approved the fatal dogleg turn in Dealey Plaza when he and the Dallas Special Agent in Charge, Forrest V. Sorels, did their dry run over the motorcade route on November 18. Thus, not only did the Secret Service plan and coordinate a turn that flagrantly violated its own rule of a minimum forty-four-mile-an-hour speed for the presidential limousine. Through orders from Washington, the agency responsible for the president's security created a vacuum of security—in Dealey Plaza, all around the limousine, and on the surrounding buildings as well...the only 'Secret Service Agents' in Dealey Plaza when the shots were fired were impostors and killers, bearing false credentials to facilitate their escape and coerce witnesses into handing over vital evidence that would vanish." [52]

Mary Pinchot Meyer

Mary Pinchot Meyer had been President Kennedy's lover and confidant, reportedly giving him LSD on one occasion. Her influence over the president was said to have been considerable. Before noon on October 12, 1964, in Washington D.C., on the Chesapeake and Ohio canal towpath, the 43-year-old scion of a distinguished American family was shot twice in

---

[50] Douglass, ibid.

[51] "Clint Hill's Warren Commission testimony and Paul Landis' report confirms that...when the shooting commenced...the limousine was slowing down from an original speed of only around 11.2 mph." Cf. Palamara, p. 10.

[52] Douglass, pp. 272-273. There were of course Secret Service men in Dealey Plaza — riding on the limousine behind Kennedy.

an execution-style murder: once in her head, and once through her back, at close range; the second shot penetrating her right lung and aorta. The .38-caliber murder weapon was never found. Her ex-husband was Cord Meyer, a CIA agent working within the CIA's Directorate of Plans under Richard Helms.

After her death her diary came into the possession of CIA executive James Jesus Angleton. A black man, Ray Crump Jr., was the scapegoat. He was charged with the crime and eventually acquitted in July, 1965. The investigative journalist on Meyer's case, Leo Damore, was found shot to death in 1995. Authorities ruled his death a suicide. His book on Meyer was nearing completion. Peter Janney's *Mary's Mosaic: The CIA Conspiracy to Murder John F. Kennedy and Mary Pinchot Meyer* (2012), is a worthwhile source of information.

Evidence Tampering

As in the hasty demolition of the Murrah building, target of the Oklahoma City bombing, and the FBI's removal of the tiny cabin of accused Unabomber Ted Kazcynski in Lincoln, Montana, against the orders of the county sheriff, to a secret district of an air base; as well as the inordinately rushed demolition of the Twin Towers in New York City in 2001, the key evidence in the JFK hit, the 1961 Lincoln Continental in which he died, was whisked away by the Secret Service and then completely gutted, rebuilt and repainted.

Folklorists often draw macabre parallels between the assassinations of Lincoln and Kennedy (such as, "Kennedy died in a Lincoln and Lincoln died in a Ford"). However, there is no comparison between the two men with regard to the fate of the scenes of their deaths. Ford's Theatre is a meticulously preserved, solemn national shrine to Lincoln, while the Lincoln limousine in which President Kennedy had been murdered was ghoulishly returned to service in 1964 where, for the next thirteen years, it ferried four presidents — Johnson, Nixon, Ford and Carter — as they and their passengers ate, drank, smoked, swore, laughed and dozed. Johnson in particular must have enjoyed quite a few laughs in the same luxury vehicle where President Kennedy's head exploded.

Aside from the grinning that such a disrespectful end for the King of Camelot's death carriage evoked within the Cryptocracy, is the fact that the Secret Service made any forensic crime scene investigation of the limousine impossible. This amounts to felony evidence-tampering.

That some Secret Service men did not care for the president is likely. The official explanation for the antipathy is Kennedy's numerous trysts with various girlfriends. Agent Tim McIntyre, who rode in the limousine behind JFK in the Dallas motorcade, "felt abused" by his service to Kennedy, claiming that JFK's adulterous acts were equivalent to liaisons with prostitutes, thereby making his Secret Service guards accomplices. On ABC-TV McIntyre stated, "...if you have a procurer with prostitutes paraded in front of you...you're asking yourself, 'well, what do they think of us?" [53] If his offended sensibility was sincere, why wouldn't a pillar of moral rectitude like Agent McIntyre quit the service? Or could it be that the tale of shocked Secret Service sensibilities is a cover for other, more esoteric sources of opposition, such as a desire to be on the winning side in the forthcoming coup [54] that would make Lyndon Baines Johnson president.

Vincent Bugliosi

Since Gerald Posner's propaganda for the government's lone nut theory (*Case Closed*) was discredited, former Charles Manson Family prosecutor Vincent Bugliosi stepped forth as the Establishment's go-to guy in support of the guilty-until-proven-otherwise, trial by media that has been used to substitute for the criminal trial Oswald never received.

In compiling his rebuttal to Bugliosi, *Reclaiming Parkland*, James DiEugenio noted the prodigious output of Bugliosi. DiEugenio waded through Bugliosi's huge tome, *Reclaiming*

---

[53] Palamara, p. 7.

[54] Two notable CIA coups: 1. in Iran in 1953 against a pro-American leader, Mohammed Mosaddeq, the elected Prime Minister whose "crime" was to nationalize Britain's oil holdings. Ryan C. Crocker, former US ambassador to Afghanistan and Iraq: "Immediately after 9/11, while serving in the State Department, I sat down with Iranian diplomats...Back then, we had a common enemy, the Taliban and its Al Qaeda associates..The Iranians were constructive...at one point they even produced an extremely valuable map showing the Taliban's order of battle just before American military action began...We forged agreements on various security issues and coordinated approaches to reconstruction. And then, suddenly, it all came to an end when President George W. Bush gave his famous 'Axis of Evil' speech in early 2002. The Iranian leadership concluded that in spite of their cooperation with the American war effort, the US remained implacably hostile to the Islamic Republic." *New York Times* (online) November 3, 2013. 2. In 1970 Richard Helms planned a coup against the president of Chile, Salvador Allende. In 1970 the CIA assassinated Chilean General Schneider. In 1973 Allende was overthrown. Cf. Johnson, *Nemesis* (2006), pp. 105-108.

History (W.W. Norton, 2007), which consists of 1600 printed pages and additional files on an accompanying CD-ROM for a total, according to DiEugenio, of 2646 pages. Bugliosi's big book has since been pared down and recycled in 2013 as *Four Days in November*. It has also been been filmed as the blockbuster Hollywood movie "Parkland," produced by Tom Hanks, accompanied by a tie-in volume, also titled, *Parkland*. A November, 2013 National Geographic television special, "Killing Kennedy" based on a silly book co-authored by Bill O'Reilly, formerly a headliner for Fox News—is evidence of ceaseless corporate support for the moronic "lone nut" theory, which the media have sought to resurrect like a rotted scarecrow from an autumnal cornfield.

This trial by media, with reporters acting as mouthpieces for crooked police, Federal agents and prosecutors, helping to convict defendants who are owed the presumption of innocence, has been the bane of our system of justice. Big Brother's preconceived assumptions of guilt are trumpeted with little skepticism or moderating shades of gray, in a process Mark Lane termed, "Rush to Judgment." Exactly one day after the president was assassinated, Captain Will Fritz of the Dallas Police Department had the chutzpah to announce that the case was already closed: "We are convinced beyond any doubt that he (Oswald) killed the President. I think the case is clinched."

Oswald was killed while under the "protection" of the government. After his death it would have been the decent, honorable and traditional American thing for the Warren Commission and the media to proceed to accord Oswald the *presumption of innocence* and a vigorous defense. The opposite occurred. As early as January, 1964 the Warren Commission presumed he was guilty, not innocent. On the day Oswald was arrested, Dallas District Attorney Henry Wade appeared on national television and stated that Oswald had killed the president. A mere 48 hours later, on November 24, the *New York Times* published the front page headline, "Evidence Against Oswald Described as Conclusive." On November 25, the Associated Press declared Oswald guilty of the assassination. One week after President Kennedy was assassinated, on December 1, the *Washington Post* assured the American people, "...all the police agencies with a hand in the investigation...insist that the case against Oswald is an unshakeable one."

Time magazine's December 13 issue asserted, "Oswald, acting in his own lunatic loneliness, was indeed the president's assassin." Newsweek rubber-stamped this "lunatic" sentiment in its December 16 issue.

When, in September, 1964, the Warren Commission released its twenty-six volumes of supporting testimony and exhibits, the *New York Times* printed a glowing review the very next day. The editors at the *Times* had somehow read and corroborated the contents of the Commission's entire gigantic opus within 24 hours. [55] Thus was born the notorious "lone nut" profile that the media and authorities would trot out for Sirhan Sirhan, James Earl Ray, Arthur Bremer, David Berkowitz, James Holmes, Stephen Paddock, Nikolas Cruz, etc.

Bugliosi and O'Reilly's literary productions and movie tie-ins are the culmination of this depressingly familiar, interminable process. What is so obtuse about prejudicial publicity, and police statements of conclusive guilt made in the immediate wake of a major arrest, is that every reporter who has worked the police beat, as well as every cop worth his salt, knows very well that *an investigation only truly begins with the apprehension of a suspect*. When some government official or news media outlet either declares, or strongly implies, that the case is "clinched" soon after the alleged perp has been arrested, it is fair to surmise that we are being hoodwinked.

Priscilla Johnson is alleged to have been a CIA-planted journalist whose disinformation about Oswald was published the weekend after the president's assassination in the pages of the *Boston Globe, Dallas Morning News* and *Christian Science Monitor*. Her 1977 book, in line with the Warren Commission's "findings," *Marina and Lee*, is in the same mold. The *New York Times* published an adulatory review. She is one of Bugliosi's major sources on Oswald.

DiEugenio states that FBI "agents in the field...got the drift: Oswald had acted alone. Therefore any evidence to the contrary would be most unwelcome. As FBI supervisor Laurence Keenan told Anthony Summers: "Within days (of Nov. 22, 1963) we

---

[55] A half century later and the *Times* was still at it: "*New York Times* executive editor Jill Abramson hijacked a large chunk of her paper's *Sunday Book Review* on November 3, 2013 to ponder the Kennedy mystery. And after deliberating for page after page on the subject, she could only conclude that there was some 'kind of void at the center of the Kennedy story' and that 'the historical consensus seems to have settled on' the lone gunman theory." -David Talbot, *Salon*, Nov. 6, 2013.

could say the investigation was over. Conspiracy was a word that was verboten. The idea that Oswald was a confederate or was part of a group or a conspiracy was definitely enough to place a man's career in jeopardy..."

Comedian Bugliosi on Hoover: "J. Edgar Hoover, since his appointment as FBI Director in 1924, at once formed and effectively ran, perhaps the finest, most incorruptible law enforcement agency in history."

Other disinformation assets in the media, such as Max Holland, Patricia Lambert, James Phelan and PBS "Frontline" reporter Scott Malone, attempted to obstruct or malign the reputation of New Orleans District Attorney Jim Garrison.

The CIA has been directly involved in planting stories and manipulating the media. An April 4, 1967 CIA directive titled "Countering Criticism of the Warren Report," is addressed to "Chief, Certain Stations and Bases." It is mainly concerned with hampering Garrison, who is referred to in the document as "the critic." It advises that the CIA should "employ propaganda assets to answer and refute the attacks of the critic." [56]

At the *New York Times*, reporter Martin Waldron is alleged by Joan Mellen to have falsified the testimony of witnesses at Garrison's trial of Clay Shaw. The *Times* even declared Garrison unfit for public office, and when its columnist John Leonard expressed skepticism toward the official Kennedy autopsy report, Leonard's column "evaporated in later editions of the *Times*."

In his own book on Mr. Bugliosi, Mr. DiEugenio is temperate and civil, and strives for objectivity, praising Bugliosi for writing he produced critical of Bill Clinton and George W. Bush.[57] Bugliosi meanwhile, employs pejoratives and invectives while denouncing as conspiracy theorists those who doubt President Kennedy was killed by a lone nut, yet Bugliosi is on record as stating, concerning the assassination of Robert F. Kennedy, "We are talking about a conspiracy to commit

---

[56] Mellen, p. 141.

[57] *The Betrayal of America*; also *No Island of Sanity: Paula Jones vs. Bill Clinton*; and *The Prosecution of George W. Bush for Murder*. The latter is a powerful indictment that deserves to be reprinted. Was it written to make amends for the disinformation Mr. Bugliosi propagated concerning the Tate/LaBianca murders and the assassination of President Kennedy?

murder...a conspiracy the prodigious dimensions of which make Watergate look like a one-roach marijuana case."

DiEugenio lists the many historically accurate points made by Oliver Stone in his movie "JFK," which Bugliosi denounces as complete fiction. DiEugenio asserts that Stone, if anything, understated the case and did not go far enough in making certain conspiracy points. DiEugenio acknowledges the inevitable dramatic license which Stone sometimes took to move the story along but which did not falsify the truth of the film's central thesis.

Future U.S. President Gerald Ford altered the Warren Report at the last minute, changing the wording of the location of Kennedy's back wound (solving the otherwise inexplicable high-exit-wound dilemma). Bugliosi says this was a benign error on Ford's part. Ford would become president after the resignation of Richard Nixon. Ford's administration was a seedbed for personnel destined to play a key role in criminal politics. Ford named George H.W. Bush as CIA director. Ford promoted Dick Cheney to White House Chief of Staff and made Donald Rumsfeld a high official in the Pentagon. The Neocon war party was energized as never before by President Ford who, together with Allen Dulles and Alan Specter, was among the most duplicitous Warren Commission members involved in the concealment of the conspiracy against John F. Kennedy.

Critics of the Warren Commission besides Jim Garrison were Gary Hart and Dave Marston of the 1975 Senator Frank Church Committee ("United States Senate Select Committee to Study Governmental Operations with Respect to Intelligence Activities"); the first chief counsel and the deputy counsel of the HSCA, Richard Sprague and Robert Tannenbaum, and their replacements, Robert Blakey and Gary Cornwell; and Jeremy Gunn, the Director and Chief Counsel of the Assassination Records Review Board (ARRB). [58] (The public furor which arose in the wake of the film "JFK" led Congress to pass the 1992 "President John F. Kennedy Assassination Records Collection Act," from which the ARRB came into existence).

Warren Commission members Rep. Hale Boggs and Sen. Russell Long, were full-fledged skeptics. Long's own private investigator, Philip Corso, did not believe that the alleged

---

[58] fas.org/sgp/advisory/arrb98/

murder weapon, the Mannlicher Carcano rifle, could have performed as alleged. Coros believed rogue CIA agents killed Kennedy. Senator Russell began to criticize the Warren Commission in public beginning on November 20, 1966. Russell did not believe in the "magic bullet" and was convinced that the FBI and CIA deceived the Warren Commission. Hale Boggs, the Commission's only Catholic member investigating the murder of the nation's only Catholic president, stated that "Hoover lied his eyes out to the Commission —on Oswald, on Ruby, on their friends, the bullets, the gun, you name it."[59] Boggs was subsequently killed in a plane crash in Alaska.

Mr. Bugliosi used the New Orleans District Attorney who succeeded Garrison, Harry Connick, as a witness against Garrison and filmmaker Oliver Stone, without mentioning that Connick was implicated in destroying Garrison's prosecution records which, by law, were left at the D.A.'s office; Connick is also alleged to be connected to rogue prosecutions in which certainly innocent defendants (such as John Thompson) were targeted for prosecution. Perhaps most damning of all, Connick had been a defense attorney for CIA asset Clay Shaw.

DiEugenio documents the corruption of Wade, the aforementioned Dallas D.A. at the time of the assassination, who is reputed to have railroaded many defendants over the years and whose office withheld twelve boxes of Kennedy assassination documents from the ARRB. Wade is praised unstintingly by Bugliosi.

DiEugenio has sections devastating to Bugliosi: on Marina Oswald, on the paraffin tests administered to Oswald after his arrest; Oswald's lack of proficiency as a marksman; the testimony of Texas School Book Depository employees Williams, Arnold and Adams; the president's autopsy, including the missing notes and the fact that the military limited the autopsy, that Humes destroyed the notes and the first draft of his own autopsy report, and the datum that the autopsy pathologists did not examine Pres. Kennedy's clothing.

John Stringer testified that he did not take the pictures of Kennedy's brain that are in the National Archives. It was Dr. Malcolm Perry who performed the tracheostomy on the president. During a press conference in Dallas and to reporters from the *Boston Globe*—Perry said three times that the wound

---

[59] *Texas Observer*, November, 1998.

in the neck was an entrance wound—but to the Warren Commission, under pressure from Secret Service Agent Elmer Moore, Earl Warren's "bodyguard," Perry repudiated his original testimony. (Bugliosi does not mention Moore in his nearly 2700 pages).

Oswald, Shaw and Ferrie

Vincent Bugliosi states that Oswald and Ferrie did not know each other and that Guy Bannister and Oswald were not connected.

Ed Voebel, Fred O'Sullivan and, according to HSCA investigators L.J. Delsa and Bob Buras, several other witnesses such as Jerry Paradis, testified Ferrie and Oswald knew each other (cf. John Armstrong's book, *Harvey and Lee*). There is a Civil Air Patrol photograph of them together.

As stated on page 187 herein, Clay Shaw, David Ferrie and Oswald were together in the summer of 1963 in two small Louisiana towns, Clinton and Jackson, in sparsely populated East Feliciana Parish, approximately 90 miles north of New Orleans. "John R. Rarick, district judge for the Feliciana parishes...was having his thick black hair cut at the Jackson barber shop of his supporter, Lea McGehee...'Oswald was here,' McGehee told Rarick. It had been late summer of 1963." [60] The FBI knew about it through Reeves Morgan, a witness who was a member of the Louisiana state legislature.

Other witnesses to the presence of Shaw, Ferrie and Oswald in East Feliciana Parish were Morgan's daughter Mary, and son Van; Gloria Wilson and Andrew Dunn, and Gladys Palmer, a woman who had worked as a stripper at Ruby's Carousel Club.

"During that summer (1963), Gladys Palmer had been seen often with Lee Harvey Oswald...Gladys had been spotted with Oswald at two bars east of Baton Rouge: the Audubon and the Hawaiian Lounge...D.J. Blanchard, an engineer at 'East' (Louisiana State Hospital), saw Gladys drive with Oswald to the Audubon...." [61]

There is no reference to Gladys Palmer in the *Warren Commission Report*.

---

[60] Mellen, p. 211.

[61] Mellen, pp. 215-216.

"As (Anne) Dischler and Fruge continued to interview the residents of Clinton and Jackson, a narrative emerged: Oswald, Clay Shaw and David Ferrie had driven into Clinton...Oswald got out of the car (a black cadillac), and joined the already long line of black people waiting to attempt to register to vote...It appears to have been September 19 (1963)..."

The registrar of voters, Henry Earl Palmer, told Garrison's investigators, "Oswald registered to vote up here." Palmer said that he allowed him to register because Oswald mentioned that he knew Cuban-American psychiatrist Dr. Frank Silva, the medical director of "East," the hospital in which Rose Cheramie had predicted that Kennedy would be killed, and where Oswald (or his double) [62] applied for a job in September, 1963.

"Maxine Kemp, who...worked in personnel, confirmed that Oswald had applied for a job...Receptionist Bobbie Dedon identified Oswald from his photograph...a 'former Army intelligence officer' told the populist writer Ned Touchstone that a man who looked like Oswald and used his name had applied for work at East. He had arrived in a big automobile 'believed to belong to a wealthy New Orleans man.' Palmer gave his description of the two white males sitting in front in the black Cadillac as it waited for Oswald. He identified David Ferrie in a photograph from his 'heavy eyebrows." [63]

A cop in Clinton identified Shaw: John "Manchester was a law enforcement officer and it was to him that the driver of the black Cadillac had shown a driver's license in the name of 'Clay Shaw.' It was to (Officer) Manchester that the driver admitted that he worked for the International Trade Mart." [64]

Witnesses Corrie Collins, Henry Palmer, and William Dunn saw Shaw, Ferrie and Oswald together in the town of Clinton.

Two witnesses died mysterious deaths — Gloria Wilson in 1964 of suspected poisoning, and Andrew Dunn, who was found hanged in the Clinton jail in 1968. "Anne Dischler discovered that Gloria had left a diary locked in her private drawer...

---

[62] "...there were quite a few men that summer and autumn who went around calling themselves 'Oswald" (Mellen, p. 209). Jim Douglass has information on Oswald's doubles: cf. pp. 221-227, 334-335; 351-354.

[63] Mellen, pp. 217; 219-223.

[64] Mellen, p. 235. In February, 1968, Hugh Aynesworth, working for Shaw's defense team, tried to bribe Officer Manchester. If he would leave Louisiana and not be a witness for the prosecution he would be guaranteed lucrative employment out of state. Manchester said no.

"When her sister Flo went to collect Gloria's possessions, the diary was gone." [65]

Mr. Bugliosi denies all of this witness testimony and charges Garrison with fraud and having removed two investigators, Francis Fruge and Anne Dischler, when it was in fact the state police who had removed those two from Garrison's staff at the same time that *Life* magazine was pressuring Louisiana Governor John McKeithen to hinder Garrison. [66]

In 1978 the House of Representatives Select Committee on Assassinations determined that there was a "clear indication" that Oswald was with Shaw and Ferrie in Clinton and Jackson, Louisiana. [67]

"Clay Shaw was a CIA operative who, as director of the Centro Mondiale Commerciale in Rome (Italy), joined fellow agents like Ferenc Nagy, who since 1948 had worked for the CIA under the direction of Assistant Director of Central Intelligence, Frank Wisner...

"In November of 1943 Shaw enlisted in the Army...Military intelligence discovered him. Never having seen a day of combat, Shaw rose to the rank of major as aide-de-camp to General Charles O. Thrasher, who was in charge of transferring German prisoners of war to the French. Thrasher was a man of such cruel disposition that he horrified the French liaison officer.

"Appalled by Thrasher's callous treatment of the German prisoners in his charge, Major William H. Haight swore out a deposition against him for the inhumane means by which he handled and transferred the Germans, who were being starved to death and were in a condition 'worse than the former

---

[65] Mellen, p. 237.

[66] Mellen, pp. 307, 319, 324.

[67] For the heroes and villains on the staff of the HSCA itself, cf. Mellen, 343-360.
"The House Select Committee on Assassinations was hastily voted into being in 1976, after some witnesses who'd been called to testify before Frank Church's earlier Senate Intelligence Committee turned up dead or missing. (Chicago's Sam Giancana was murdered while cooking sausage in his basement, five days before he was scheduled to testify, wounded around the mouth and throat to signify the price of becoming an informant; Jimmy Hoffa disappeared; and Vegas's Johnny 'Mr. Smooth' Rosselli, who'd mediated between the CIA and the mob in plots to kill Castro and who evidently, in closed session, had been overly forthcoming to the Church Committee about the Kennedy plot, was discovered floating—legless, stabbed, and shot—in an oil drum in Dumfoundling Bay, north of Miami...the CIA, aided by a fishy liaison named George Joannides, held back from the House Select Committee a raft of relevant documents..." (Nicholson Baker, op. cit.).

German concentration camps.' Shaw moved with ease through an Army Counterintelligence group called the 'Special Operations Section.' Still without having stepped onto a battlefield to face enemy fire, he was to receive a Croix de Guerre, and a Legion of Merit from France, and a similar decoration from Belgium.

"Returning to New Orleans, he joined a CIA proprietary, the Mississippi Shipping Company, run by a fellow homosexual, Theodore Brent. When the (Central Intelligence) Agency sponsored the first of its international trade centers in New Orleans (there would be another in Rome), its 'principal backer and developer' was a lawyer named Lloyd J. Cobb, who had received his Covert Security Clearance from the CIA in October 1953...The International Trade Mart was run by CIA operatives...The Trade Mart donated money to CIA asset Ed Butler...Every consulate within its bowels was bugged...(Shaw) hired fellow single men and could be spotted in his Thunderbird convertible filled with boys...when Theodore Brent died, he left Shaw a legacy, a legal defense fund for gay men that Shaw dispensed as 'Clay Bertrand.'" [68]

David Ferrie piloted the plane which flew Shaw to Cuba in 1959 as part of a CIA project to refine Cuban nickel at a Louisiana refinery through the Freeport Sulphur company, which Vincent Buliosi does not mention. L.P. Davies Jr., Charles Krop and Betty Rubio also testified to seeing Shaw with Ferrie. Bugliosi does not mention them.

According to Prof. Mellen, "Shaw knew Oswald's mentor David Ferrie so well that he co-signed a loan for a him a week before the assassination so that Ferrie could rent a plane and fly to Dallas." Ferrie was never called to testify before the Warren Commission.

Lyndon Johnson

Recent findings of Kennedy assassination conspiracy investigators such as Phillip F. Nelson, point to Vice President Lyndon Johnson having had a significant or even decisive hand in the murder, which appears to have been managed by operators who had the cooperation of clandestine networks tied to two CIA heads, former director Allen Dulles and future

---

[68] Mellen, pp. xvii and 130-132.

director Richard Helms, as well as CIA Deputy Director of Plans Richard Bissell. Strong suspicion has also been cast on Air Force General Curtis LeMay.

In 1966 Helms was named CIA director by President Johnson. (Dulles and Bissell had been fired by JFK). Helms ran the CIA until 1971, when he was replaced first by James Schlesinger and in 1973 by the reform-minded William Colby, who had acted criminally in Vietnam, but for whatever reasons was attempting to make amends by exposing Helms and discharging "James Jesus Angelton and the entire top brass of the (CIA's) counterintelligence division." Colby implicated Helms in the CIA overthrow of Salvador Allende, which led to Helms being convicted of having perjured himself before Congress.

Colby died under mysterious circumstances April 27, 1996 in Maryland. Though he was no longer with the Agency at the time of his demise, "the CIA had exclusive control of the death scene." [69]

Decades after King-Kill/33, investigators like Jim Douglass say they still do not know who in the Cryptocracy gave the direct order to assassinate the president. Others, including Phillip F. Nelson in his powerful work, *LBJ: The Mastermind of the JFK Assassination,* believe that Lyndon Johnson was the ring-leader. Our own best surmise is that without the Vice President's knowledge and consent the November coup could not have gone forward. We now know that Johnson faced imminent political ruin and removal from the 1964 ticket, if Kennedy was not killed or incapacitated. "His involvement in scandals with his aide Bobby Baker and business tycoon Billy Sol Estes were about to make headlines. During the summer of 1963, *Life* magazine had been developing a major feature story concerning Vice President Johnson and his scandalous dealings. The in-depth story was scheduled for publication in late November...The story, according to James Wagenvoord, at that time the chief assistant to *Life*'s Publishing Projects Director, Phil Wooton, had been researched by members of the senior staff at *Life* who had a direct line to Bobby Kennedy...On (President) Kennedy's death, research files and all numbered

---

[69] On Colby's strange death and the aftermath, cf. Randall Woods, *Shadow Warrior* (2013), pp. 2-5.

copies of the nearly print-ready draft were gathered up...and shredded." [70]

According to his foremost biographer, Robert Caro, in *The Path to Power (The Years of Lyndon Johnson, Volume 1)*, pp. 275 and 535, Johnson's lifetime obsession was to be President of the United States.

In 1966 the "Grassy Knoll Press" published *MacBird* by Barbara Garson, a modern play penned in mock-imitation of Shakespeare's various tragedies, with special emphasis on *Macbeth* ("Macbird"), who is meant to represent Lyndon Baines Johnson. In Shakespeare's play, the witches anticipate Macbeth's murder of Duncan, King of Scotland and prophetically greet Macbeth as Thane of Cawdor and "king hereafter." In *MacBird* the witches say, "All hail MacBird that shall be President!" Garson's play, in line with Shakespeare's, has Johnson as the guilty killer going slowly mad, and "Robert" (Kennedy) as JFK's avenger. *MacBird* sold over half a million copies as a book and had over 90 stagings worldwide. Theater critic Dwight Macdonald writing in the December 1, 1966 *NY Review of Books*: "...the murder in Dallas paralleled the one in Dunsinan— Johnson-Macbeth contrived the murder of Kennedy-Duncan."

Here was the Killing of the King story being further imprinted on the psyche of the American people, with the boldface parallel between Lyndon Johnson and Macbeth, after having John F. Kennedy identified as the leader of Camelot. Is this another "hide in plain sight" gambit of the Truth or Consequences revelators?

Assassination Conspiracy: Right Wing or Left?

Oswald was made to look like a commie pinko. The original intent of this set-up was to fan the flames of US/Soviet tensions which JFK had been seeking to extinguish. Kennedy assassination conspirator Lyndon Johnson discarded the part of the script that had Oswald acting on behalf of Castro or Krushchev. The general impression of Oswald as a Communist was left to fester however (where it remains today), but no move was made on the part of Johnson's administration to hold Communist governments responsible for the president's death.

---

[70] Peter Janney, *Mary's Mosaic,* 307-308.

From the Left comes the idea that Kennedy was killed by a Right wing conspiracy. DiEugenio, misquoting Joan Mellen in her book, *A Farewell to Justice*, (p. 227), claims that White Citizens Council publisher Ned Touchstone, who opposed JFK when he was alive and was a self-admitted associate of the Kennedy-hating General Edwin Walker, intimidated a key JFK conspiracy witness (Gladys Palmer) into silence.

DiEugenio: "Others (witnesses) like lawyer Billy Kline, were intimidated by the aforementioned rightwing forces in the town...There was also Gladys Palmer, a potentially very important witness, who was talked to by local rightwing heavies Jack Rogers and Ned Touchstone. She then forgot all about seeing Oswald." DiEugenio cites Prof. Joan Mellen's book, p. 227, as his source.

Here is what Joan Mellen actually wrote on p. 227: "On August 22, Fruge and Sciambra found Gladys at her home on Evangeline Street. She had already been interviewed by Jack Rogers and Ned Touchstone, she said testily. She did not know anything 'that would lend any assistance.' She had never seen or heard of Lee Harvey Oswald 'in her life' before the assassination. She had never heard of Jack Ruby until he shot Oswald."

It's quite a leap for Mr. DiEugenio, who in other respects is an astute investigative journalist, to say "rightwing heavy Ned Touchstone" talked to Gladys, and then in the very next sentence state, "She then forgot all about seeing Oswald," as if her feigned amnesia was connected to Touchstone — a connection which Mellen, who seems to accept Touchstone as a sincere JFK conspiracy investigator (cf. Mellen, 210-211), did not make. Mr. Touchstone spent much of his journalistic career supporting Jim Garrison and denouncing the Warren Commission. Another key witness who was not intimidated was McGehee. Ned Touchstone was married to June A. McGehee. [71]

Something that both James Douglass and James DiEugenio don't take the time to refute are theories by Left-wing groups who are known to affiliate with Gerald Posner, claiming that Jim Garrison's investigation was an operation of the extreme Right wing in America.[72]

---

[71] In another JFK synchronicity, Touchstone's daughter Lia, married a man named Tippit.

[72] Cf. for instance, mcadams.posc.mu.edu/clinton4.htm

DiEugenio and Douglass seem oblivious to this canard. Douglass and many other Kennedy conspiracy investigators insist that the president was killed by a Right wing CIA that benefited from hate-propaganda against him stirred up by radical Right groups like the John Birch Society, one of whose leaders was among those who placed an advertisement in the *Dallas Morning News* of November 22, accusing the president of treason (for the text of the advertisement cf. Douglass, 369-370). The ad was placed by Bernard Weissman, Larrie H. Schmidt, William Burley III and John Birch Society coordinator Joseph P. Grinnan, who was a Texas oilman, under the name of a fictitious organization, "The American Fact-Finding Committee" (Douglass, p. 483).

By means of this advertisement, the JFK assassination conspiracy yet again becomes all things to all people: what was a supposed Left-wing plot on the part of Oswald in the CIA's planted Soviet "expatriate" and missionary for Castro performance, becomes a Right-wing plot involving Birchers and Texas oilmen. Choose your poison.

The oft heard canard about the involvement of H.L. Hunt and "Texas oilmen" has a CIA origin: "In March of 1968 D.A. Garrison was given a manuscript, variously titled 'The Plot' and 'Farewell America' which was a 'ragtag jumble of disinformation designed for no other purpose other than to distract Jim Garrison from naming the CIA as his chief suspect...' The book pinned Kennedy's killing on 'Texas oil interests and the Hunt family.' The...litany of false sponsors appears: Drennan, Wheat and Gale, Minutemen and Birchites...The author, Herve Lamarre, turned out to be...a scion of French intelligence doing the CIA a favor." [73]

To what degree was the "Right wing hate propaganda" that greeted President and Mrs. Kennedy in Dallas, a put-up job by the Cryptocracy? If Oswald was a patsy made to look like a Left wing conspirator, why is it so improbable that there were Right wing patsies made to look as though they were behind the JFK assassination?

Jim Douglass comes out of the Catholic Left for whom a Communist war criminal like Nikita Krushchev, who butchered, at the very least, hundreds of thousands of Ukrainians, was a partner for peace.

---

[73] Mellen, 293-294.

When Mr. Douglass posits the CIA as "Right wing" he should distinguish between the military-industrial complex's Establishment Right, and the anti-Establishment populist Right of leaders such as Willis Carto and Ned Touchstone. Carto published and promoted the work of Kennedy assassination researcher and attorney Mark Lane. Carto's Liberty Lobby and *Spotlight* newspaper were sued for defamation by CIA conspirator E. Howard Hunt for having printed an exposé of Hunt provided by former CIA agent Victor Marchetti. Mark Lane, who successfully defended Liberty Lobby in court, provides a valuable account in his 1991 book *Plausible Denial*. [74]

Some Left-leaning Kennedy assassination investigators make the knee-jerk assumption that the U.S. government in the 1940s, '50s, '60s and '70s was a bastion of sincere conservative anti-communism. A study of top U.S. government operative George C. Marshall's role in protecting Maoist Communism in China from defeat, [75] as well as the machinations of Operation Keelhaul, the assassinations of General George Patton and Secretary of Defense James Forrestal, among numerous instances of U.S. intervention on behalf of international Communism, puts paid to this illusion about the Federal government.

Carto and Touchstone and other American populists objected to many of Jack Kennedy's policies before his death, but after he was killed they presciently espied an emerging shadow government. These men realized that *if the*

---

[74] Also cf. Michael Collins Piper, *Final Judgment* (1995), published by Willis Carto. Mr. Piper provided seldom discussed evidence of the Israeli-connections of intelligence operatives associated with the assassination conspiracy.

[75] An early front was opened by the Cryptocracy through its agent Gen. George C. Marshall, Chief of the U.S. Army during World II and no less influential under the administration of President Harry Truman. In 1946, by misdirecting Chiang Kai-shek's pro-western Nationalist forces, Marshall engineered the victory of Mao Tse Tung's mass murdering army: "Marshall was to perform a monumental service to Mao. When Mao had his back to the wall...in late spring 1946, Marshall put heavy— and decisive— pressure on Chiang to stop pursuing the Communists into northern Manchuria, saying the U.S. wouldn't help if he pushed further...Marshall's diktat was probably the single most important decision affecting the outcome of the civil war." (Jung Chang, *Mao: The Unknown Story* [Random House, 2005], p. 289). The Cryptocracy moved again to protect Mao's tyranny when its asset Truman deliberately failed to prosecute and win the Korean War—rejecting General Douglas MacArthur's request for permission to attack Communist supply bases in China, north of the Yalu River. In 1951, Truman relieved MacArthur of his command. The hold of Mao's closest ally, the Communist Kim dynasty, over North Korea was thereby cemented.

Commander-in-Chief could be murdered with impunity in Dallas, then all future presidents, out of fear of the same fate befalling them, would take their orders from the intelligence services. Who can gainsay this observation?

Distinctions about the Right wing should be easier to make in our time when Neocon "Rightists" engineer the Afghan and Iraq wars and support a domestic police state, while the populist, "Paleo-Right" seeks to restore our Constitutional Republic and reject overseas empire.

Labeling without qualification the CIA and the forces arrayed against John F. Kennedy as "Right wing," is an erroneous generalization which contributes to further confusion concerning who killed our president. A sloppy researcher could go so far as to deduce that Ferrie and Shaw were KKK operatives because they shared a private flight to Canada with Jules Kimble, a Klan member. But in truth Kimble was an FBI informant who had infiltrated the racist organization.[76]

Right/Left labels are largely meaningless in this context. The shape-shifting Cryptocracy appears as a Leftist phantom to Right wingers and a Right wing bogey to Leftists. A similar charade functioned smoothly for Lyndon Johnson, who ran as a liberal peace candidate in the 1964 presidential election against Senator Barry Goldwater and who, after defeating Goldwater, emerged as a Right wing interventionist who would commit 500,000 U.S. troops to a Southeast Asian civil war. Johnson was clearly Left wing with regard to domestic policy, such as the Civil Rights movement and his "Great Society," with its socialist programs.

If he really had been an anti-communist ideologue however, rather than an accomplice of the military-industrial complex and the Israeli lobby, during the Vietnam conflict he would have fought Maoist China and North Vietnam the way the U.S. had fought Nazi Germany, which would have resulted in the end of the regimes of Mao and Ho Chi Minh. The Cryptocracy had no such objective in place. Nor do we advocate that Johnson should have pursued such an objective, in that the war in Vietnam from the outset was a needless, Cryptocracy-initiated alchemical cauldron which processed the American people through a stage of degenerative psychological

---

[76] Mellen, p. 135.

transformation. Making war on a North Vietnamese nation that was an enemy of Communist China was a catastrophe. Invasions of sovereign nations whether by Bush or Johnson inevitably motivate even a potentially friendly or neutral population into fierce patriotic opposition to the invaders.

In addition to Oswald's sojourn in the Soviet Union, his alleged attack on Edwin Walker, a prominent Right-wing activist, decorated combat veteran and retired U.S. Army Major General, is the other supposed evidence which is put forth to finger him as a committed Leftist extremist.

Suspicious anomalies are present in this Cryptocracy-scripted Walker sideshow, however. The Warren Commission accused Oswald of having attempted, on April 10, 1963, the assassination of General Walker, at Walker's Texas home, as a prelude to the violence Oswald would supposedly perpetrate on November 22.

As Gerald McKnight demonstrates in his book, *Breach of Trust*, the Dallas police referred to the bullet fired into Walker's house as a steel-jacketed 30.06, as indicated in a report filed by Dallas Police Department officers Van Cleave and McElroy.

DiEugenio: "In less than three weeks after the assassination (of JFK), the FBI changed the bullet (fired at Walker) to a 6.5 caliber, copper-jacketed bullet; which meant that they could link this projectile to Oswald. And, in fact, the bullet today in the National Archives, allegedly tied to the Walker case, is copper coated. Yet none of the Dallas police officers who handled the slug were called to testify before the Warren Commission."

In a March 27, 1964 memorandum to the FBI, forensic investigator Henry Heiberger tested the lead alloy of the bullet recovered from the attempted shooting of General Walker. Heiberger testified that it was different from the lead alloy of a bullet fragment from the auomobile in which Kennedy was shot. The Warren Commission did not call Heiberger to testify.

An eyewitness to the shooting at General Walker's home, Kirk Coleman, identified two assailants, neither of whom resembled Oswald.

Bugliosi claims that Oswald confessed to shooting at the Walker house and that nothing further is required to substantiate the charge. His alleged source for this supposed confession was Oswald's widow, Marina.

CE 399: The Magic Bullet

Which brings us to Warren Commission Exhibit ("CE") 399: "Commission Exhibit 399...the infamous Magic Bullet — the projectile that the Warren Commission says went through two people, President Kennedy and Governor John Connally, making seven wounds and smashing two bones, yet emerging from this travail in almost pristine condition...

"O.P. Wright, who was head of Parkland Hospital Security, was shown a photograph of Commission Exhibit 399 by investigative reporter Josiah Thompson. 'President Kennedy was rushed to Parkland Hospital for emergency treatment after he was shot, and that is where CE 399 was (allegedly) discovered.' The photo 'depicting a copper coated, round nosed, military jacketed bullet' was not the one Wright 'turned over to the Secret Service. He said he had turned over a lead colored, sharp-pointed hunting round...Thompson wrote that if this was true, it indicated that either the FBI or the Secret Service had switched the bullet and therefore the assassination was, at least in part, an 'inside job.'

"It is clear from his footnotes that Bugliosi knows about the...Thompson interview because he read Thompson's 1967 book *Six Seconds in Dallas*, but he left this particular interview out of his book...in any real crime scene investigation, Dealey Plaza would have been immediately cordoned off and then details of Dallas Police offiers, supplemented by FBI technology, would have been channeled into the entire area. There would have been a foot-by-foot systematic check for shells, bullets, weapons and anything else lying around from the shooting. That did not happen...

"One of the more interesting discoveries of the ARRB, was an FBI evidence envelope from Dallas. As Michael Griffith points out, although the envelope was empty, the cover indicated it had contained a 7.65 mm rifle shell found in Dealey Plaza after the shooting. The envelope was dated December 2, 1963, so the shell was found sometime between November 22 and December 2, 1963. This important piece of evidence was hidden for three decades..." [77]

---

[77] DiEugenio, op.cit. "Once it closed shop, the Assassinations Records Review Board (ARRB) declassified about 2 million pages of records...there are still scores of records that were not declassified or located by the ARRB." The CIA alone is still concealing some 1,500 documents in defiance of the 1992 JFK Records Act.

Legacy

In the name of national security, in the 21st century the policies of the Federal government are manipulated by CIA and Mossad acts of terror made to appear as though they emanate from Iran or Hezbollah. On Russia's border the CIA formed the now discredited "Orange Freedom Movement" intended to unite Ukraine with NATO against the Russians. After 9/11 the Patriot Act extended the nascent police state into "Homeland Security." Under the George W. Bush administration, claims were put forth of the president's worldwide authority to "render" (kidnap) any person on earth, even a U.S. citizen, and hold them in military custody for months or years without trial.

In December 2011, President Obama signed the 2012 National Defense Authorization Act (NDAA), codifying indefinite military detention without trial into law for the first time in American history. The NDAA's detention provisions authorize the president — and all future presidents — to order the military to seize and indefinitely imprison people, including American citizens, apprehended anywhere in the world, far from any battlefield.

In the name of "national security" the government engages in assassinations at an extraordinary rate, both through drone technology as well as more traditional methods. If any foreign power were to kill a former CIA director, or the former Chief of Intelligence for the FBI, those assassinations would be considered terrorism and the American people would be persuaded to pay billions if necessary, to pursue the assassins anywhere in the world.

In point of fact, recent evidence indicates that the erstwhile CIA director William Colby was assassinated by the U.S. government in Maryland, and FBI Chief of Intelligence William C. Sullivan was shot to death by government agents when he was "mistaken for a deer" while standing on the porch of his home.

Since 1963, assassination chic has creeped into American culture. The *Wall Street Journal* has advocated the assassination of Bashir Assad in Syria *and his family*. In Georgia, Andrew Adler, publisher of the *Atlanta Jewish Times*, in the newspaper's January 13, 2012 edition, allegedly advocated the Mossad assassination of President Obama.

On March 6, 2013 Republican Rand Paul filibustered on the floor of the Senate against the confirmation of John O. Brennan as CIA director, and the prospect of government assassinations of American citizens on American soil. In news reports from the Orwellian corporate media, the word assassination is seldom employed in connection with U.S. government operations. The preferred cosmetic euphemisms spoon-fed to the infantilized public are "drone strikes, targeted killings" and "lethal military force." God forbid reporters or officials would utter the words *"U.S. government assassinations."*

Elie Hobeika, a Lebanese former collaborator with Israeli forces and a key witness in the Sabra-Chatila war crimes case being prosecuted in 2002 in a Belgian court against Israeli Prime Minister Ariel Sharon, was blown up outside his home in Beirut on January 24, 2002, together with three bodyguards and a civilian bystander. The car-bomb was the work of professional assassins in the employ of Mossad, the Israeli secret service. The bombing occurred two days after Hobeika agreed to give evidence against Sharon in Belgium. Hobeika had met with Belgian Senators Josy Dubie and Vincent van Quickenborne in east Beirut, agreeing to be a witness at any trial of Sharon for the Sabra and Chatila massacre.

Belgian human rights lawyers seeking to indict Sharon expressed their "profound shock" at Hobeika's murder. "Mr Hobeika had several times expressed his wish to assist the Belgian inquiry on the massacres at Sabra and Chatila," the lawyers said. "His determination to do so was reported widely on the eve of his assassination. The elimination of the key protagonist who offered to assist with the inquiry is an obvious attempt to undermine our case."

Marwan Hamadeh, the Lebanese minister for refugees stated, "My initial evaluation is that of course Israel doesn't want witnesses against it in this historic case in Belgium..."

In 1963 and 1973 Americans would have been nauseated and angered by Israeli assassinations. Decades after Kennedy's murder and many Americans believe that such gangland rub-outs are justified.

Since 2007, seven Iranian scientists have been assassinated and in some cases their family members killed or wounded, in terrorist acts perpetrated by hit teams sponsored by the U.S. and the Israelis.

Beginning in 2005, certain assassins covertly dispatched to Iran were trained at the Department of Energy's Nevada National Security Site by the U.S. government's Joint Special Operations Command (JSOC).[78]

Murders committed by the U.S. government are vindicated by threadbare logic from Wonderland, namely that terrorist acts such as assassinations are appropriate against whomever we deem to be terrorists. (No doubt JFK and his brother were "terrorizing" the military-industrial complex and the Mafia). Many decades after King-Kill/33 and many more Americans now believe in the morality of the government assassinating "bad guys."

Of course, once you open Pandora's box and engage in extra-judicial executions by U.S. "special forces," and "our Israeli allies" in the Middle East, then the genie is out of the bottle and the principle that "bad people can and should be assassinated," is spread throughout the land, which begs the question, who in the government defines a "bad" person and by what criteria?

Was Dorothy Kilgallen a bad person? What of Bill Hunter of the *Long Beach Press-Telegram*? He interviewed Jack Ruby's roommate and was subsequently shot to death "by accident" by a cop who claimed he had been practicing his fast draw when his handgun discharged in the direction of Mr. Hunter.

On May 22, 2013, Ibragim Todashev was very likely murdered by the FBI, probably to keep him from testifying to his belief that the accused Boston Marathon bombers, the Tsarnaev brothers, had been, in his words, "set up."

The FBI has radically altered its original story of how and why Todashev died, and the inconsistencies and anomalies are so preposterous as to merit an independent congressional investigation, and sleuthing from multiple newspaper, magazine, and television outlets. Most Americans don't seem particularly troubled by this execution by the Federal government of a witness in a terrorism case.

The presumption of the guilt of the Tsarnaevs is the proper belief. The authorities and the media have insinuated this belief, and Americans believe properly.

Welcome to the Brave New World initiated in Dealey Plaza, in the darkness just past noon, of November 22, 1963.

---

[78] Seymour M. Hersh, *The New Yorker,* April 6, 2012.

"Allen Dulles, Richard Helms, Carmel Offie and Frank Wisner were the grand masters. If you were in a room with them you were in a room full of people that you had to believe would deservedly end up in hell. I guess I will see them there soon."

—James Jesus Angleton, Associate Deputy Director of Counterintelligence Operations, Central Intelligence Agency.[79]

---

[79] Cf. Joseph Trento, *The Secret History of the CIA* (Prima, 2001), pp. 478-479.

Select Bibliography

Armstrong, John, *Harvey and Lee* (Quasar Books, 2003).

Brown, Walt, *Master Chronology of the JFK Assassination* ("Kindle" book; multiple volumes)

Cranor, Milicent, "Trajectory of a Lie," history-matters.com/essays/jfkmed/TrajectoryOfaLie/TrajectoryOfaLie.htm

Davy, Bill, *Let Justice Be Done* (Jordan Publications, 1999)

DiEugenio, James, *Reclaiming Parkland* (New York: 2013)

Douglass, James W., *JFK and the Unspeakable* (Orbis, 2008)

Downard, James Shelby, and Hoffman, Michael, *King-Kill/33* (St. Petersburg, Florida, 1977)

Feister, Sherry, *Enemy of the Truth: Myths, Forensics, and the Kennedy Assassination* (2012)

Fonzi, Gaeton, *The Last Investigation: What Insiders Know about the Assassination of JFK* (New York: 2013)

Garrison, Jim, *On the Trail of the Assassins* (1988)

Janney, Peter, *Mary's Mosaic: The CIA Conspiracy to Murder John F. Kennedy and Mary Pinchot Meyer* (New York, 2012)

Lane, Mark, *Plausible Denial* (New York: 1991)

Lane, Mark, *Rush to Judgment* (Holt, Rinehart, 1966)

McKnight, Gerald, *Breach of Trust* (Univ. of Kansas, 2005)

Melanson, Philip, *Spy Saga* (New York, 1990)

Mellen, Joan, *A Farewell to Justice* (New York: 2013)

Nelson, Phillip F., *LBJ: The Mastermind of the JFK Assassination* (New York: 2013)

Newman, John, *Oswald and the CIA* (New York: 2008)

Palamara, Vincent Michael, *Survivor's Guilt: The Secret Service and the Failure to Protect President Kennedy* (2013)

Piper, Michael Collins, *Final Judgment* (Wolfe Press, 1995)

Prouty, Fletcher, *JFK* (Kensington, 2004)

Savage, Gary, *First Day Evidence* (1993)

Tague, James J., *LBJ and the Kennedy Killing* (Trine Day, 2013)

Thompson, Josiah, *Six Seconds in Dallas* (Random House, 1967)

Turner, Bill, *Deadly Secrets* (Thunder's Mouth Press, 1993)

Ventura, Jesse, *They Killed Our President*, (New York, 2013)

Bobby Kennedy and Thane Eugene Cesar

Statement of Robert F. Kennedy Jr.

"September 11, 2019 — Thane Eugene Cesar died today in the Philippines. Compelling evidence suggests that Cesar murdered my father.

"On June 5, 1968, Cesar, an employee in a classified section of Lockheed's Burbank facility, was moonlighting as a security guard at the Ambassador Hotel. He had landed the job about one week earlier. Cesar waited in the pantry as my father spoke in the ballroom, then grabbed my father by the elbow and guided him toward Sirhan. With 77 people in the pantry, every eyewitness said Sirhan was always in front on my father at a 3 - 6 feet distance. Sirhan fired two shots toward my father before he was tackled. From under the dog pile, Sirhan emptied his 8 chamber revolver firing 6 more shots in the opposite direction, 5 of them striking bystanders and one going wild.

"By his own account, Cesar was directly behind my Dad holding his right elbow, with his own gun drawn when my dad fell backwards on top of him.

"Cesar repeatedly changed his story about exactly when he drew his weapon. According to the coroner, Dr. Thomas Noguchi, all 4 shots that struck my father were "contact" shots fired from behind my Dad, with the barrel touching or nearly touching his body. As my father fell, he reached back and tore off Cesar's clip-on tie.

"Cesar sold his .22 to a co-worker weeks after the assassination, warning him that it had been used in a crime. Cesar lied to police claiming that he'd disposed of the gun months before the assassination.

"Cesar was a bigot who hated the Kennedys for their advocacy of civil rights for blacks. I had plans to meet Thane

Eugene Cesar in the Philippines last June until he demanded a payment of $25,000 through his agent, Dan Moldea.

"Ironically, Moldea penned a meticulous and compelling indictment of Cesar in a 1995 book and then suddenly exculpated him by fiat in a bizarre and nonsensical final chapter.

"Police have never seriously investigated Cesar's role in my father's killing."

End quote from RFK, Jr.

When interviewed, Cesar stated that he had indeed pulled a handgun at the scene of the shooting, but insisted the pistol was a Rohm 38 caliber, not a .22. The bullets which killed John F. Kennedy's brother came from a .22 caliber gun. Cesar also claimed that after the first shot he was knocked down and was unable to fire his weapon.

The Los Angeles Police Department (LAPD), which interviewed Cesar shortly after the shooting, did not regard him as a suspect and *did not ask to see his gun.*

Cesar stated that he did own a .22 caliber Harrington & Richardson pistol. He showed it to LAPD sergeant P. E. O'Steen on June 24, 1968. This gun was not confiscated and no ballistic tests were conducted on it.

When LAPD officers interviewed Cesar in 1971, he claimed that he had sold the gun before the assassination to an individual named Jim Yoder. In October 1972, William W. Turner located Yoder. Mr. Yoder had saved the receipt for the sale of the H&R pistol, which was dated September 6, 1968, and bore Thane Cesar's signature, indicating that Cesar had sold the pistol three months *after* Robert F. Kennedy's assassination, contradicting his 1971 claim that he had sold the weapon months before Bobby's murder.

The 9/11 Terror Attacks as Alchemical Ritual

> "Let us never tolerate outrageous conspiracy theories..."
> —President George W. Bush
> Speech to the United Nations • November 10, 2001
>
> Tim Russert: "You (and John Kerry) were both in Skull and Bones, the secret society."
> George W. Bush: "It's so secret we can't talk about it."
> —*Meet the Press*, February 8, 2004
>
> "Our enemies are innovative and resourceful, and so are we. They never stop thinking about new ways to harm our country and our people, and neither do we."
> —George W. Bush
> Defense Appropriations speech • August 5, 2004

Those who aspire to teach can determine the effectiveness of their instruction by determining whether or not anyone has come along to extend or elaborate on what was taught. In the case of our book *Secret Societies and Psychological Warfare*, finally completed in mid-2001, we were gratified to see that the author of the 2013 volume, *The Most Dangerous Book in the World: 911 as Mass Ritual*, S.K. Bain, a former staff member of *Oxford American* magazine and the *Weekly Standard* newspaper had in many respects, built upon our own work.

We don't share all of the premises of Mr. Bain's metaphysical teleology, but we're heartened that he was inspired by some of our ideas on civic magic and the reality that current events can, on many occasions, be more than politics, statistics, armies and navies, budgets and lobbying — that "something more" being esoteric messages embedded in ritual crimes that "speak" to our subconscious as a form of human alchemical processing.

When we say "he took," we note that he did so by crediting us by name and mentioning our own book by its title. Our work has been used by others, not just by Mr. Bain, but almost always as an act of covert plagiarism, and plagiarists, particularly on the Internet, do not give credit — they take it — and the hell of that act of intellectual theft is it denies researchers the opportunity to examine the source and follow-up on the originator of the information. Moreover, many plagiarists do not comprehend the concepts they are "borrowing." Consequently, they sow confusion, which is an act friendly to the Cryptocracy. As Bain writes, "Many...of the components of the 9/11 script were *designed* to confuse, to distract, to mesmerize..and suck investigators and conspiracy theorists alike down a bottomless rabbit hole of misinformation...We are bombarded with such volumes of conflicting information that our ability to meaningfully process it is overwhelmed...we give up trying to figure it out...we shut down..."

Bain's *The Most Dangerous Book in the World: 911 as Mass Ritual* introduces the reader to psychological warfare as it "incorporate(s) a wide variety of occult symbols." He proposes that the 9/11 terror attacks were not only an inside job and a black op, they were "...an ultra-powerful mind control...weapon —a psychological warfare tool of enormous proportions— infused with techno-sorcery and deep-level occult programming."

It's one thing to pronounce so ambitiously on so startling a proposition (sorcery, no less), it is quite another to deliver the goods. For the most part, Mr. Bain backs up his assertions with considerable evidence, marshaled step by step as an act of *disenchantment*, the signal characteristic of Mr. Downard's *gestalt*, in a society where the pursuit of self-deception in the form of fairy tale enchantment is threaded throughout our culture's literature, cinema and advertising, resulting in widespread acceptance of virtual and consensus "reality."

If Americans possessed the intuition of early medieval people, most would laugh to scorn the corporate media's official 9/11 tale. What might be the intuition of an early medieval human? First, it would be likely to be close observation and contemplation, which is increasingly abandoned in an Internet Age that offers a deluge of information and misinformation, along with entertainment, amusement, erotica and every other distraction. The aperture is opened so wide it takes a sage to filter it to a manageable point.

When we were with the Amish, we stayed with Ben S. at his home in a settlement in the foothills of New York's Adirondack mountains. After Ben fed and bedded down his cattle and horses, he had the leisure to go out on clear nights to pursue his entertainment: studying the evening sky, the venerable hobby of countless shepherds, hunters and other truly *human* beings. As Ben pointed out various constellations and planets to us one evening, we noted that he also had committed to memory the orbits of many satellites, and even the space station itself, with no assistance from "apps" or computers. He was a keen observer and his observations were not mediated by an "expert" who told him what he was or was not seeing. Whereas, in modern society, almost everything we see, or think we see, is mediated by an authority of some kind. The Emperor has no clothes? The experts say he does. 9/11 was a conspiracy? The "experts" at *Popular Mechanics* say it was not.

Having over the years watched a half-dozen or so films of controlled demolitions of buildings prior to the morning of September 11, 2001, we recognized the collapse of the Twin Towers as being the same kind of direct drop to the ground that we observed in the case of buildings that were razed by the strategic placement of demolition explosives. We didn't need to ask the high priests at *Popular Mechanics* to approve our observation.

As previously noted in this writing, during the Half-Time Show at the National Football League's 2012 "Super Bowl XLVI," pop singer "Madonna," surrounded by Egyptian-Pharaonic props, acted the part of an occult goddess in a ceremony broadcast to hundreds of millions of people. Most Americans didn't see an occult personage. Was an occult ritual being televised, or not? Do we need to ask the "experts"? What does the Revelation of the Method tell us? What do facts as plain as those satellites and space stations that flew across Amish Ben's night sky, reveal to a person whose thoughts are not controlled to any significant degree by the thoughts of others?

Mr. Bain informs us that none other than the co-chairmen of the 9/11 Commission itself, Thomas H. Kean and Lee H. Hamilton, in their 2006 book, *Without Precedent,* charged that the 9/11 Commission was "set up to fail." John Farmer Jr., the Commission's senior counsel, stated that the Air Force decided not to tell the truth about 9/11 and that, "The (NORAD) tapes told a radically different story from what had been told to us (the Commission) and the public." Kean agreed that what NORAD told the Commission, "was just so far from the truth." (NORAD, America's air defense command, somehow could not put a single interceptor fighter-jet in the air over Manhattan during the seventeen minutes the Twin Towers were under attack). [1]

Bain informs us that FBI agent Robert Wright, who worked out of the FBI's Chicago office assigned to tracking Osama bin Laden's financing, gave a speech to the National Press Club in which he stated, "The FBI allowed 9/11 to happen. FBI management intentionally and repeatedly thwarted and obstructed my investigations..."

From Bain we also learn that Andreas von Bülow, a member of Germany's Schalck-Golodkowski investigation committee which tracks financial crimes, "...estimated that insider profits surrounding 9/11 totaled approximately $15 billion."

We see in 9/11 a coverup as flagrant as the daylight assassination on 11/63 at "Bloody Elm Street" of a president whose Secret Service and other forms of protection had been to a certain significant extent, withdrawn.

The contradiction between what our mind and spirit tell us is true and what the legion of professional liars, official spin doctors and prestigious disinformation specialists impose upon us, becomes fertile ground for our processing. When some of us doubt the veracity of the Establishment-propagated official facts about the September 11 terror, we are repeatedly apprised by the "authorities" that only a goofball "truther" kook, or a mentally imbalanced individual, would be skeptical.

A psychic tension arises in the discrepancy between our perception and the force by which the authorized tale is foisted, and we either become a witness against the System which perpetrated the falsehood or we live with the tension. To

---

[1] "At least six air traffic controllers who dealt with two of the hijacked airliners on September 11, 2001, made a tape recording a few hours later describing the events, but the tape was destroyed by a supervisor without anyone making a transcript...The recording included statements of five or ten minutes each by controllers who had spoken by radio to people on the planes or who had tracked the aircraft...A quality-assurance manager...destroyed the tape several months after it was made, crushing the cassette in his hand, cutting the tape into little pieces and dropping them into different trash cans...Although the matter had been referred to the Justice Department...prosecutors said they had found no basis for criminal charges." Cf. "Tape of Air Traffic Controllers Made on 9/11 Was Destroyed," *New York Times*, May 7, 2004, p. A29.

relieve the stress we are prodded into shoulder-shrugging conformity and therefore made complicit in the spectacular crime—partnered with the criminals by the fact of our indifference to what they perpetrated. Our humanity is radically diminished in the course of this process.

Black Jack 21 alchemy is achieved partly through the ceremonial manipulation of hypnotic cues and subconscious archetypes and symbols, comprising the Twilight Language which communicates with our subconscious mind and lately, our waking mind. The American people are far gone in the depths of this processing. Psychologically, they have the status of defeated and demoralized prisoners of war. They have cut a deal with the System: they won't contradict the Cryptocracy's flimflammery, in return for the Cryptocracy allowing them to "get on with their lives," pursue a career, marry a trophy wife, raise and educate one or two children, root for the stadium sports team of their choice, acquire a boat, an RV and a second home. In the course of this quid pro quo, they pretend they are concerned about the state of the nation and their children's future, while their souls are dissolved in the face of the lie they are living. It bears repeating: Americans have been marching in the direction the Cryptocracy has been taking us since the Creation and Destruction of Primordial Matter at the Trinity Sight in 1945, the immolation of the King of Camelot near the 33rd degree line in 1963, and the alchemical union of the sun and the moon with the Apollo 1969 moon mission. The 9/11 attacks of 2001 represent the fourth stop on this masonic *Jornada del muerto*. S.K. Bain picks up the trail:

"The Pet Goat"

"The Goat of Mendes, or Baphomet, is a goat-headed deity, being formed of both male and female principles, with Mercury's Caduceus for its phallus. One arm points up and one down, with the Latin '*Solve et Coagula*'...("breakdown and reform"—Hoffman)..."This is...a symbol of the ancient alchemists...(Satanist Aleister) Crowley asserted that Baphomet was a divine androgyne and the 'hieroglyph of arcane perfection...'"

Bain ushers us into a scene on the morning of September 11, 2001 when George W. Bush, the 43rd President of the United States, was visiting Sarasota, Florida, listening to a group of children reciting the juvenile tale, *The Pet Goat,* when his Chief of Staff, Andrew Card, announced that the Twin Towers had been struck by a second airliner. *Mr. Bush continued to sit and listen to the children's* Pet Goat story *for several minutes as the Twin Towers burned.*

From *Alice in Wonderland* to the 1939 classic movie, "The Wizard of Oz," juvenilia is sometimes a vehicle for conveying adult messages. Mr. Downard claimed that in the Kennedy King-Kill/33, Jack *Ruby* represented "the powerhouse of Oz." In Hebrew *Oz* denotes strength. In "The Wizard of Oz," the most potent magic resided in the *ruby* slippers.

According to Albert Mackey in volume two of *The History of Freemasonry* (New York, 1906, pages 363-364), Pythagoras is a formative character in the mythology of the Freemasons. In *The Wizard of Oz* the Scarecrow recites for the wizard a garbled version of Pythagoras' Theorem.

When in Kansas, the Oz protagonist Dorothy runs away from the family farm and encounters the campsite of "Professor Marvel." The itinerant showman fools her into thinking he discerns her predicament with the assistance of his crystal ball, which he informs Dorothy is, "...the same genuine, magic, authentic crystal used by the Priests of Isis..."

Diabolist Aleister Crowley's *Book of the Goat* was titled, *Liber Oz*.

Mr. Bain writes that while it's ostensibly a children's story about a girl and her ruminant playmate, "*The Pet Goat* was in reality a strategically employed device used to introduce this key occult element into the 9/11 MegaRitual...this children's story is an allegory of the Luciferian Doctrine: The Father is an overbearing hyper-authoritarian...The goat's aggressive behavior and destructive tendencies at first appear problematic...but in the end render the goat uniquely qualified to serve as savior..and the goat—whose initial poor behavior is, in broader context, relatively benign—saves the day. Praise the Goat.

"...In the class's reading of *The Pet Goat*, the Direct Instruction method was utilized. The teacher pounded out the syllables with a pen on her book and read in unison with the children, the overall effect being not unlike the ritualistic chanting of a religious ceremony.

"You...need to see the YouTube video to get the full effect)...there sits Bush as the Satanic High Priest...listening to little black children...chant out a humorous story about a pet goat—which is actually a thinly veiled simplification of the Luciferian Doctrine—while people burn to death in the North Tower and UA175 slams into the South Tower in New York City. Crowley's *Liber 175*, 'the book of Uniting to a particular Deity by devotion,' outlines precisely what the perpetrators are seeking to accomplish at that exact moment through their sadistic, homicidal ritualistic acts — unite themselves with Satan.

"And although the locations for these two events are separated by hundreds of miles, the two acts are bound together in an ingenious and sophisticated manner by a cohesive ritual unity.

"There is yet another...disturbing aspect to the selection of Sarasota as backdrop to the Bush-Baphomet Black Mass...Of the hundreds of flight schools in the United States, Mohamed Atta, the (alleged) ringleader of the 9/11 terrorists and the (supposed) hijacker-pilot of the first plane to hit target on the morning of September 11, 2001, attended a school located in the very city President Bush was visiting that same fateful morning, where he was presiding over the...Goat Ritual...This is neither coincidence nor synchronicity, it is yet another example of the twisted humor and sophisticated logistics employed..." (end quote).

This occult "twisted humor" in Sarasota is exacerbated by the fact that in 2001 (and for years prior), Ringling Brothers Barnum and Bailey circus hosted a clown college at its Sarasota headquarters. In legend Barnum is made to say, "There is a sucker born every minute."

The idea that George W. Bush was tied into occult goat-craft is a hypothesis we are free to accept or reject. As noted however, occult rituals are above all psychodrama—pattern theatre—and they weave tales from myth and literature as a way of programming us.

Baphomet, the hermaphroditic goat, is a sigil of the alchemical transformation of humanity.

The goat tale that kept President George W. Bush so entranced that he would not interrupt it even to take command during a terror attack as chief of the nation's armed forces, is certainly an intriguing factor and may even be, as S.K. Bain claims, part of the "Mega-Ritual" that was 9/11.

From Levi's *Transcendental Magic*.
BAPHOMET, THE GOAT OF MENDES.

"**Baphomet: The Goat of Mendes**," a viral hieroglyph engraved by Éliphas Levi that became the representative symbol of the western occult, revisioning Michael Maier's "Emblem 33" Rosicrucian image of alchemical transmutation. [2]

---

[2] From Levi's *Dogme et rituel de la haute magie* (1855). "Levi was born Alphonse-Louis Constant in 1810...Levi's enormous impact on esotericism throughout the Western world is indisputable, and influential later authors like H. P. Blavatsky and Aleister Crowley are heavily indebted to him...his books were instrumental in bringing about the occult revival of the mid and late nineteenth century." (Per Faxneld, *Satanic Feminism: Lucifer as the Liberator of Woman in Nineteenth-Century Culture* [Oxford Univ., 2017], p. 131). It pains us to state that Levi was a "traditional Catholic" whose occultism was shielded against all interference and any charges of demonism or heresy by every church authority we located in the annals of the pontificate of Pope Pius IX. Madame Blavatsky complained that "Levi was yet too subservient to his Roman Catholic authorities." This did not deter her however, from continuing to defer to Levi for inspiration and direction. Levi led the attack on the Bible as the Word of God. *Wizard of Oz* author L. Frank Baum's mother-in-law, Matilda Joslyn Gage, referred to "Levi's laudable occult understanding of the Bible." Levi "was...a major source of inspiration for...(the) counter-reading of Genesis 3...the Devil...is given a most generous portrayal." (Ibid. pp. 134-136).

In the forehead of Baphomet, "the Goat of Mendes," we observe the five pointed star or pentagram, which is incorporated into the architecture of that other "magic powerhouse," the Pentagon, target of an alleged terror attack by a jetliner supposedly flown by a clown named Hani Hanjour, who would have had difficulty flying a teacup at Disneyland. Hanjour supposedly eluded all of the U.S. government's formidable radar and surveillance, including the E-4B "Venus77" government spy plane that was aloft over the Washington D.C. area on September 11 (cf. Mark H. Gaffney, *The 9/11 Mystery Plane*).

The very talented pilot of Flight 77 executed a remarkable 330-degree spiral turn clockwise to descend toward the Pentagon, after which Hani Hanjour completed his spectacular aerial feat by supposedly crashing the huge airliner into the 5-sided edifice, causing major damage to the west wing of the nerve center of the U.S. military.

When Mr. Bain refers to twisted humor we think of Sir Francis Dashwood's Hell Fire Club where sadistic occult "pranks" were played for the amusement and edification of the high society initiates, a custom which reflects the Satanic nose-thumbing which embodies the spirit of certain acts of ceremonial magic when conducted in broad daylight before millions of people, and which are contemptuously mounted as an insult to our God-given intelligence and reason; intended to be doubly insulting to Christians who are supposed to possess the gifts of the Holy Spirit after Pentecost, including the gift of discernment.

In our recorded lecture, *Masquerader's Jest,* we analyzed the satirical mocking conducted by George W. Bush in the role he played as "commander in comedy" at the Radio and Television Correspondents dinner on March 24, 2004,[3] in the wake of the U.S. invasion of Iraq, after it was revealed that there were no weapons of mass destruction ("WMD") in that Arab nation.

At the dinner, the president, as "commander in comedy," had the audacity to perform a contemptuous charade, clownishly pretending to search the White House for the weapons of mass destruction which had been his sworn alibi for the war against the sovereign nation of Iraq.

---

[3] As of 2021, a video of his malevolent clowning was online at c-span.org.

> Hermes was the muse responsible for inspiring the rhetoric of salesmanship; he had a modest musical talent; and he was an adept of the daring and elaborate prank.²¹

This prank by a member of the Skull & Bones secret society, was a bold public mockery of the millions of Americans who had believed their president's story about WMD, as well as sneering at the U.S. troops who fought and died, along with the countless tens of thousands of Iraqi civilians who perished. [4]

His consummate Hell Fire Club jest, generally applauded by the media, put the finishing touches on Mr. Bush's post-9/11 masterpiece: the human sacrifice that was the Iraq war.

S.K. Bain is concerned with the psychology and epistemology behind the 9/11 rituals: "In the context of the occult script, all of the inconsistencies, suspicious facts and blatant lies make perfect sense — it was a huge, multi-faceted operation involving so many different working parts that the conspirators never expected to be able to cover it all up, or even cared about doing so. In many instances, they didn't even try, or, worse still, were so bold and arrogant that they mocked us to our faces by leaving clues in plain sight."

What does this arrogance tell us? What does the Cryptocracy thinks of us? These elitists always regarded the rest of us non-initiates, in *any era,* as being born somewhat less than human: "ghostly homunculi," e.g. *"goyim,* gentiles, *kelipot,* cowans." The "Cambridge (University) Apostles," who produced a slew of Soviet spies who defected to the Soviet Union, styled themselves the "realities," in contrast to the rest of humanity who they termed mere "phenomena."

Before the modern age, the Cryptocracy's low estimation of the American people was concealed, for the reason that virile, perspicacious, pre-modern yeomen had a tendency to rise against wicked tyrants when they were identified as such, and

---

[4] Bain informs us that at a previous, 2002 White House Correspondents' Association Dinner, President G.W. Bush invited Oz man "Ozzy" Osbourne, lead singer of "Black Sabbath," a "Heavy Metal" rock band. At this "fun-loving" event, Bush stated: "The thing about Ozzy is, he's made a lot of hit recordings— 'Party with the Animals, 'Bloody Sabbath,' Facing Hell,' 'Black Skies' and 'Bloodbath in Paradise'— Ozzy, Mom loves your stuff!" (End quote from Bush; cf. Bain, pp. 62-63). Bush neglected to mention Ozzy's other song, "Mr. Crowley," inspired by Aleister Crowley. The video game "Fallout 3" reproduces the lyrics to Ozzy's song in the lead into "You Gotta Shoot 'em in the Head." A "Mister Crowley" is a character in the game.

summarily pitchfork, club and hang them expeditiously. Even in the Victorian era, in the wake of the Trafalgar riots, British Freemasons perpetrated the "Jack the Ripper" butchery with the utmost secrecy. Now they are so contemptuous of us, so extremely confident of their invulnerability and immunity, "so bold and arrogant," that on *9/11 "they mocked us to our faces by leaving clues in plain sight."*

We contend that at some level of their collective psyche, the American people have an inkling that George W. Bush had a hand in the 9/11 terror attacks that killed 3,000 of their countrymen. But since The Power has signed off on this betrayal of "the phenomena" by "the reality," it has been decided that we "ghostly homunculi" are to haunt the stage of our masters' alchemical theatre, by "living the good life" of getting and spending, the glamor and glitter of fine clothing and travel; ogling the flesh that is peddled to sell soap and automobiles, and the pound of flesh that is extracted by the barons of banking. We have been programmed to drown our intuition of a soul-shriveling truth about our leader, by immersing our snouts in the amusements and distractions of the Renaissance-humanist Abbey of Thelema, where we are governed solely by our own free will, the only law being, *Fais ce que tu voudras* ("Do your own thing").

Twenty years ago in *Secret Societies and Psychological Warfare* it was necessary to explain this process of alchemical dissolving-and-rebuilding (*solve et coagula*), in detail and at length, to a startled audience in order for them to grasp it fully. At present, Americans are so far "down the (laboratory) tubes," that many will recognize the alchemical process without prompting, because *they are living it.*

In the Black Jack 21 era Americans exhibit the mental effects of the shock-and-awe doctrine, which is applied not only as military warfare, as in Iraq, but by domestic conspirators who wage psychological warfare as part of what anthropologist Joseph Campbell termed, *"mysterium tremendum et fascinans"* (a mystery before which man both "trembles and is fascinated").

Fascination is immobilizing. The fact that not a single one of the masterminds behind King-Kill/33, Oklahoma City '95, or 9/11, has ever spent so much as a day in jail for their monstrous, world-historic crimes, leads the masses to kneel in *trembling and fascination* before their prowess and potency.

We regret to say that Americans have become degenerate voyeurs who desire to be fascinated by more of these spectacular criminal prodigies, a supplication which will surely be fulfilled in the maelstrom that lies ahead, unless we change our ways by cooperating with the grace of God.

Misdirection of what energy there is, is the order of the day. The Golden Dawn initiate William Butler Yeats predicted a future in which "the best lack all conviction, while the worst are filled with passionate intensity." The unprecedented apathy we are witnessing serves as consent for the hell-on-earth that has been scripted and needlessly imposed upon us as "The Future," like it or not.

Many of us, even while on the golf course, at the shopping mall or the tailgate party, can glimpse, out of the corner of our eye, the harbinger of this end game. Edgar A. Poe drew its contours when he crafted a scene in which people become gradually aware of the presence of a horrifying reality that they had repeatedly denied and ignored—as the "Masque" finally dropped from the visage of "The Red Death": "...before the last echoes of the last chime had utterly sunk into silence, there were many individuals in the crowd who had found leisure to become aware of the presence of a masked figure which had arrested the attention of no single individual before. And the rumor of this new presence having spread itself whisperingly around, there arose at length from the whole company a buzz, or murmur, expressive of disapprobation and surprise — then, finally, of terror, of horror, and of disgust."

By then it was too late, as "...the throng of the revelers...gasped in unutterable horror..." at the reality of the monster that stood among them — a monster that had been present from the beginning of their revels. Poe states that the horror is so terrible it cannot be described or spoken of; it is "unutterable."

In line with Mr. Poe's dictum, this writer stands mute in the face of the extraordinary clockwork that has ticked out the inversion of good and evil, while contemporary Americans, like Esau of old, sell their birthright for a bowl of digital dung.

The "Literary Game" of the Rosicrucian Brotherhood

For the Alchemical Marriage of Magic and Science

Groundwork for a *Transhuman* Century 21:

EMBLEMA XXXIII. *De secretis Naturæ.* 141

Hermaphroditus mortuo similis, in tenebris jacens, igne indiget.

EPIGRAMMA XXXIII.

*Ille biceps gemini sexus, en funeris instar
 Apparet, postquam est humiditatis inops:
Nocte tenebrosâ si conditur, indiget igne,
 Hunc illi præstes, & modò vita redit.
Omnis in igne latet lapidis vis, omnis in auro
 Sulfuris, argento Mercurii vigor est.*

S 3   Ex

The two-headed being possessing both male and female genitalia, depicted by Michael Maier in "Emblem 33" of his *Atalanta Fugiens* ("Atalanta Fleeing"; 1617). [5]

---

[5] In *The Metamorphoses* of Ovid, *Atalanta* and her male consort Hippomenes, are rivals in a contest. Hippomenes achieves the victory over Atalanta with assistance from Venus, who bestows upon him three golden apples.

Title of the illustration on the preceding page:

"Emblem 33. The Secrets of Nature. The Hermaphrodite, as though a dead person lying in the shadows, requires fire."

The caption below the illustration reads:

"This two-headed being of double sex, funereal in aspect, gains this image when starved of dampness: hidden in the shadowy night, it craves fire. If you provide it with fire, it instantaneously revives. All the power of the stone is hidden in the fire, All the power of sulphur, [6] in gold; that of mercury in silver."

In the Hermetic fugue, the transit of one thing into another is the motive principal that powers the world, as demonstrated in the texts and the illustrations of *Atalanta Fugiens* by Dr. Michael Maier. [7]

James Shelby Downward gave consideration to the likelihood that the container designated "Jumbo" at the nuclear Trinity Site housed a mannikin that was animated by the bomb's atomic energy.

In the text accompanying "Emblem 29" of Maier's alchemical treatise, we read: *"Ut Salamandra vivit igne sic lapis."* ("Like the Salamander the Stone lives in the fire").

The caption under emblem 29 states, *"Degit in ardenti Salamndra patentior igne...Sic quoque non flammarum incendia saeva recusat, Qui fit asidduo natus in igne Lapis."*

("The Salamander lives more vigorously in the heart of the fire...Like her, our Stone, born in everlasting fire, does not attempt to flee from the relentless flame").

---

[6] Sulfur in this alchemical context is a code word for semen. Cf. Michael Maier, *Atalanta Fugiens,* emblem, 44: *"Isis adest soror et conjunx ac mater Osiris, Cujus membra Typhon dissecat, illa ligat. Defluit at pudibunda mari pars, sparsa per undas, Sulphur enim, Sulphur quod generavit, abest"* ("Isis, wife, sister and mother of Osiris, unites his sacred limbs torn apart by Typhon. But the phallus is lost out to sea by the waves, the sulphur which generated the sulphur is there no longer").

[7] M.D., Basle University; born in 1569 in Kiel, Holstein, Germany; died in 1622 in Magdeburg. Maier was Count of Palatine and a member of the Rosicrucian Brotherhood.

Whether or not Mr. Downard's surmise was correct, in our Century 21 we are experiencing the public fulfillment of the age-old alchemical *magnum opus* in its full spectrum: the racial, [8] sexual, [9] agricultural [10] and *transhuman* assault on nature.

The Rosicrucian Brotherhood

Michael Maier's Rosicrucian alchemy synchronized with the furore generated by the European intelligentsia's frenzied fascination with the recently published "Rosicrucian Manifestos" (*Fama Fraternitatis* [1614], *Confessio Fratenitasis* and *Consideratio brevis* [1615]), which served to announce the debut of the Brotherhood on the public stage, together with an embarkation upon a perception of science as inextricably tied to alchemical objectives.

The *Fama* and the *Confessio* are believed to have been authored by Johann Valentin Andreae and his "Tübingen Circle," including Johann Arndt, Tobias Hess, and Abraham Hölzel, among others. [11]

---

[8] The dissolution of racial differences and the amalgamation of the distinct races into one is the focus of Maier's Emblem 43: *"Audi loquacem vulturem, qui ne utiquam te decipit. Montis in excelso consistit vertice vultur Assidue clamans; Albus ego atque niger, Citrinus, rubeusque feror, nil mentior"* ("Hearken unto the talking vulture, he will not deceive you in any way. Atop a lofty mountain a vulture calls without ceasing; It is said that I am White and I am black; I am also Yellow and red and I do not lie").

[9] In addition to the hermaphroditic aspect, there is also the unnatural use of semen, as limned by Maier, in "The Philosophical Child Who Knew Three Fathers" (Emblem 49): *"...Phoebus, Vulcanus et Hermes in pellem bubulam semina quod suerint; Tresque Patres fuerint magni simul Orionis."* ("Phoebus, Vulcan and Hermes placed into the hide of an ox, semen from each one of them, and the three at the same time became the father of great Orion").

[10] Genetically modified (GMO) crops consist of *plants that could not occur in nature*. In combination with the application of artificial herbicides and pesticides, the fertility of the soil upon which human life depends, has been assaulted by these alchemies. Moreover, healthy soil nurtured through regenerative agriculture can hold more carbon dioxide than plants or the atmosphere combined. Naturally fertile soil can help to substantially remove carbon from our air. For a blueprint cf. the 2020 documentary film, "Kiss the Ground."

[11] Another foundational Rosicrucian text is *The Chemical Wedding of Christian Rosenkreuz (*1605), also by Johann Valentin Andreae and the "Knights of the Golden Stone." It has sometimes been alleged that Protestant founder Martin Luther had sympathy for the Rosicrucian occult because his escutcheon was a rose cross. This was a matter of the Rosicrucians hitching their wagon to a symbol that predated their occult fraternity by decades, similar to Adolf Hitler's appropriation of the swastika, a good luck charm that had been an ancient symbol of the sun in motion. Because Hitler made it synonymous with his Nazi movement, it would be folly to claim that Native American tribes or Hindus, or anyone who embraced swastikas prior to Hitler, were Nazis. It is equally fallacious to equate Luther's (or Dante's) rose symbols with the Rosicrucians.

"Both works were published by Wilhelm Wessel, the court printer of Kassel, with the explicit permission—perhaps even on the orders of the ruler, Landgraf Moritz of Hessen." [12]

These texts proclaimed the existence of the "Fraternity of the Rose Cross" and the dawn of a new age of "Magic, Alchemy and Cabala" (Kabbalah), working partly through the employment of Twilight Language, with a view toward the *expansion of man's power over nature*.

The Rosicrucian manifestos reflected Paracelsus' anticipation of the capacity of human brain power to take "command over the stars" and create "new forms of life," as the *"Anima Mundi"* (Spirit of the World) dictates (cf. the identification in 2 Corinthians 4: 3-4).

Here we see launched a major axis of the Cryptocracy, whose subsequent influence on our world is in some respects inestimable:

Rosicrucian alchemist and visionary Dr. Michael Maier, 1617

"Andreae's extraordinary concept, a *'literary game,'* or *'Ludibrium'* (as he would later call it), the creation of a secret society, combined with a very serious call for a radical new reformation that would incorporate science...That the sciences are thought of in Renaissance Hermetic-Cabalist terms as related to 'Magia' and 'Cabala', is natural for the period." [13]

---

[12] Joscelyn Godwin, *Rosicrucian Trilogy: Modern Translations of the Three Founding Documents* (2016), pp. 35-36.

[13] Frances Yates, *The Rosicrucian Enlightenment* (Oxford University, 2002), p. 67.

Roland Edighoffer: "The authors of the *Confessio Fraternitatis* agree with the astrologers that their epoch is entering into the sign of Mercury, who was assimilated by Michael Maier with Hermes. In his *Choephoroi*, Aeschylus has Electra define Hermes ('Mercury') as the mediator par excellence between gods and men, a function also ascribed to him by the alchemists and by Heinrich Khunrath...

"Thus it is normal for astrologers to regard Mercury as 'the lord of the word,' and for the *Confessio Fraternitatis* to proclaim the coming of 'the age of the Tongue.'

"Jacob Boehme, in his *Morgen-Röthe im Auff- gangk* ("Rising Dawn," 1612), wrote that in the man who is fulfilled, the planet Mercury gives rise to an inspired language...In the same way, the *Confessio* states that the time has come to speak...the Adamic language, i.e. the primordial idiom...which allowed Enoch to converse with angels. The Rosicrucians claim to already possess the knowledge of this language, but they make it plain that ...(it) cannot be read and understood except by a minority.

"They proclaim 'the age of the tongue,' but they impose the law of silence on whoever rallies to them...secrecy is a fundamental element in the *Confessio Fraternitatis*, which mentions it at least ten times...certain realities...are held to be inaccessible without a long initiation... Hermes Trismegistus says to Asclepius: 'It is an impious thing to divulge to the masses a teaching filled with the divine majesty'...the 'true philosophy' that the *Confessio* extols is Hermetist..." [14]

Frances Yates: "To the pseudonymous author 'Philip a Gabella' (Cabala) was attributed the *Consideratio brevis*, or 'A Short Consideration of the More Secret Philosophy.'The historical Rosicrucian movement had its origins within the Hermetic, and specifically Paraclesian, tradition that was so pervasive in Renaissance Europe, from its beginnings in Italy initiated by Marsilio Ficino and Pico della Mirandola.

"However, the Rosicrucian movement of the early 17th century was particularly influenced by the English mathematician John Dee, as evidenced by the publication of

---

[14] Edighoffer, "Rosicrucianism I: First Half of the 17th Century," in Wouter J. Hanegraaff (ed.), *Dictionary of Gnosis & Western Esotericism* (Brill Academic, 2006), p. 1011.

'Gabella's *Consideratio brevis* (a work based on Dee's *Monas hieroglyphica*) alongside the first edition of the *Confessio*...

"Rosicrucian in this purely historical sense represents a phase in the history of European culture which is intermediate between the Renaissance and the so-called scientific revolution of the 17th century. It is a phase in which the Renaissance Hermetic-Cabalist tradition has received the influx of another Hermetic tradition, that of alchemy. 'Rosicrucian manifestos' are an expression of this phase, representing, as they do, the combination of 'Magia, Cabala, and Alchymia' as the inference making for the new enlightenment." [15]

A clear premonition of the infernal marriage of scientism with "Magic, Alchemy and Cabala"—"the capacity of human brain power to take command" which was initiated by the occult imperium in its Rosicrucian manifestation—is afforded by the accelerating creation in our Century 21 along lines of Egyptian-type chimera of millennia ago (humanoid animals such as Anubis and Set), and the legendary Babylonian man-headed fish being Oannes, called Dagon in the Bible. [16]

In our "21" Age of Revelation, comparatively little dissembling is required to propagate public acceptance of laboratory-conceived monsters. Not only is the abomination acknowledged, but after a pro forma nod to anxiety about "unproven forms of intervention and the unintended consequences," these abominations are promoted as the fulfillment, in the words of Nathaniel Rich, [17] of the "lost reverence for the wonders of the natural world," citing conservationists such as Aldo Leopold.

In the *Wall Street Journal* of May 1, 2021, [18] Mr. Rich candidly explains the utopian blandishments entailed within the process by which acceptance of the Frankenstein horrors will be achieved: "Only after the public has warmed to the tools of synthetic biology and land regeneration, enticed by cruelty-

---

[15] Yates, op.cit., pp. 63; 65.

[16] In I Chronicles 10:10 King Saul's head is taken by the Philistines and "fastened" in their "temple to Dagon."

[17] Mr. Rich is the author of *Second Nature: Scenes from a World Remade* (2021).

[18] The article is sub-titled, "Altered and cloned creatures invite us to confront a future in which technology manipulates nature as never before —to save it." This is tantamount to saying we will engage in sexual intercourse to "save" virginity.

free meat and flood-resilient coastlines and Covid immunity, will we be prepared to undertake uncomfortable conversations over hybrid species, bespoke fetuses..."

Concerning this alchemy he writes: "In...recent scientific milestones you can make out the sharpening contours of our unnatural future...researchers in La Jolla, California, and Kunming, China, announced that they had successfully implanted human cells into macaque monkey embryos. The experiment suggested it would soon be possible to engineer a novel hybrid species: a human-monkey chimera.[19]

"...scientists have created transgenic species for decades. We've already seen 'humanized' pigs, cows and rats, and the first Covid vaccines available in the U.S. were initially tested on mice implanted with human genes.

"Scandal-averse scientists prefer to speak of these creatures as...'models," as in the language on the website of Jackson Labs in Bar Harbor, Maine: 'The latest model, the humanized NSG™-IL15, is now also available in limited quantities." [20]

"...The word 'monster' comes from Latin *monere*, 'to warn, remind,' a root shared by 'premonition.' The future now emerging is one of unabashed, targeted interference in natural processes, through the manipulation of genetic codes...

"The act of interference is not itself alarming—it's as old as civilization...What's novel today is the effort to use these tools to reverse some of the harm we've done....monsters serve a crucial function. They invite us to confront what's coming, to accept techniques for reshaping reality..." (end quote).

"*...unabashed, targeted interference in natural processes...*"

---

[19] Cf. Tao Tan, Jun Wu, Juan Carlos Izpisua Belmont, et. al, "Chimeric contribution of human extended pluripotent stem cells to monkey embryos ex vivo," *Cell*, vol. 184, no. 8, April 15, 2021: "Interspecies chimera formation with human pluripotent stem cells (hPSCs) represents a necessary alternative to evaluate hPSC pluripotency in vivo and might constitute a promising strategy for various regenerative medicine applications, including the generation of organs and tissues for transplantation. Studies using mouse and pig embryos suggest that hPSCs do not robustly contribute to chimera formation in species evolutionarily distant to humans. We studied the chimeric competency of human extended pluripotent stem cells (hEPSCs) in cynomolgus monkey (Macaca fascicularis) embryos cultured ex vivo."

[20] From the website (jax.org) of The Jackson Laboratory, May 3, 2021: "Humanized Mice Solutions. Humanized NSG™ represents an innovative and cost-effective platform to simulate trials, evaluate multiple drugs alone or in combination, and produce predictive data. Now, you can request a quote or start an order today. Our portfolio of humanized mice support the development of functional cellular components of the human immune system. Mouse models with human immune cell engraftment represent ground-breaking platforms to evaluate compounds to treat a variety of human diseases."

"The Tarot Card Killer"
The D.C. Sniper

A good deal of nonsense has been be penned about this case, and others like it, by writers who reach into a New Age grab-bag of dementia and disinformation. The CIA terms this distraction "noise" and the spooks are delighted to help propagate it. We term it "X-Files"-style muddying of the watergate that opened in the Age of Aquarius, wherein so many hypotheses and rumors were posited that the people imbibed the sense that everybody killed Kennedy; that everything causes cancer. In which case, how could JFK's killers be brought to justice if everyone is guilty? If everything causes cancer then it's futile to clean the environment. What's the point? Futility is born from the notion that we have no enemies among conspiracy theorists, only among the agents of the Cryptocracy. It hasn't occurred to some folks that a considerable portion of conspiracy theory may have been driven by the Cryptocracy itself, as cognitive infiltration.

In the D.C. Sniper theater of October 2002, there were reports of a suspicious white van with the letters, "Total Recall" printed on the vehicle, which was supposedly spotted at the scene of the sniper's "Exxon shooting." Since one of the goals of the Cryptocracy is the inculcation of apathy, amnesia and abulia in the target population, "Total Recall" would seem to be an antidote to the Cryptocracy's plan.

Let's endeavor to pursue this objective by *totally recalling* that we don't just see words, we hear them. Might it be that "serial" killer is heard as "cereal" killer (from Ceres the vegetative goddess of human sacrifice) in our collective mind?

We didn't coin the word "serial" killer for ritual murder, the U.S. government's FBI profilers did. Their "profile" is sometimes a script. A better name for some of them might be FBI scripters. They point the way out of amnesia into last-minute recall, ceremonially, like the sacrificial victim whose hands are bound and who is being led through an October cornfield. She is jolted into total recall when she sees the altar or pyramid, or wicker man of immolation, in the middle of the mow.

Another news report wanted us to know that the white "Total Recall" van was seen near the scene of the "Exxon sniping."

Can the script be interpreted to be received in the brain of percipients as: "X on Total Recall" i.e. cross out (cancel) Total Recall?

The advertising industry is a medium where the practical application of the Cryptocracy's mind control meets commerce. Advertising agencies are paid millions of dollars to conjure names such as Exxon because those ruthlessly pragmatic businessmen know that sub-rosa manipulation of the Group Mind pays large dividends in sales and profits. One of the most important branches of this epistemology is operated by the symbolic "Dr. Syntax," who features in masonic engravings depicting him giving a lecture at Freemason's Hall. What the masons called word magic, scientists today call neuro-linguistics. Advertisers term it "branding."

Some examples: the written word "serial" is transformed into the phonetic sound "cereal" in the synapses of the brain which link the raw sounds to new meanings not denoted in the textual rendering of the word. These raw sounds are known to the creators among advertising executives, as "phonemes."

The 21st century telecommunications corporation which goes under the brand name "Verizon" paid a large sum in order for that name to be conjured. In terms of textual denotation, Verizon means nothing. It's "just a name," like Lee Harvey Oswald was "just a lone nut." But the sound of that name inside one's head conjures a subtle sense of a rising sun, a new beginning, a "True Horizon." What is common knowledge in elite circles of American advertising, is the datum that to influence the masses with a brand name, one must pay attention to how letter combinations sound, because the advertising executives are cognizant that "In the beginning was the Word...faith cometh by hearing..." and the universe is sustained by sound.

In October, 2001 we witnessed a most highly charged image of the World Trade Center attacks—a burning tower spewing flames with people jumping to their deaths—in the form of the number 16 Tower card from the Rider-Waite Tarot deck.

In October, 2002 the Establishment massively publicized and reproduced another card from the Tarot deck, the number 13 Death card, in connection with the "D.C. Snipers."

Newsweek magazine featured this Tarot card on the front cover of its October 21, 2002 issue, and dubbed the mysterious sniper(s), "The Tarot Card Killer."

All Hallows Eve was around the corner and the movie "Red Dragon," featuring a fictional serial killer named Hannibal (i.e. Hani*baal*) *Lecter* (from the Latin root word for an ecclesiastic whose duty consists in reading "the lessons"), was being exhibited on the nation's silver screens, as snipers' bullets commenced the ceremony by which coercion and control are maintained.

The System's media drew attention to the "FBI profilers" who were supposed to have been concentrating on the sniper's "geography," in other words the Downardian realm of Mystical Toponomy (Greek: *topos* [place] + *onuma* [name]), which was notably relevant in the JFK assassination and the Jack the Ripper murders. The Establishment dismisses toponomic connections in those cases, but touts them when employed by the FBI when supposedly on the trail of Washington D.C.'s snipers.

Some of the FBI's behavioral psychologists ("profilers") are sometimes the guiding light for ritual murderers and "serial" killers. Perhaps we should extend the FBI "the benefit of the doubt" and surmise that there are only a handful of these bad actors inside the bureau and they are "rogue FBI employees."

However, it is a matter of the documentary record that the FBI's HRT ("hostage rescue team") committed the most infamous sniper murder in memory, FBI agent Lon Horiuchi's shooting of Mrs. Vicky Weaver at Ruby Ridge, Idaho, as she cradled her infant daughter. [1]

And the FBI most certainly played a criminal role in the Unabom murders.

Did they shepherd the D.C. area sniper(s)? It does appear that the snipers were monitored by the government until Revelation of the Perp time "came 'round again" — on the 6 o'clock news.

One of the police road blocks shown on national television and allegedly maintained to apprehend the sniper(s), was manned by a purported police officer wearing a full face mask. The roadblock was close to the Exxon sniper kill site.

Why would a policeman in 2002 be masked? What Hell-Fire Club jest on the gentiles is conveyed when the cops dress like the robbers?

Assassination of Federal Agent

What was Linda Franklin, a Federal agent who CNN described as "an intelligence operations specialist for the FBI," doing at the Seven Corners shopping mall October 14, when the sniper(s) were stalking there? Just a coincidence?

FBI agent Franklin was subsequently assassinated and the media attributed her death to "the sniper."

Police officials said *the sniper's alleged murder of the FBI intelligence operations specialist had no particular significance and was just a coincidence*:

---

[1] *Ambush at Ruby Ridge: How Government Agents Set Randy Weaver Up and Took His Family Down* (1995), by Alan W. Bock, is, as of this writing, easily the best study of the Federal government's murder of Mrs. Vicki Weaver and her son. In an interview conducted by Alisha Haridasani Gupta of the *New York Times* (Jan. 8, 2021), Seyward Darby, author of the *Times*-endorsed volume *Sisters of Hate*, insinuated that Vicki Weaver was not an innocent non-combatant: "...when people think about Ruby Ridge, they don't even think of Vicki's name per se, they think, 'Oh, that situation where the government was dealing with the separatists and they shot and killed a woman.' That's what it gets boiled down to, and any normal person would hear that and think, 'Oh, wow, that's a really terrible thing.' But it obviously strips important context. As I understand it, from my research, Vicki Weaver wasn't a bystander." We don't know if Ms. Darby's statement signifies that Mrs. Weaver did something that caused her to deserve to be killed while holding her infant daughter inside her home. If she wasn't a bystander that might imply she was guilty of somehow being a participant in what appears to have been a one-sided encounter with an elite FBI sniper. What, pray tell, is the "context" that would render her murder anything other than a "really terrible thing"? The *Times* reporter made no request to view Darby's "research" and exhibited no curiosity about the reference to a "context."

"Charles Moose, the police chief of Montgomery County in neighboring Maryland, said Franklin, an FBI intelligence analyst, was not involved in the sniper investigation and was therefore considered yet another random victim." (Reuters, October 15, 2002). Another "random victim"—the explainers' default dismissal.

The spectre of Arab terrorism is introduced into the Idyll

How could the police chief know with confidence that this particular killing (of Linda Franklin) had been "random" when the possibility of Islamic terrorism had not been ruled out?

"Federal investigators refused Tuesday (October 15) to rule out the possibility that organized terrorist groups are behind the shootings that have left some residents apprehensive all around the nation's capitol. 'The communities are terrorized,' said the Homeland Security Director, Tom Ridge, who said federal investigators don't know whether the sniper might be a domestic or international terrorist...Asked whether there were links to al-Qaida or other foreign terrorists, Ridge said, 'I don't think we can foreclose that. Certainly, nobody in the FBI or the White House has foreclosed that." (Associated Press, October 15, 2002).

If the sniper case was a possible foreign terrorist operation —and the Homeland Security Director refused to preclude the possibility—then how could Police Chief Moose know for certain that the shooting of FBI official Linda Franklin was "random," rather than deliberate?

Spot the farce?

One clown sticks his head out from behind the curtain and shouts, "Random killing!"

Then another clown pokes his head out and speaks his line, "Might be a terrorist!"

The normal reaction of an audience would be to laugh. But there's nothing humorous about the death of Linda Franklin, except to mentally sick people who stage macabre civic comedies at the expense of murder victims.

Furthermore, how was it that the shooters had the guile, meticulous planning, control and prudence to elude massive police roadblocks and dragnets, allegedly travel day in and day out to the murder scenes in the same light-colored "Astro van" [2] with a defective tail light and a telltale silver ladder on the roof, as the media reported?

Of course, when the suspects' actual vehicle was finally impounded it turned out to have not the faintest resemblance to a light-colored truck or van of any kind. Someone within the Establishment had consistently circulated false descriptions of the killers' vehicle, providing them with excellent cover.

What happened to the October 11, 12 and 13 focus on a large white commercial truck with the words "Total Recall" on the side?

Those words emblazoned on the truck have faded from the official record and the two trucks, the tradesman's large white truck pictured in the Sunday *New York Times* of October 13, and the astral "Astro van," back in the limelight as of October 14, appear and disappear from the list of suspect-connected vehicles, episodically, like a flashing signal.

At the very least, the invocation of the Tarot card in the sniper case indicates that the System wants us to think occult thoughts, perhaps along Hannibal/Red Dragon lines (as noted, the sniper shootings debuted close to the time when the latest Hannibal Lecter movie, "Red Dragon" debuted). It seems as though the Game Players sought to maintain the American Group Mind pressure cooker on "high."

Arcane considerations of this nature were germane long before the era of FBI profilers and are hardly unique to the FBI's "psy-war specialists.' What is unique is that under the aegis of "FBI profiling," occult elements heretofore dismissed by the Establishment as the phantasmagoria of "conspiracy kooks," have lately been held aloft as both credible and relevant in elite police homicide "investigations," bringing occult themes of sub-rosa processing and "Satanic" symbolism to stage center.

This process plays bipolar havoc with the mentalities of those who thought the Establishment wanted them *not to believe* that psychological warfare entails manipulating the archetypes of the public's subconscious.

A year before the D.C. snipers' October, 2002 reign of terror, in October of 2001, America was in the grip of an "Arab

---

[2] A celestial vehicle, since the root of the astro is from the Greek, ἄστρον, denoting a star in the sky.

terrorist" anthrax scare that kept hundreds of thousands of children indoors on Halloween and made millions of Americans apprehensive about opening their mail.

Sniper Halloween 2002 fit the same pattern: "Too Spooked to Trick-or-Treat: This year the monster lurking in the shadows is real..." [3]

That's a headline of the "says it all" variety: monsters lurking in the shadows are real and it's understandable that they would "spook" us into suspending our activity.

Maryland's *Enterprise* newspaper published a front page story directing readers' attention to a pentagram pattern allegedly formed by the snipers' shooting locales.

The *Enterprise* article, sub-titled, "Last leg of pentagram could point to Michaels in St. Mary's," states:

"Among the theories considered in an ongoing hunt for a Washington D.C. area sniper is the possibility that he has targeted places near a chain of craft stores, in a star pattern...'It's just one theory of many,' St. Mary's sheriff's Captain John Horne cautioned...but he noted the pentagram created by the location of four Michaels stores in areas where many of the shootings have occurred...'When you add ours in, that completes (the five points of) the star,' Horne added... 'The pentagram star is a familiar part of Satanic cult activities, the sheriff's captain said." [4]

The public's attention and alertness to these themes are switched on and off. It's permissible to think along these occult-symbol lines if FBI profilers, sheriff's captains or Establishment newspapers are doing so in specifically circumscribed areas of concern. But to apply this heightened consciousness at all times to all areas of criminology and pathology without Establishment authorization, is strictly forbidden, and the "conspiracy nut" and "grassy knoll" labels will be cranked out on cue and applied to whoever dares violate the protocol.

Hence, for someone to take Captain Horne's statement about the pentagram being "a familiar part of Satanic cult activities" and apply it to the U.S. military's five-sided, star-shaped headquarters known as the Pentagon, would invite

---

[3] *Washington Post*, October 24, 2002, p. B-1.

[4] *The Enterprise*, October 18, 2002, pp. 1 and A-13.

media derision, or even a one-way ticket to the funny farm. Much in law enforcement display a pentagram as their badge of identification and authority, and it's emblazoned on their patrol cars. In Russia the pentagram was daubed red to represent the bloody terror of Bolshevism. The red star pentagram was retired by Russia in the 1990s, but was resurrected as the nation's emblem by Vladimir Putin.

The D.C. Sniper/Tarot Card Killer caper also featured major broadcast media hosting various former detectives who had "investigated" the "Son of Sam" killings in 1976 and 1977. This was mockery. These "astute investigators" retailed a moldy pack of lies, including the preposterous claim that David Berkowitz was the "lone nut" responsible for all Son of Sam-connected fatalities. In fact, the Sam case, which we investigated and reported in *Secret Societies and Psychological Warfare* 2001, was the among the spectacular ritual murders the Cryptocracy mounted in the 1970s. The Son of Sam killers were part of a larger ceremonial series that included the Hillside Strangler in Los Angeles, Kenneth Bianchi, and the "alphabet" rape/murder of little girls in Rochester, New York that came to be known as "Double Initial." [5]

"Total Recall" Triggers "Puzzling Amnesia"

We have seen that the Feds issued repeated disinformation about a white van. As previously noted, they issued a report that the white van exhibited the words "Total Recall" and that this vehicle was spotted at the scene of "the Exxon shooting." "Total Recall" is the title of a film from a science fiction novel by Phillip K. Dick about a "zombie" programmed with hidden commands to execute a specific mission. The movie depicts a company named "Recall" implanting false memories.

In the wake of the "Total Recall" truck sighting, the police were said to possess only a "composite" picture of the truck and that "witnesses cannot agree on the writing that they saw on the white truck, nor can they come up with a license plate number." One correspondent referred to this as "puzzling amnesia."

---

[5] In May of 2021 Netflix cable television debuted a four-part documentary series, "The *Sons* of Sam." Part 2 shreds the official tale of Berkowtiz being the only shooter. At least three NYPD detectives are guilty of having participated in the cover-up. In Parts 3 and 4, a devil angle, which misled investigator Maury Terry, is emphasized. "Sam" was executive action by elite controllers operating behind a "Halloween" cover.

In the October 13 edition of the *New York Times* a photo of the suspect white truck was shown with the phrase "Unknown Words" printed on the side. The significance of words in connection with the sniper case was being emphasized by the *Times*, though the words themselves were evanescent, flashing on and off, leaving almost no trail (until the profilers decide to script a more tangible trail for us through their mouthpiece media).

FBI profilers market brand names to the public. "Unabom" was the name the FBI scripters gave to the purported environmental fanatics who bombed corporate polluters and academic computer gurus, and who eventually were said by the FBI to consist solely in the person of the lone nut Dr. Theodore Kaczynski. But why this odd spelling, Unabom? The FBI brand name "Unabom" is incomplete. The letter "b" has been dropped from the end of the word. This omission telegraphs to us the fact that something is being omitted; the matter is incomplete.

(It should be noted for the record that the phoneme mechanism is a neutral technology that cuts both ways. Someone on the Right came up with a phoneme in the 1980s alleging a "Zionist Occupation Government" which they abbreviated as "ZOG," invoking the sound and image of a monstrous idol and false god).

During the sniper shootings the emotional energy of the nation's Hive Mind was focused like a burning light in a mirror. Scott Thornsley, a "criminal justice scholar" said that the shooter "is planning how to increase the thrill level" (Associated Press, Oct. 15, 2002). The question is, whose "thrill level"—the snipers' handlers, or the masses, or both?

The spotlight was on, and the American people were paying strict attention to the urgent need for surveillance cameras and ubiquitous satellites, military assistance and intervention in domestic affairs, 400 assigned detectives, random traffic stops by police who harassed citizens in white vehicles. The mounting tension, fear, anxiety and expectation in connection with the sniper were palpable, commensurate with the simultaneous, melodramatic "Countdown to War with Iraq," which the media were presenting.

This was all building to a spasm of ecstatic release—the anticipated thrill of the imminent capture of the fiendish culprit(s) and the post-spasm euphoria of a mystery solved and the "case closed."

Those who have been programmed to kill on cue are often also programmed to self-destruct or self-incriminate on cue. In the aftermath of the most notorious masonic murder in American history, the assassination in New York of writer William Morgan in 1826, the investigators of that era remarked on the tendency of the "mesmerized" perpetrators to incriminate themselves or commit suicide. They dubbed the phenomenon "Masonic apoplexy."

The D.C. Sniper case is not a matter of good vs. evil. It is about cryonic, freeze-thaw Revelation of the Method amid the clamor of adrenaline-pumping thrills. It is a medieval mystery play for the Pepsi Generation, a sobering parable about the crying need for a benevolent Super-State, an army of cops and a digital All-seeing Eye to "keep us safe." After all, this is the 21st century! "Life is not so simple anymore."

During the sniper killings this writer was contacted by a Department of Defense official who has been known to us for some time, but this was the first time he was willing to speak this candidly:

"As you know from my other e-mail I work for the Defense Department...While I am a well compensated member of the military-industrial complex I have had growing concern over the years about the direction of our government and who is really controlling it. I wrote you recently about the D. C. Sniper asking you if you believed this killing spree was an occult black arts operation and this has initiated e-mail from you on the subject.

"...This would be the first time that very sophisticated U.S. Military intelligence assets would be used against a (supposed) U.S. citizen in violation of the Posse Comitatus Act of 1877. Thus we see the real reason for the D.C. Sniper — to get our military to conduct operations against U.S. citizens with the approval of those citizens...

"...I'm very concerned about the erosion of the Posse Comitatus division between police and military work in the U.S.. Military assets have been used in the past few years to digitally map with infrared sensors most of the major cities of the U.S. I've overheard a lieutenant general in Army intelligence speak of the fact that all 21st century wars will be urban wars since most people in the world will soon live in urban areas. This may explain the need for a war with Iraq. Our leaders want our military to have a Stalingrad or Berlin house-to-house battle in Baghdad in order to train them for coming events...(some of those events will be here in the U.S.)

"...It looks like Secretary Rumsfeld wants the people to know that the U.S. Military will 'save' them from the sniper so they will welcome military intrusion into their lives. As the French say, sometimes the poison and the antidote are concocted in the same laboratory."

The last time we witnessed a police dragnet comparable to the one in Maryland, was when neo-Nazi terrorist Buford Furrow—after shooting up a defenseless Judaic daycare center on cue—was being hunted by the LAPD. Like the sniper(s) in Maryland, he expertly eluded the formidable Los Angeles police and their intensive manhunt, tiptoed through the roadblocks and chopper spotter beams, traveling all the way to Las Vegas, where he promptly reported directly to personnel at the Las Vegas FBI headquarters. Talk about Revelation of the Method.

Some disinformation in the D.C. Sniper killings came from outside investigators—sloppy or intellectually dishonest researchers who proliferate in this field. For example, conclusions were floated at the point when the shooter(s) had allegedly killed nine and wounded 11 (9/11). Some Internet scribes fell for this rush-to-judgement pitfall by proclaiming a 9/11 sniper signature or message. One must be prudent and avoid forcing data to fit one's own personal prejudices or pet theories. Wishful thinking is a trap for investigators.

The Feds play pranks on independent investigators and the public and we would characterize at least some of the reports about this case which appeared on October 21 and 22, 2002, as telephone pranks and deliberate misdirection, such as what a stage magician uses. For example: "the white van parked at the pay phone with two dark-skinned, Hispanic suspects." It was said these two were definitely not involved. Yet, the pay phone where their van had been parked had, according to the media, been used "by the sniper(s)" to make a call *to the police.*

Moreover, it is the police who routinely confirmed that all the shooting victims were victims of the same sniper(s), based on bullets allegedly extracted from bodies and subsequent ballistic tests. So-called expert criminologists who automatically proceed from the assumption that the police are retailing infallible truth about the victims and the bullets, are about as sophisticated as the kids who whitewashed Tom Sawyer's fence. Without *independent* corroboration of police ballistics tests, we do not see how any authentic criminologist or journalist can assume anything about who killed the victims grouped and ascribed to "the sniper." [6]

One may wish to study the Pentagon's Urban Warfare Doctrine to learn the role which "information superiority" and control of the media play in manipulating a target population. PSYOP, according to the Pentagon's doctrine, entails having the media disseminate only the "approved message...modifying attitudes and behavior of selected audiences." [7]

The System did get its requisite "Muslim monster," John Allen Muhammad, a U.S. Army veteran, into theatrical custody. The supposed "sniper" was indeed struck with that ancient, self-incriminating malady, masonic apoplexy: "The link to the two Washington men came in part from a call from the suspected sniper himself. In the call, the sniper told investigators to look into an incident in Montgomery, Alabama, a federal law-enforcement official said." [8]

Did the snipers turn themselves in on hypnotic cue?

Reading a carefully drafted, cryptic message to the snipers, Chief Moose said:

"You have indicated you want us to say and do certain things. You want us to say, 'We have caught the sniper like a duck in the noose.' We understand that hearing us say it is important to you."

A few hours after Chief Moose's conveyance of this seemingly hypnotic cue in public, the suspects were found conveniently asleep in the wanted car, at a public rest stop, not far from I-70, a heavily-traveled Interstate highway.

Sleep well, America. The Manchurian candidates have emerged from the shadows. A "Manchurian candidate" is defined as: "A group of American soldiers brainwashed into becoming sleeper agents."

After this possibly hypnotic cue had been conveyed to Mr. Muhammad, the Cryptocracy required a story to conceal the cue.

---

[6] Cf. John F. Kelly and P.K. Wearne, *Tainting Evidence* (1998).

[7] *Joint Publication 3-06: Doctrine for Joint Urban Operations* (Pentagon, 2002).

[8] *Seattle Times*, October 24, 2002.

They deliberately intended for that story to be absurd. Why? So they could mock the credulity of the dupes who would believe a sheerly stupid explanation solely because it was retailed by the credentialed Establishment Media. Half of occult ritual consists in mockery of We the People, we who our processors consider morons richly deserving of contempt and exploitation.

Having assessed the reaction in advance, the Overlords chose not to suppress their sneers. They did this by presenting to the American people a "folktale expert" who "solved the riddle" by explaining that Chief Moose's statement was just an old Cherokee Indian story about a rabbit that goes hunting for a duck. [9]

The System will have a tougher time however, explaining away and solving the riddle behind certain revelations, such as the datum that well before the sniper murders occurred, police in the state of Washington, as well as Federal agents there, received numerous red flag warnings concerning the suspects, including information concerning Mr. Muhammad's acquisition of an illegal silencer for his weapon.

According to the *Seattle Times*, ATF Special Agent Patrick Berarducci stated that the ATF learned of Muhammad and the silencer, but took no action. Neither did the ATF act against the gunshop where some say the sniper rifle was obtained. The rifle cannot be traced any further than this gun shop, to Muhammad or anyone else, because the record for this rifle and hundreds of other rifles are missing.

The teenaged Jamaican national, "Malvo," the alleged sniper's accomplice, was designated an illegal alien in 2001, but was allowed to remain in the U.S. after a top official of the INS intervened, and overturned the U.S. Border Patrol's deportation advisory.

Or how about this revelation: "According to several news reports, authorities spent so much time trying to collect forensic evidence from the (sniper's) letter, which was retrieved from Saturday night's shooting site in Ashland, Va., that they missed a deadline the sniper had imposed." (*Seattle Times*, October 24).

---

[9] No allegation of wrong-doing on the part of Chief Moose is here alleged. He may have been only a messenger innocently retailing a communication above his comprehension.

A Fable for Our Times

Sniper's Message Cites Cherokee's Tale
Associated Press (AP), October 24, 2002

"The last cryptic message from Montgomery County Police Chief Charles Moose to the Washington-area sniper referred to a Cherokee Indian story about an arrogant rabbit that was duped by the duck he tried to catch...

"In the ancient story, passed down through generations of Cherokee Indians, a rabbit brags that he can catch a duck. He throws a noose over the neck of a duck, but it flies away with the rabbit hanging on. Eventually the rabbit must let go, landing in a hollow tree stump.

"The conceited animal has to eat his own fur for food and is embarrassed by his appearance when he finally escapes. 'His boastfulness got him in trouble and eventually destroyed him,' said Tera Shows, spokeswoman for the Cherokee Nation, based in Tahlequah, Oklahoma" (end quote from the AP). [10]

Chico Marx: "Why a duck?" [11]

Sheriff Daggett: "The Duck of death, says I." [12]

---

[10] This does not have verisimilitude, even as mythology. Rabbits don't catch ducks. Birch bark canoes of some North American Natives (for instance the Passamaquoddy tribe), were occasionally adorned with images of a confident, pipe-smoking rabbit on one side and a mountain lion on the other. The Mad River Canoe company featured this rabbit mascot, explaining that the pipe-smoking rabbit is a symbol of freedom from fear of one's natural enemies. The legend is prominent in the 1997 film "The Edge," written by David Mamet. In the movie, the owner of a wilderness lodge (played by L.Q. Jones), bets New York billionaire Charles Morse (Anthony Hopkins), that he can't guess what's on the back of a canoe paddle that features an image of a panther on the front. Morse answers directly, "A rabbit smoking a pipe." He adds, "The rabbit is not afraid, because he knows he's smarter than the panther." This Native proverb foreshadows the film's subsequent key action sequences. In the finale, after a harrowing life-and-death ordeal, Charles and the lodge owner revisit the aphorism. Hopkins's character says, "We are all put to the test, but it never comes in the form or point we would prefer..."

[11] A line from a 1929 Marx Brothers movie.

[12] The Daggett character was portrayed by Gene Hackman in the movie "Unforgiven" (1992), directed by Clint Eastwood, who also directed "American Sniper" (2014).

Certain Anomalies in the Case of 33 Deaths in the Virginia Tech Terror
April 16, 2007

Joseph Paul Watson writes: "Charles Mesloh, Professor of Criminology at Florida Gulf Coast University, told NBC 2 News that he was shocked that Seung-Hui Cho, an undergraduate (Korean) student at the university, could have killed 32 people with two handguns absent expert training. Mesloh said the killer performed like a trained professional, 'He had a 60% fatality rate with handguns.'

"In the two hour gap between the first reported shootings and the wider rampage that would occur later in the morning, Cho had time to videotape his confession, transfer it to his computer, burn it onto a DVD, package it up, travel to the post office, post the package, and travel back to his dorm room to retrieve his guns, and then travel back to the opposite end of the campus to resume the killing spree." (End quote from Joseph Paul Watson)

The campus was not shut down after the first shooting of student Emily Jane Hilscher, and Ryan Clark, the resident adviser at the dorm. Lame excuses have been put forward but the fact is, in August, 2006, during a hunt in the vicinity of Virginia Tech for an escaped convict accused of killing two people, classes were canceled and students were told to stay in their rooms (that was the first day of the school year at Virginia Tech, August 21, 2006, so one can describe the shock and fear mined that day as the opening scene in the play that would climax on April 16, 2007). Two people were killed in August off campus and Virginia Tech is shut down and students placed on alert, in defensive posture. The first two people killed by Cho in April and the college continued operating as though nothing was amiss. Why?

It's our hunch that campus security and local law enforcement were misled by assurances from officials higher up that the first two killings, of Hilscher and Clark, were a domestic matter involving a man romantically involved with Hilscher. The profile on cases like that indicates that bystanders are seldom at risk. The local officials took the fatal bait and did as they were told— they relaxed their vigilance.

State officials, notably Virginia State Police Col. W. Steven Flaherty were still saying as of the early morning of April 18 as follows: "...investigators were not ready to conclude that the same gunman was responsible for both episodes..." [1]

This follows the initial insistence of the University President on April 16: "Charles Steger, president of the university, said at a later afternoon news conference that 31 people, including the gunman were killed at Norris Hall and two others died at the dorm. He said there was no connection between the two shootings."

On the morning of April 17, President Steger definitively labeled the Korean as the second shooter: "He was one of our students,' Charles W. Steger, Virginia Tech's president, said this morning on CNN. Offering the most detailed official description so far, Mr. Steger said the shooter at Norris Hall was an Asian male student who lived on campus in one of the dormitories. The suspect was called the 'second shooter." [2]

What of the fact that the sound of a shotgun being fired inside Norris Hall, scene of 30 of the murders and one alleged suicide, was heard by a witness, Wayne Neu? The shooter is said to have been armed only with hand guns. The discharge of a hand gun is very different from the report of a shotgun. If a shotgun was discharged we must ask by whom and at what target?

We have cell phone service being obstructed on campus the morning of April 16. This was explained as due to heavy calling on that day. Gosh, service was obstructed even *before the massacre* in Norris Hall commenced? How odd that cell phone service was on the blink on that day. The school's website was down intermittently too, during the shootings. Not enough bandwidth, it seems. One might venture to say it appears that Cho and whomever may have assisted him, had to be allowed to mow down 30 people in addition to the first two victims. The green light was on for the massacre, even if certain essential services on campus were out of order.

We are informed that Cho was on unspecified "prescription medications," like so many schoolyard shooters and Manchurian candidates; that portion of the script has not been

---

[1] "Two-Hour Delay Is Linked to Bad Lead," *New York Times,* April 18, 2007.

[2] "Massacre in Virginia: The Day After," *New York Times,* April 17, 2007.

altered. He was also programmed the way millions of American kids are programmed for mayhem and violence, with ultra-violent and highly profitable digital games: "Several Korean youths who knew Cho Seung Hui from his high school days said he was a fan of violent video games, particularly 'Counterstrike,' a hugely popular online game published by Microsoft, in which players join terrorism...groups and try to shoot each other using all types of guns." [3]

The media reported that the phrase "Ismail Ax" was scrawled on the shooter's arm. Later it was reported that the inscription on his arm read "Ismale Ax." Were they going to work a Muslim (Ishmael) angle, but then dropped it?

In his chilling, videotaped tirade broadcast on television, Mr. Cho spoke of being humiliated, saying, "You forced me to dig my own grave. You shoved trash down my throat." Masonic initiations by secret society groups like Skull-and-Bones involve mock burials in coffins and graves and humiliation involving excrement and sexual fluids (as portrayed in the Revelation of the Method movie, "The Good Shepherd").

The hastily assembled post-massacre "public convocation" at Virginia Tech with President George W. Bush and First Lady Laura in attendance put a funerary pall over the proceedings on a day that should have been a time of intense police investigation—but one doesn't ask questions during a funerary rite, one mourns—and thus as the trail got cold, tampered with, destroyed and manipulated, our attention was focused elsewhere, on the instant mourning rite. This one-day respite in the immediate aftermath of the slaughter gave the Cryptocracy the opportunity to manage and arrange the scene of the crime; to stage it like a realtor stages a house for sale. As the magicians distracted us with the mourning rite, the Cryptos took care of cleaning up the evidence; how convenient.

Their staging differs in certain respects from past scenarios. For example, the case was not entirely presented as open-and-shut. The Cryptocracy released to the media a report of a couple of puzzling items, contradictory data and ambiguous loose ends that gave the massacre the aura of lingering mystery, like acrid gunsmoke hanging in the air. Their allowance for mystery was a safety valve. It enhanced the credibility of the official account. Instead of giving an

---

[3] Cf. "Centreville Student Was Va. Tech Shooter," *Washington Post*, April 17, 2007.

impression of absolutism in an age of uncertainty, they allowed for uncertainty, conveying a "Gee, some of this is as mystifying to us, as it is to you," message. An attempt to abruptly claim the Virginia Tech case was closed, as was preemptively done with the Son of Sam and Unabom murders, would tax the government's credibility in the year 2007, which was steeped in an Iraq war quagmire in which Americans were becoming distrustful of official malarkey. Far better to allow for an uncertainty principle, which the System can then manage in the direction it wants the investigation to proceed.

The media reported: "Up until today, the deadliest campus shooting in United States history was in 1966 at the University of Texas, where Charles Whitman climbed to the 28th-floor observation deck of a clock tower and opened fire, killing 16 people before he was gunned down by police. In the Columbine High attack in 1999, two teenagers killed 12 fellow students and a teacher before killing themselves. The shooting at Virginia Tech came just four days before the anniversary of the Columbine High School slaying."

The Korean Cho replaced Texan Charles Whitman as the top campus killer of record. We're shown a timeline, we're looking beyond Virginia Tech. Many other "lone nut" type of "violence-is-as-American-as-apple-pie" killings were being summoned, like ghosts to a seance table, making the third week in April of 2007 a haunted one. Spines were being collectively tingled; we were on alert, not quite so drowsy. We were in "teachable" mode. The Virginia Tech massacre of April 16 was electrifying in itself. This was doubled in light of the imminent arrival of the commemoration service on the April 20 anniversary of the 1999 Columbine school massacre, also allegedly perpetrated by medicated, violent video gamers.

We were "teachable" that week in April, 2007. But what were we being taught?

1. That Cho's sister Sun Kyung worked for the U.S. government in the State Department's Iraq Reconstruction Management Office and that her office "was set up by President Bush."

2. That we didn't care enough about innocent life to prevent another Columbine, by banning access to pharmaceutical substances that lower inhibitions against killing fellow human beings. That we didn't care enough to take on Hollywood's slaughter/slasher movies exhibiting depraved indifference to

human life, and "humanitarian-philanthropist" Bill Gates's Microsoft and their unconscionably profitable traffic in ultra-violent and dehumanizing digital games.

23 is the reported age of the alleged perpetrator.

33 is the number of the total who died: the shooter killed 32 plus himself.

Significant numbers 23 and 33, whether by design or CCC (Cosmic Coincidence Control), were seared into the Group Mind.

Less than two months earlier, on February 23, 2007, movie star Jim Carrey produced and took the lead in the movie, "The Number 23."

The significance of number 23 as a chaos integer was not so well known beyond fans of the writings of William Seward Burroughs, that is until Mr. Carrey's movie debuted in the U.S. on 4/23/07 (4 + 23 +7 = 34, presaging April's 32 to 33 victim progression at Virginia Tech).

On February 27, four days after "The Number 23" movie debuted, a "suicide" bomber blew himself up near where Vice President Cheney was staying in Kabul, Afghanistan. The headline of the February 28 edition of the *New York Times* read, "A Mile from Cheney, Afghan Bomber Kills At Least 23."

Three separate cases of murder-suicide in Houston, Texas, including one at the Johnson Space Center, followed the killings at Virginia Tech.

The third death in the series took place on April 23.

One of the killers was age 33.

And where is Black Jack in all this?

Where's the tunnel to the 21 Gateway?

According to a British newspaper, Cho's dorm room was numbered 2121. [4]

---

[4] "The Killer of Room 2121," *The Observer*, [UK], April 22, 2007.

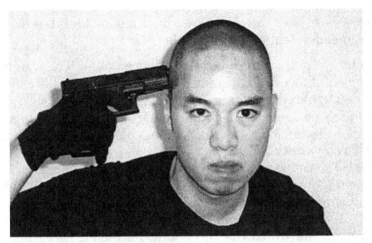

Copycat Videogram to America's Youth

Why was the video containing Cho's gruesome and perverted death manifesto televised?

Why not issue a transcript of his statements and spare the nation the spectacle of making a Videodrome celebrity out of a mass murderer while disseminating his death message to millions?

There was a macabre kamikaze glamor to the video: a demented nerd was transformed into a deadly, potent and instantly famous ninja by the power of his homicidal/suicidal rage. The repeated broadcast seemed like a recruitment piece soliciting copycats. [5]

The Willard Factor: when Israeli civilians massacre Arabs, they are usually described as mentally ill. When Arab civilians massacre Israelis, they are commonly referred to as terrorists. Cho Seung Hui was presented as mentally ill. This deflates speculation that he was directed to do what he did, or that he perpetrated his crimes for defined political, racial or occult motives. Mental illness smothers a multitude of leads: "He was a lone nut. That's all there is to it."

Under that cover story, programming him with drugs becomes "the administration of medication."

---

[5] Cf. Loren Coleman, *The Copycat Effect: How the Media and Popular Culture Trigger the Mayhem in Tomorrow's Headlines* (2004).

He was a lone nut so there's nothing to investigate, other than "incompetent college officials." [6]

Violence from on high begets violence below. The Columbine killings followed President Bill Clinton's indiscriminate, NATO-partnered bombing of ancient churches, cities, trains and buses packed with civilians in Orthodox Christian Serbia. Violence is a form of contagion, particularly the state-sponsored variety.

NATO's carnage was approved by our moralists and statesmen even as loads of Serb civilians were burned alive on the altar of the god of collateral damage. The casual violence of the U.S. government and NATO in Serbia, and the disregard for human life which the two homicidal teenagers exhibited in Littleton, Colorado, are linked.

Depravity and mockery are compounded when slaughterer-in-chief Bush goes to Virginia Tech to "minister" to the victims of an epidemic of violence, of which he himself was a prime instigator through his Skull-and-Bones contempt for human life in Iraq.

---

[6] Cho's "psychiatric records had been missing from the university counseling center for years..." (*Telegraph* [UK], August 21, 2009).

Red Dawn at Midnight
The Aurora, Colorado "Batman" Massacre

On the 43rd anniversary of the Apollo Moon Landing, a mass shooting at the midnight screening in Aurora, Colorado of Christopher Nolan's Batman movie, "The Dark Knight Rises" which premiered *nationally* on July 20, 2012, bore eerie similarities to a scene from the 1986 comic book, *Batman: Dark Knight Triumphant,* down to the killer's red hair.

In the comic strip, a crazed, gun-toting loner walks into a movie theater and opens fire, killing three in the process. The scene in the comic concludes with the media blaming Batman for inspiring the shooting, though he is not involved in the incident.

The 1986 illustrations, written and drawn by Frank Miller, were allegedly a key inspiration for the Batman movies. They supposedly helped to re-imagine the character away from his kiddie cartoon image and into a darker, more macabre incarnation. The point of the scene in Mr. Miller's *Batman: Dark Knight Triumphant* was to show just how far Gotham city had gone berserk since the Batman had retired.

Was one of the Aurora shooters (James Holmes) imitating this scene? In the comic book the shooter is portrayed as inspired by his disgust at the breakdown of American society: its pornography and inhuman rock music. [1]

In magic, the highest ritual imprinting of the Group Mind is accompanied by blood sacrifice. The bat has not traditionally been associated with goodness, but rather the opposite, from the bat of the "Dracula" mythos, to the masonic bat caves of New Mexico and the Bat Towers of Florida and Texas. But in America, where heads-is-tails and sinners are saints, the sinister bat image has been reversed and transformed into a crime fighter.

A depraved pattern of media corruption was repeated a mere several hours after the Colorado massacre. Like with Lee Harvard Oswald and David Berkowitz, when the investigation should have begun in earnest the *Washington Post* (online July

---

[1] As of this writing the illustrations can be viewed at: washingtonexaminer.com/was-the-batman-movie-shooting-imitated-from-scene-in-1986-comic

20, 6:47 p.m.) closed the case by issuing the infamous, omniscient lone-nut declaration:

"The only near-certainty is that the gunman (James Holmes) acted alone and not as part of a terrorist group or other conspiracy."

The *Post* knew this with "near-certainty" and publicized it a little over eighteen hours after the crime had been committed.

It sure is a relief to have clairvoyant, credentialed Establishment sources of information serving the people's right to know and protecting us from the "recurring paranoia" of "discredited conspiracy theories" which, thank goodness, ever-vigilant Twitter, Facebook and YouTube have the good sense to ban.

As with Oswald, a similarly ludicrous, all-knowing declaration was issued by the establishment media in 1977 in the immediate aftermath of the apprehension of "troubled loner" David Berkowitz as New York City's one and only "Son of Sam" shooter—brazen mendacity which the hierarchy of the NYPD buttressed.

As we have detailed, years later this frozen "certainty" was thawed when it was decided it was Revelation of the Method time.

Reports by eyewitnesses of an accomplice of Holmes who was seen inside the Aurora theatre is down the memory hole, replaced by the incontestable dogma that Holmes was another "disturbed loner." [2]

A name-game question: they caught Holmes. Where's Dr. Watson? Perhaps he's dating actress Katie *Holmes,* after she divorced Scientologist Tom Cruise. It was James Holmes who knocked Katie Holmes off the front page of the entertainment news in July.

According to Internet Movie Database (IMDB), Katie Holmes starred in the 2005 Batman film, "Batman Begins." Katie Holmes also has a JFK connection. IMDB reports that she portrayed Jacqueline Kennedy in "The Kennedys" television mini-series. The name Holmes, from Sherlock to James to Katie, has caught the attention of the establishment media in our "maddened land."

---

[2] Batman movie star Gary Oldman portrayed "lone nut" Lee Harvey Oswald in Oliver Stone's "JFK." In "The Dark Knight Rises" he portrays Gotham's Police Commissioner, James Gordon.

"Names have always been the subject of magical thinking — the ancient Romans buried lead tablets invoking the names of spirits, gods or the dead in order to curse their enemies, so perhaps it shouldn't be too surprising that many people think uttering the name 'James Holmes,' like an unguarded mention of the name "Voldemort" in J.K. Rowling's *Harry Potter* series, will cause bad things to happen...

"The curse invoked by Holmes' name, according to some, will take the form of other mass shootings. Indiscriminate killers seem to crave fame and notoriety; take those away, the theory goes, and there will be no reason for troubled loners of the future to strap on weapons and shoot up the local post office/mall/campus/movie theater." [3]

The establishment media were having quite a struggle deciding how to refer to James Holmes in the wake of his massacre. They didn't know whether to imprint him as "the Dark Knight shooter" or "the Joker" (a name which Holmes, a PhD. candidate in neurology, the science of the mind, supposedly called himself according to police at the scene of his crime).

Perhaps they intended to alternate between the two. The description "the Batman shooter" was out for some reason.

Who makes these editorial choices, and why? Are these assigned monikers mundane, or coincidental preferences on the part of a group of copy editors around the nation who are somehow unanimously united into one one mind? Or are people, places and events sometimes deliberately named for special effect, by media executives?

For example, how did "same sex marriage" become a ubiquitous description of homosexual nuptials, and then morph almost overnight in the national media into "marriage equality"? Will the drive for legalizing the marriage of incestuous couples be granted the dignity of the term "marriage equality"? Who among our Overlords decides to confer a name or a phrase and turn it into a nationally mandated expression?

In the nineteenth century, German philosopher Friedrich Nietzsche, among others, termed Alchemy the "gay science." How did homosexuality come to be termed "gay" and the name universally assigned?

---

[3] *Los Angeles Times,* July 26, 2012.

The name-game is played for high stakes in the battle for Orwell's Newspeak. On September 14, 2020 the Associated Press "Style Book" which is referenced and usually heeded by media executives throughout the English-speaking world, damned the word "transvestite": "Use the term cross-dresser instead of the outdated term transvestite for someone who wears clothing associated with a different gender, and only when the subject identifies as such."

Damn a word as being "outdated," which is not the same as inaccurate, and then consign the forbidden word to oblivion. When modernity replaces accuracy as the criterion for the use of a word which signifies a thought, then as George Orwell warned in the appendix to *1984,* that thought itself gradually becomes impossible to think.

The movie "The Dark Knight Rises" does not contain any blatant Cryptocracy symbolism (at least to these eyes), save for the Batman himself — he is of course the physical image of darkness. At the end of the movie a statue of Bruce Wayne/Batman is unveiled, which conveys this darkness, although supposedly signifying formidable power on behalf of what is good, along with selfless dedication.

What the film does exhibit is a number of initiatory, reality-is-not-what it-seems reversals: prisoners who set up their own rendition by the CIA; Catwoman's use of a fugitive's cell phone to launch a police SWAT team assault; the assumed identity of the child who climbed out of the prison turns out to be another person entirely.

Children are no longer suckled

The word *wayne* is a derivative of the Old English word *wean*: "To cease to be suckled; to accustom a child to the loss of its mother's milk." Bruce Wayne, the man of light, wears the disguise of a man of darkness whose familiar is the bat. *Wayne* has other gender-bending and twilight language connotations.

The 39th Degree of Heartbreak in the Heartland

The 39th degree of the Mizraim (Egyptian) rite of Freemasonry is called Knight of the Red Eagle. Colorado denotes the color red. Aurora denotes dawn. Hence, Aurora, Colorado signifies "Red Dawn."

In 1999, nineteen miles southwest of Aurora, during the orgy of bombing violence which the U.S. and NATO inflicted on the civilian population of Serbia and its ancient Christian centers of learning and worship, thirteen people were massacred at Columbine High School.

Those two Colorado massacres, in Aurora and Columbine, occurred on what is known as "the heart line" — the 39th degree of north parallel latitude—which runs through America's heartland.

Denver International Airport, known for its strange architecture and arcane symbolism, is also situated on the 39th degree. Of all the macabre iconography at that airport, the most intriguing was a large, 70-ton, 26-foot statue of Anubis, the Egyptian jackal-headed god, a personification of the star Sirius, in the constellation *Canis major*. The dog star was at the theological center of the state religion of ancient Egypt. According to the Babylonian Talmud, "Ten measures of magic came into the world. Egypt received nine of them, the rest of the world only one" (BT Kiddushin 49b).

With Aurora's location on the 39th degree line in mind we read in Jim Brandon's [4] *Weird America* (Dutton, 1978): "*The Sirius Mystery*...explores the role of the star Sirius in the mystical and religious affairs of the earliest civilizations of the Mideast and Mediterranean. In his fifth chapter, on the geodetic locations of the various oracle shrines of the ancient world, Temple points out that these places were arranged along *nine* bands of latitude..." (from the 31st to the 39th).

Dodona, one of the "oracle shrines" in Greece, dating from the Mycenaean era (1900 B.C.), is, like Aurora Colorado, on the 39th degree line of north parallel latitude. Dodona was first dedicated to the goddess Isis. Jason, while searching for the golden fleece, sailed in the "Argo," and in *The Argonautica*, Apollonius of Rhodes writes that the Argo possessed the gift of prophecy because it contained an oak timber from Isis's shrine at Dodona. Isis and Sirius are linked. Anubis is the guard dog of Isis and the personification of Sirius.

The Batman theatre shootings occurred during what is known as the "Dog Days" of summer, associated with the "heliacal" (i.e. rising at dawn) of the star Sirius, a sacred date on the ancient Pharaonic calendar: "...the star most important to the Egyptians was Sirius, or Sothis, as the Greeks rendered

---

[4] Pen name of William N. Grimstad.

its Egyptian name, and its heliacal rising was taken as the first day of the proto-dynastic era's lunar calendar..." [5]

The slayings in Aurora occurred while America's heartland, bisected by the 39th degree, was being parched and scorched in a Dog Days' drought. "In ancient Greece the heliacal rising of Sirius coincided with the intense midsummer heat...hence its classical Greek name, *Seirios*, meaning 'glowing one' or 'the scorcher.' Its heat-laden fierceness was considered an aspect of the star's malign influence." [6]

"Throughout Latin literature there are many references to 'the Dog Days' which followed the heliacal rising of Sirius in the summer. These hot, parched days were thought at that time to derive some of their ferocity and dryness from the 'searing' of Sirius. Traditions arose of Sirius being 'red' because it was in fact red at its heliacal rising, just as any other body at the horizon is red. When making rhetorical allusions to the Dog Days, the Latins would often speak of Sirius being red at the time, which it was." [7]

Heliacal rising of Sirius = Red Dawn. The symbolic connection of Anubis, which stood like a beacon at the Denver Airport, to Sirius, is not easy to miss. Robert K.G. Temple: "The heliacal rising was the occasion when Sirius again rose into visibility in the sky after a period of seventy days of being out of sight, during which time it was conceived as being in the *Duat*, or underworld. A further connection with Anubis comes in here, as Anubis was conceived of as embalming Sothis for these seventy days in the *Duat*. An embalmed mummy is supposed to come alive again. And this is what happened to the mummy of Sothis. Sothis (Sirius) is reborn on the occasion of her heliacal rising."

The Egyptians and all subsequent Hermetic systems constructed their elaborate and obsessive religio-astronomic observances around Sirius. The importance of Sirius to the global pagan psychodrama beggars description. By psychodrama we are referring to the process wherein a cultural mnemonic consisting of archetypes, subliminals, synchronicity

---

[5] Richard A. Parker, *The Calendars of Ancient Egypt* (University of Chicago Press).

[6] Reitha Pattison, "J.H. Prynne's 'The Corn Burned by Syrius" (sic), *Glossator 2*, p. 92.

[7] Robert K.G. Temple, *The Sirius Mystery* (1977).

and memes are attracted by a type of scientific sorcery pioneered by Anton Mesmer.

In the case of neuroscience PhD. candidate James Holmes we have a scientist of the mind who simultaneously was the "peak soldier" who supposedly perpetrated this bloody invocation, which is presented to the public through a media filter of mental illness, gun control and Second Amendment controversies. The theurgic character of the rite is overlooked and suppressed when it emanates from independent scholars and researchers. The exception is in the realm of "pattern-detection" and "profiling," concepts which have entered American culture in connection with television and cinema centered around U.S. intelligence data-mining, and the FBI. Profiling as presented to the public is usually limited to a psychological analysis, even though profiling has a great deal to do with "predictive programming," which is essentially a literary phenomenon (cf. *Secret Societies and Psychological Warfare*, p. 205).

Pattern detection, to be most effective, must take note of highly charged symbolism, which for millennia have been the province of sorcery of the kind at work in Pharaonic Egypt. Pattern detection ought to discern tales freighted with intentional significance. Aurora is one such narrative in the mesmeric "magnetism" and "charm" tradition of the old masonic Rite of Memphis and Mizraim.

Not to put too fine a point on it, but *if* the erection of the statue of the Egyptian god "*An*-ubis" at the Denver airport, on the 39th degree of latitude, which it shares with the Dodona oracle and the Columbine and Aurora massacre sites, has significance to the enchantment under consideration, then it behooves us to inquire into what evil directs the adepts we are investigating. Kenneth Grant, a leader of the Ordo Templi Orientis (OTO), states in *The Magical Revival*:

"In the Arcane Tradition, the vast star, Sirius, symbolizes the sun behind the sun, i.e. the true father of our Universe. Sirius was the primordial star of all time, as the duplicator or renewer (of time cycles). He was known in Egypt as the Doubling One, therefore a Creator or reflector of the Image. Sirius, or Set, was the original 'headless one' — the light of the lower region (the South) who was known (in Egypt) as *An* (the dog), hence Set-an (Satan), Lord of the infernal regions, the place of heat, later interpreted in a moral sense as 'hell.'"

When the image of Anubis ("*An* the dog") was placed on the south side of one of our nation's largest airports, were "our" civic officials ceremonially paying homage to Satan?

Or was this merely *coincidental,* being largely a colorful stunt from the world of promotion and advertising?

In response to that familiar bromide, let us quote Police Commissioner Gordon (Gary Oldman) in the "Dark Knight Rises" movie, in theaters during the Dog Days of 2012:

"You're a detective now. For you there are no more coincidences."

In the first century A.D., the Roman Marcus Manilius crafted *Astronomica,* a poetic catalogue of the stars. Manilius wrote the following verse associating Sirius with "opposite extremes":

> Next barks the Dog, and from his Nature flow
> The Most afflicting Powers that rule below,
> Heat burns his Rise, Frost chills his setting Beams,
> And vex the World with opposite Extremes.
> He keeps his Course, nor from the Sun retreats,
> Now bringing Frost, and now increasing Heats:
> Those that from Taurus view this rising Star,
> Guess thence the following state of Peace and War,
> Health, Plagues, a fruitful or barren Year.
> He makes shrill Trumpets sound...

Alexander Pope shall have the last word in this Sirius matter:

> The dog-star rages! nay 'tis past a doubt,
> All Bedlam, or Parnassus, is let out:
> Fire in each eye, and papers in each hand,
> They rave, recite, and madden round the land.

The Aurora Shooter's Cryptocracy Connection

According to Kurt Nimmo of Infowars.com, investigative journalist Wayne Madsen claims that James Holmes had a number of links to U.S. government-funded research centers, including the Defense Advance Research Projects Agency, (DARPA). Holmes was one of six recipients of a National Institutes of Health Neuroscience Training Grant at the University of Colorado's Anschutz Medical Campus in Denver, Madsen writes in the *Wayne Madsen Report*. "The Anschutz Medical Campus is on the recently de-commisioned site of the U.S. Army's Fitzsimons Army Medical Center and is named after Philip Anschutz, the billionaire Christian fundamentalist oil and railroad tycoon, who also owns the neo-conservative *Weekly Standard*," Madsen reported. "The Anschutz Medical Campus was built by a $91 million grant from the Anschutz Foundation."

Holmes also worked as a research assistant intern at the Salk Institute, at the University of California at San Diego in La Jolla. The Salk Institute partnered with DARPA, Columbia University, University of California at San Francisco, University of Wisconsin at Madison, Wake Forest University, and the candy bar company Mars, "to prevent fatigue in combat troops through the enhanced use of epicatechina, a blood flow-increasing and blood vessel-dilating anti-oxidant flavanol found in cocoa and, particularly, in dark chocolate," according to Madsen's research.

The DARPA program was part of the military's "Peak Soldier Performance Program," which involved engineering brain-machine interfaces for battlefield use and other bionic projects. In addition, James Holmes' father, Dr. Robert Holmes, allegedly worked for San Diego-based HNC Software, Inc., a company reputed to be allied with DARPA in developing "cortronic neural networks" that enable machines to translate aural and visual stimuli and simulate human thinking.

DARPA was the government agency that developed the supposedly now defunct, "Total Information Awareness" (TIA) program. But according to James Bamford in a report in *Wired*, "Inside the Matrix," (April, 2012), the TIA has been secretly revived by the National Security Agency (NSA) and is based at its vast, newly constructed "Utah Data Center," near Bluffdale, Utah, in what Bamford calls, "the heart of Mormon country."

TIA was originally developed by Reagan's Iran-Contra co-conspirator, Admiral John Poindexter (whose 26-year-old grandson Zach killed the admiral's 51-year-old son, Navy Captain Alan Poindexter, in a bizarre accident off Pensacola Beach, July 1, 2012).

Using the Batman shootings as another stepping stone to a police state, the *Wall Street Journal,* in a July 25, 2012 editorial, suggested that the government should revive the TIA program: "Aside from privacy considerations, is there anything in principle to stop government computers...from algorithmically detecting the patterns of a mass shooting in the planning stages?"

Just five days after the massacre and the media were not interested in investigating the shootings and the questions surrounding it. They preferred to insinuate that the shooter was a crazed kook without accomplices. DARPA's revived TIA was put forth as the American people's defense against mass-shooters like James Holmes, without mentioning that Holmes and his father allegedly had ties to DARPA. Can a kingdom divided against itself stand? Can DARPA cast out DARPA?

A week after the Batman theatre attack in Aurora, on July 27 (the Judean holy day of *Tisha B'av)*, ceremonies for the Olympic Games commenced in London, England with the theme, "Isles of Wonder." One of the ceremonies included a speech by Prospero's slave, Caliban, from Shakespeare's *The Tempest,* wherein Shakespeare offers a sympathetic portrayal of John Dee, thinly disguised as Prospero and set on an enchanted island. The ceremony included video of the modern 007 (actor Daniel Craig who portrays 007 James Bond on screen), escorting a grim-faced Queen Elizabeth II to the Olympic ceremony. One might deduce from this symbolism that Dr. Dee was the intended guiding spirit of the London Olympics.

As readers are aware by now, mathematician John Dee, Elizabeth I's astrologer referred to himself as 007. Elizabeth II's son, Prince Charles, has written about this original 007 and his code-number nickname:

"(Marsilio) Ficino's highly influential book, *Platonic Theology,* found its way to England shortly after it was published and eventually, some 90 years later, into one of the most important libraries in Elizabethan London, owned by Dr. John Dee, Queen Elizabeth I's astrologer...

"He coined the term 'British Empire' as part of his vision of creating a world-wide religion that emphasized the unity of all things, and was a close adviser to the queen. Intriguingly, he may have been a spy for Elizabeth when he traveled to Poland and Prague.

"I am told that when he wrote to her from such places he signed his letters with a curious combination of symbols: two zeros, sometimes connected by a bridge, implying he was her 'eyes,' followed by an elongated 7, which happens to be the alchemical symbol for Mercury. As Mercury was the messenger of the gods, the implication is rather clear. Dee was the Queen's secret and mercurial messenger." [8]

As we elucidate in *The Occult Renaissance Church of Rome*, Rev. Fr. Ficinio was one of the Vatican's prime Neoplatonic occult agents and initiates, and here we observe the belt of transmission between Renaissance papalism and its rival, the arch-Protestant regime of Elizabeth I.

Moreover, the credibility of the sales pitch of Prince Charles regarding Dee's new spin on catholic (universal) religion (the *prisca theologia*), emphasizing the alleged origin of *all* religions in a harmonious ancient "wisdom tradition," is undermined by the impolitic fact that the Pirate Queen Elizabeth was the first English monarch to put the African slave trade on a firm footing, with the assistance of her swarm of skilled buccaneers.

Was Advance knowledge of the Aurora and Sandy Hook shootings embedded in a major Hollywood movie?

We're interested in the possibility of deliberately planted theatrical numerology and twilight language symbolism which may perhaps point to the possibility of the scripted nature of serial killings and ritual murders.

"Batman: The Dark Knight Rises" references "Sandy Hook" *prior* to that school massacre in Newton, Connecticut. It can be glimpsed at approximately one hour, 58 minutes into the

---

[8] HRH The Prince of Wales, with Tony Juniper and Ian Skelly, *Harmony* (HarperCollins 2010), p. 132.

movie. It appears as tiny penciled words on a map which a police official is using to select his target.

Furthermore, in the same film the word "Aurora" is prominently displayed in a scene of a skyscraper ablaze with that lighted word, against a backdrop of darkness.

Necromancy in Parkland

Parkland in the context of President Kennedy's murder (he died at Parkland hospital) and this mass murder on Valentine's Day, February 14, 2018 suggests Twilight Language, when taken together with the infamous 1929 "Saint Valentine's Day Massacre" from the annals of gangland.

The origins of Valentine's Day are not happy if the fate of its namesake, Saint Valentinus, is any guide: "According to the official biography of the Diocese of Terni, Bishop Valentine was born and lived in Interamna and while on a temporary stay in Rome he was imprisoned, tortured, and martyred there on February 14, A.D. 269."

In 2018 February 14 was also the 73rd anniversary of the Allied massacre in Dresden, where Americans assisted the British in slaughtering at least 100,000 German civilians. Then there is the abortion holocaust to which the media are oblivious. They cherish abolitionist John Brown for declaring in 1859 that our nation had to be purged with blood for slavery: "I, John Brown, am now quite certain that the crimes of this guilty land can never be purged away but with blood." (December 2, 1859).

But the System will not countenance the possibility that America is being purged for its mass murder of the most helpless and dehumanized in our society—unborn children. We are *certainly not* suggesting that the innocent souls massacred in Florida deserved to die, or anything approaching such a reprehensible equivalence. If Nikolas Cruz was indeed the perpetrator he seems to have been demon-possessed, or at the least, a *pharmakos* (drugged, enslaved) individual, one of many resident in the haunted house that is the United States of America.

Whether at Parkland in Florida or the "Route 91 Harvest" shootings in Las Vegas, we are being forced into attendance upon a ceremonial *Dia de Muertos* on a national scale, like the Aztec and Egyptian people of old. In the words of H.P. Lovecraft "...*behind it all I saw the ineffable malignity of primordial necromancy.*"

The Cryptocracy has seeded the "crisis actor" meme (the claim that shootings are staged and victims non-existent) among activists otherwise rightly skeptical of the official government and media narratives. This "crisis actor" allegation however, is automatically assigned to nearly every mass shooting in the U.S. by dupes and irresponsible conspiracy theorists. When confronted with a lawsuit, conspiracy talk show host Alex Jones recanted his claims of staged shootings in the Sandy Hook Elementary School massacre in Connecticut in 2012.

There is no doubt in our mind that the Parkland, Florida slaughter was real and that those who designate the victims, or all the witnesses, as "crisis actors," are doing the Cryptocracy a favor by bringing discredit on investigations that are independent of the government's mouthpiece media.

Chuck Baldwin's Analysis

Dr. Chuck Baldwin (chuckbaldwinlive.com), director of Kalispell, Montana's Liberty Fellowship, is one of the independent investigators, and the Parkland conspiracy he posits is evidence-based and reasonable. Pastor Baldwin makes the following points in his essay, "Florida School Massacre Proves Police Are Worthless In Protecting Us." He writes:

"...courts have consistently ruled that it is not the responsibility of a police officer to protect the citizen. It is the responsibility of the citizen to protect himself. The job of the police officer is to gather evidence, apprehend the suspected criminal, and bring him to a court of law for a fair trial where they are presumed innocent until proven guilty.

"All of this talk about cops protecting us is a myth—a fabrication and misrepresentation. Almost every lawyer and judge in the country knows it. The only ones who don't know it are most of the American people. So, think about it: under our Constitution and laws, police officers have no obligation to protect the American citizenry. But at the same time, our politicians, news media, and most public school administrators and police chiefs insist that the American citizens should not be allowed to protect themselves. If this isn't madness, there is no such thing."

Dr. Baldwin cites anomalies in the Parkland shooting: "Did you watch the eyewitness testimony of the teacher who saw the shooter from a distance of only twenty feet?

"Stacey Lippel, a language arts teacher at Marjory Stoneman Douglas High School where the killings occurred, said at first

she thought the shooter was a police officer because of the way he was dressed 'in 'full metal garb' complete with helmet, face mask and bulletproof armor. 'I'm staring at him thinking, Why is the police(man) here? This is strange,' she said. 'And I'm just looking at him, but I'm still getting the kids (to safety), knowing this is an emergency.' The teacher also said that the shooter was carrying a type of rifle that she had 'never seen before.'

"Ms. Lippel's eyewitness testimony contradicts the official story that the 19-year-old shooter was wearing street clothes and a backpack and carrying a black duffel bag containing extra ammunition, which he discarded when he casually walked out of the school with the other students, and was later arrested in a nearby residential neighborhood. (I have not seen reports stating exactly where authorities found the discarded rifle, backpack, and duffel bag.)

"If this teacher saw Nikolas Cruz, the 19-year-old kid (who we are told was the sole shooter), could he really have carried all of that armored police gear to the school (remember he was supposedly driven to the school by an Uber driver), quickly put on all of the gear (no easy task unless one is very familiar and practiced with this kind of equipment), go through the school, shooting everyone in sight, then take off the body armor and tactical gear without being seen, and casually walk out of the school with the other students, without being recognized, blending with them and raising no suspicion by police officers as he walked away from the scene?

"Apparently, that is what we are expected to believe. What happened to all of the armor the shooter was wearing? Not a word has been said about it. The more plausible explanation is that Ms. Lippel saw a second shooter—someone professionally trained and equipped with sophisticated military and police tactical gear. Furthermore, it's difficult to believe that the teacher wouldn't know what an AR-15 rifle would look like. But military units carry a plethora of combat weapons that most civilians have never laid eyes on. That's a whole different subject, isn't it?

"It is more than curious that according to students and teachers at the school: 1. *the U.S. Secret Service conducted drills (plural) at the school, and 2. teachers and students had been told by police that they would be conducting active shooter drills at the school that very week and that they would be firing blanks during the exercises (many students and faculty members thought police had begun the drill when they heard the shots ring out);* and 3. according to one student's testimony, she actually walked out of the building with the alleged shooter Nikolas Cruz. Obviously, Cruz was not wearing police armor. The girl said *she heard shots coming from another part of the school at the same time that she was walking out with Cruz* and is certain there had to have been a second shooter.

"Another troubling question: since when does the Secret Service conduct drills at public schools in different states? What a coincidence that police had told the school to expect an active shooter drill at about the same time as the actual homicidal live shooting took place. I don't believe in coincidences when it comes to mass shootings. Isn't it convenient that the government is razing the entire Parkland school building—just like in Waco, the Twin Towers and the Murrah building in Oklahoma City etc.?[1] Destroy the building (crime scene) and you destroy the evidence, which is a crime" (end quote from Dr. Chuck Baldwin).

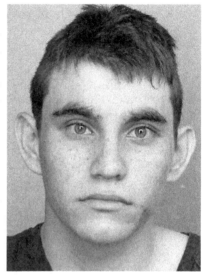

Banning "assault" guns has little or nothing to do with actually preventing mass murder sprees in America. The eighth-deadliest shooting in the U.S. was perpetrated by Charles Whitman at the University of Texas in 1966, killing 17 and wounding 31. Whitman used basic hunting rifles in the course of his massacre. He would have killed more people, but armed Texas civilians repeatedly shot back at him, pinning him down. Soon after the Parkland school massacre, a man shot and killed himself outside the White House in our nation's capitol. There would seem to be a connection between increasing homicidal psychosis among the American people and mass murders like Parkland which transmit a subtle, anxiety-producing hint of a conspiratorial role by a higher power.

---

[1] As of this writing (2021), the school building was closed but remained standing.

A guard with an "assault rifle" protects U.S. senators. Washington, D.C., March, 2021

The corporate media suppress the common sense fact that disarming the American people makes us more vulnerable to the psychotics our society produces and the killers "our" government itself dispatches.

As noted, dehumanizing violence to human beings inside the womb (60 million aborted children in the U.S. since Roe v. Wade), breeds similar violence outside of it, a reality the virtue-signalers will not acknowledge.

Furthermore, when politicians and the media call for a radical reduction of gun ownership in America, they're not referring to the guns they possess by special permit or hidden loopholes in the law; or the heavily armed guards that ringed Congress in early 2021, or the armed security people who shield Biden, Bill and Hillary and more billionaires than we can name. Deep State bureaucrats have a mandate to disarm Americans, while plutocrats, politicians, and lawyers with status or connections continue to have access to high powered weapons or elite guards licensed to carry them.

Gun control is a euphemism for disarming the common people, not the Overlords and the "connected." Their lives are viewed by the Cryptocracy as being worth more than ours. These would-be godlings of the ruling class will always be protected by gunmen who possess automatic or semi-automatic firearms, or even more advanced, exotic weaponry unknown to the public. *There is no gun control for the Overlords.* Their privileged position will not be altered when a "ban on assault rifles" specifically, or strict limits on firearms generally, are enacted in the name of "gun control."

Hoodwinked "progressives" don't know or don't wish to entertain the fact that so-called gun control is poor people control. In these schemes, the elite (or their guards) remain heavily armed, while the peasants are disarmed on the faulty supposition that rendering them nearly helpless renders madmen and criminals harmless. It's Plato's dual law system: one law for the putative higher-souled human beings and another for those designated as lower-souled.

Texas Church Shooting:
Congregant Fires Back, Stopping a Murderer

December 29, 2019—Jack Wilson, 71, of rural Hood County Texas, a member of the West Freeway Church of Christ in White Settlement, shot and killed Keith Kinnunen after Kinnunen opened fire on the congregation, murdering two Christians, Rich White, 67, of Westworth Village, and Tony Wallace, 64, of Fort Worth.

"The events at West Freeway Church of Christ put me in a position that I would hope no one would have to be in, but evil exists and I had to take out an active shooter in church," Mr. Wilson said.

Accompanied by gun-carrying bodyguards, billionaire Michael Bloomberg addressed the shooting at West Freeway Church of Christ during a speech in Montgomery, Alabama on New Year's Day, 2020:

"It may be true that someone in the congregation had his own gun and killed the person who murdered two other people, but it's the job of law enforcement to have guns and to decide when to shoot,' the former New York mayor said, adding, "You just do not want the average citizen carrying a gun in a crowded place."

Jack Wilson replied, "Mr. Bloomberg—had we operated by his standards or his wishes, the carnage would have been significantly greater....If Mr. Bloomberg would have his security detail turn their arms in and not guard him, he would be in the same situation as many American citizens are every day."

Manifestations of End-Time Burnout in the Alchemical Theater of Thanatos

In the wake of the mosque attack in March, 2019 in New Zealand by the "Knight Templar" Benton Tarrant, and in Poway, California in April, 2019 on a synagogue by adolescent John T. Earnest, we were asked why we didn't analyze them and accord them the investigative rigor that we have undertaken in other mass murders. The reason we did not is because of the transparency of these shootings. We seldom point out the obvious. Tarrant and Earnest were *patently* tools of the Cryptocracy.

The ISIS terrorists who massacred 321 mostly Christian Sri Lankans and wounded another 500 on Easter Sunday, 2019 are also under the direction of the Deep State, via what was Donald Trump's favored nation of Saudi Arabia. The theology of the ISIS mass murderers happens to be Salafist Wahhabism, the state religion of Saudi Arabia. The Saudis are Israeli allies. With that laurel there was no evil they perpetrated that would register in the Trump White House.

The U.S. Government Nurtures Enemies and then Organizes the American People to Fight Them

In May, 2015 Judicial Watch procured by means of a federal lawsuit, formerly classified official U.S. intelligence related to Syria. One of these documents, from President Obama's Defense Intelligence Agency dated August 12, 2012, "anticipates the rise of Islamic State" and "seems to suggest it would be a desirable development from the point of view" of those in the U.S. government "seeking regime change in Damascus."

In section 8c the Defense Intelligence Agency document looks forward to establishing in Syria a "principality" of the Islamic terror state of ISIS: "If the situation (in Syria) unravels there is the possibility of establishing a declared or undeclared Salafist principality in eastern Syria (Hasaka and DerZor) and this is exactly what the supporting powers to the opposition want, in order to isolate the Syrian regime."

Notice that in this document, which the government fought to avoid disclosing, American intelligence sounds no alarm about ISIS gaining a caliphate ("principality") in Syria. Observe too that it does not report that the Salafists (ISIS) will establish this principality, only that it's possible that it will be established. By whom? By the "supporting powers to the opposition" to Syrian President Bashir Assad. In other words, American "allies" Saudi Arabia and the United Arab Emirates, those two Sunni Salafist monarchies.

The United States government under Obama viewed ISIS and the al Qaeda proxy Jabhat al-Nusra, as useful auxiliaries in the drive for regime change in Syria, eliminating Israeli nemesis Assad, the protector of Syria's minority Christian community. *The U.S. viewed an ISIS takeover of northeastern Syria as a positive development.* The only nation that foiled the U.S. plan for the overthrow of the Christian-protecting Muslim leader by al-Qaeda and Islamic State terrorists was Putin's Russia, denounced ever since as the shameful and dastardly oppressor of Syria. This is as upside-down as Senator Bernie Sanders demanding the government keep its abortion laws off a woman's body, while at the same time asserting that the government has the absolute right to inject that body with a vaccination serum. The British elevated the House of Saud and its Wahhabbist theology to power on the Arabian peninsula. The United States has been the Saudis' chief enabler since World War II.

Daniel Lazare reports on the U.S. government's role in creating modern jihadism:

"Kosovo, where the United States joined forces with Saudi-backed jihadis in support of the secessionist movement of Hashim Thaçi; Chechnya, where leading neocons such as Richard Perle, Elliott Abrams, Kenneth Adelman, Midge Decter, Frank Gaffney, Michael Ledeen, and R. James Woolsey championed Saudi-backed Islamist rebels...the United States pronounces itself—*shocked!*—at the results, while pocketing the winnings. This is evident from a famous 1998 interview with Zbigniew Brzezinski, who, as Jimmy Carter's national security adviser, did as much as anyone to invent the modern phenomenon of Islamic jihad. Asked if he had any regrets, Brzezinski was unabashed:

"Regret what? That secret operation was an excellent idea. It had the effect of drawing the Russians into the Afghan trap, and you want me to regret it? The day that the Soviets officially crossed the border, I wrote to President Carter: We now have the opportunity of giving to the USSR its Vietnam war....What is most important to the history of the world? The Taliban or the collapse of the Soviet empire? Some stirred-up Muslims or the liberation of Central Europe and the end of the Cold War?' Or, as Graham Fuller, former deputy director of the CIA's National Council on Intelligence and later a RAND Corporation analyst, put it a year later: The policy of guiding the evolution of Islam and of helping them against our adversaries worked marvelously well in Afghanistan against the Red Army. The same doctrines can still be used to destabilize what remains of Russian power..." (end quote from Brzezinski). Lazare continues:

"...the need to prosecute the so-called 'War on Terror,' was never about terrorism per se, but about terrorism unsanctioned by the United States. The goal was to arrange for jihadis only to strike at targets jointly approved by Washington and Riyadh (the capital of Saudi Arabia)...Eastern Syria...became part of the Caliphate declared by ISIS—the recipient of 'clandestine financial and logistic support' from both Saudi Arabia and Qatar, according to no less an authority than Hillary Clinton— in June 2014.

"...As part of its alliance with the Saudis, the United States encouraged the growth not only of jihad but of Wahhabism in general...how could Washington object when the kingdom vastly expanded its missionary effort in 1979, spending anywhere from $75 billion to $100 billion to spread the word? King Fahd, who ruled from 1982 to 2005, bragged about all the religious and educational facilities he built in non-Muslim lands—200 Islamic colleges, 210 Islamic centers, 1,500 mosques, 2,000 schools for Muslim children, etc." [1]

These "King Fahd Centers" produce the suicide bombers who plague the world and target enemies of the Israelis such as the Christian communities of the Third World (Syria, Egypt, Sri Lanka), as well as Shiites in Lebanon, Pakistan and of course, Iran.

Benton Tarrant's profile as a Manchurian Candidate is a common one on the "racist Right"

The same profile of Earnest, the 19-year-old synagogue shooter in California in April, 2019 was exhibited by some of the "white nationalist" marchers in Charlottesville in August, 2017: single white men alienated from women, marriage and the family, who despise the Old Testament and very likely the New, and who identify either with Social Darwinist scientism, or certain memes of the western occult. Men fitting that profile are targets for recruitment by Deep State actors. The prototype is Anders Breivik, the Norwegian Freemason and partisan of Israeli Zionism who murdered dozens of his fellow Norwegians *while they were holding a convention devoted to protesting and highlighting Israeli war crimes in Palestine.* This context is often omitted. For example, Breivik has been transformed into a neo-Nazi by the *New York Times.* His crimes were indeed Nazi-like, but his ideology was masonic-Zionist.

After Tarrant struck in New Zealand, by way of providing background, the *Times* published a photo of Breivik giving the Nazi salute and described him as the inspiration for white racist terrorism around the globe. A photo of him attired in his masonic regalia was not published. *What kind of white racist terrorist murders only Nordic whites on behalf of the Israeli state?*

In the midst of these massacres, Acura automobiles were being marketed in American television commercials broadcast

---

[1] Daniel Lazare, "How The US-Saudi Marriage Gave Birth to Jihad," *Swarajya* magazine, Nov 6, 2017

during the "March Madness" college basketball playoffs, using a soundtrack consisting of an excerpt from the famous rock-and-roll song, "Sympathy for the Devil." Acura chose the devil tune presumably to highlight the otherworldliness and devil-may-care attitude of its latest automobile, the RDX. In 2019 invoking Satan to endorse your SUV was a successful marketing strategy. It remains so.

The trend is not confined to any one pocket of the political spectrum. Evangelical Christians protest abortion but they have no problem with Israelis killing Palestinian children after they emerge from the womb. Alabama is in the "buckle of the Bible belt" and opposes abortion and rights for homosexuals. Yet it has one of the most God-forsaken prison-systems in the U.S.A., where rape is regarded (off-the-record) as one of the suitable punishments for writing a bad check or stealing a car. Upstate Idaho is one of the most heavily churched regions in the nation yet the legislature allows for unconscionable usury rates approaching 500% on loans.

In 2001 in *Secret Societies and Psychological Warfare* we foresaw the ascendance of an American man and woman so heavily processed, neutered and psychologically enthralled that they would be equivalent to masonic initiates. Large swathes of white America are now, in masonic parlance, "on the level."

What is the purpose of pointing out the extent of occult symbolism and Twilight language in America, when in 2021 these things are in the open and utilized in television commercials for automobiles and insurance, without concealment? America consists of a population of virtual masonic initiates immersed in the occult. From 2001 to 2021 is a long time in the high speed zone. Much innocence has been lost, while much knowledge of the self-indicting and obligating kind, has been acquired. *Americans reside in a Twilight Zone daily existence where blatant occult cues and indoctrination are so profuse they're shrugged off as unremarkable.* Attempting to expose what is already in front of our eyes becomes an exercise in "camp" (failed seriousness). The futility serves a clown-like function within The Process itself.

We inhabit an open-air occult laboratory. Our children go to the movies and see witches ("Harry Potter") doing good deeds, and a demon ("Hellboy") accomplishing heroic feats of benevolence. At the opening Mass of the Synod on Youth in 2018, Pope Francis carried a staff in the form of a 'stang,' an object used in occult rituals.

The role of False Prophesies in Contributing to Mind Control and End-Time Burnout

One source of the current state of the process is to be found in relentless false prophesying of "The End."

The first significant End of the World falsehood in the U.S. was by William Miller in 1844. The second was mounted by the Jehovah's Witnesses organization, predicting throughout most of the 20th century that "Millions now living will never die," and "Confidence in the Creator's promise of a peaceful and secure new world before the generation that saw the events of 1914 passes away." What had been the central prophecy of the Jehovah's Witnesses for decades was quietly dropped in 1995 when the people alive in 1914 were increasingly dying off with each passing year. More recently we have witnessed:

• 1971: *The Population Bomb* sells more than two million copies and goes through twenty reprints. Prof. Paul Ehrlich's prediction: "The battle to feed all of humanity is over. And humanity has lost....Hundreds of millions of people will starve to death." In 1968, in the first edition of his book, Ehrlich predicted, "Unless humanity cuts down its numbers—*soon*—all of us will face mass starvation on a dying planet."

• The Chastisement: a prophecy circulated among Catholics of three days of darkness when half of humanity will perish.

• The Rapture (*Left Behind* according to Tim LaHaye).

•Comet Hale-Bopp apocalypse that was set for Spring, 1997.

•Gary North's Y2K end-of-civilization-as-we-know-it of 1999.

• Harold Camping's Armageddon prophecy for 2011.

- The Mayan apocalypse predicted for December, 2012.

•The Climate Apocalypse" forecast for 2031 according to Rep. Alexandria Ocasio-Cortez (D-NY), and seconded by Greta Thunberg. Ocasio-Cortez stated on January 22, 2019: "The world is going to end in twelve years if we don't address climate change."

There is something about the nuclear age and the prospect of "instant extinction" that has produced a madness that sets dates, promotes predictions and builds expectations which, when they are not fulfilled, slowly rot people in mind and spirit. After the prophecy fails, they become enervated and barely have energy to act for more than a limited period of time. While the false prophecy remains current they have a schedule and they expect that within the schedule which they impose on history, it will "All come to a shattering climax never before seen!" Anticipation of the arrival of this unprecedented event is their psychological motivation—not truth or God—but a spine-tingling, hair-raising thrill to end all thrills.

In addition to the spectacular, big-ticket false prophecies, there is a sustained monthly chatter concerning this or that hurtling asteroid, flood, mass murder or hurricane which will be a supposed definitive sign that, "The End is Near." When people cry wolf and wolf tickets are sold, and the wolf doesn't appear, what is the effect on the human mind? The "sky-is-falling" prophets seldom study this particular constituent factor from the laboratory of human conditioning, and how it is that their false prophesies contribute to mind control and occult hegemony.

Every jolt of the month is labeled an extraordinary, fraught-with-harrowing-significance, "seismic shock." The insinuation is always that a massive upheaval is imminently careening toward us. Many of these lesser prophecies turn out to be not even close to the hyped expectations by which they were seeded; or they're completely untrue.

When there is a surfeit of these false alarms, people attuned to gaining knowledge about criminal conspiracies learn nothing. Instead, they become numb, cynical and exhausted—exactly where the Cryptocracy wants them. Afterward they can't be roused when a genuine emergency arises. This is the service which some conspiracy theorists provide to the Cryptocracy.

Short-sighted persons fail to observe the cyclical nature of history. The Book of Revelation is not the completion of a linear history. It is an *intervention in the cycles of history and as such its ultimate fulfillment is outside of time.*

We who should take the lead in guiding the world, look around at its enormous challenges and shrink into a crippled, stunted claustrophobia, of which "The End Times" is one symptom of our shrunken souls. Yes, Judgment Day and the End are coming, perhaps tomorrow, or 500 years from now. A personal terminus is coming for all of us in the grave, and we never know when. Young, healthy people die every day. It could be any one of us. Should we succumb to nervous apprehension and despair in view of this fact of daily life?

Gauging the Extent of our Hypnotic State

The American people look around. They see a demon named Hellboy idolized on megaplex 3-D movie screens and they hear "Sympathy for the Devil" employed to sell new cars—and yet life goes on. The sky does not belch flames. We have our jobs, the pawns reason. The shopping malls are still open. We go out for pizza. The grass is still green. The world is still here. *Somebody lied to us.*

Guess who is apportioned the blame for the lie? *The dissidents who reveal the evil of the System, the corruption of the courts, the Money Power's occupation of the government.* In the Cryptocracy's human behavior laboratory we are tarred with the stigma of the false-prophet conspiracy theorists, even when we are not implicated.

The American *goyim* have a subconscious sense that, Satanic or not, for all its foibles and imperfections, the System in America will persevere and continue to deliver the wonders of technology and many aspects of "the good life."

We inhabit a *post*-"Secret Societies and Psychological Warfare" world. 2021 is aftermath. *What this writer presented at the 2001 gateway to the "Black Jack" century 21 seemed like high strangeness at the time. Now it is the "new normal."*

It is at this juncture that we might wish to pause and place these deeply troubling developments in accurate historical perspective. The linear view of history perceives these abominations as a progression of ever more extreme phenomenon, inevitably culminating in an apocalyptic climax from which there will be no return. The historian has a different viewpoint. He sees the Roman empire dissolving into unimaginable chaos and degeneracy, yet the decaying corpse fertilizes a rebirth of life and law, and the love of God.

Turning to medieval Europe we know the people experienced a "Black death" (bubonic plague) which eliminated fully one-third of the population, yet it was the survivors who constructed the edifices that to this day make our hearts soar, from the burned but still standing Notre Dame Cathedral in Paris, to York Minster in the north of England, and many more of these astonishing and ennobling wonders of architecture.

Furthermore, some of the assaults upon us in the 21st century are not necessarily on our subconscious twilight mind, but on common sense itself: blatant, in-your-face lunacy. What needs to be decoded? Everything is not occult. If it were, then nothing would be.

In "Sympathy for the Devil," Lucifer says, "I shouted out, 'Who Killed the Kennedys?'—when after all it was you and me." Observe the playbook: if everyone killed the president and his brother then no one did.

The Internet can be a force for good or evil. At present, for a majority, immersion in the Internet has unleashed the power of distraction. Information is *not* power. It is the ability to *detect fraud* that empowers us. People flit from theory to theory, from cause to cause and leader to leader; from web page to podcast to video, lingering for moments or hours and then jumping to the next mesmerizing web page or video. Their distraction has scattered and confused them. They are spectators more than doers, and have difficulty discerning worthy leaders and genuine facts from fools and deception.

While the scientific consensus is still unclear, it appears that "surfing the Internet" daily for hours on end interferes with the brain's ability to read deeply. The great books are not being studied and digested cover to cover, as they once were. People have been hoaxed into thinking that "Almost everything I want to know is online." Even if that were true, the act of consuming it online seems to hinder our brain's capacity for deep thought and analysis.

The bellwether is the eerie paralysis setting in. "The best lack all conviction while the worst are filled with passionate intensity." Many of the former have succumbed to comprising an audience whose *raison d'etre* is to "see what happens next." The corroding enchantment of the "Society of the Spectacle" is upon them.

Authentic Christians are at radical variance with the ways of the god of this world. Followers of the Jesus of the Bible are profoundly counter-cultural. For those believers Spectacular Society does not attract, it disenchants.

Listening to a reading of John Bunyan's *Pilgrim's Progress*, or reading the text, we comprehend the beauty and the splendor of navigating a parallel that is the inverse of the processed majority. We do this not out of a Pharisaic superiority. Penetrating the glamor of this system of things with the power of the disenchanting grace of Jesus Christ, is to see our own transgressions first, after which we perceive the operating engineer behind the shimmering curtain that is Oz in the 21st century.

The "Joker" [movie 2019]
Mental Illness and Misfortune in the U.S.A.

"Perhaps the bleakest assertion of 'Joker,' is the one that's hardest to disprove: that the ghastly world (the Joker) inhabits, and by extension ours, is the one we deserve." — John Wenzel

Early in 2019 we were asked to write an introduction to a new book examining occult symbolism in America. We declined. In our judgment the author was mistaking mundane phenomena for occult conspiracy. He didn't see that if everything is occult then nothing is. The inability to make the distinction is reflected in the reception that the 2019 "Joker" movie has received from some researchers who attempt to study the intersection of the arcane and the Cryptocracy in popular media.

These researchers, along with some celebrity movie critics, decided that Warner Brothers and Village Roadshow had created a sequel to Heath Ledger's unrelievedly evil Joker character in Christopher Nolan's 2008 film, "The Dark Knight." Without having seen the 2019 "Joker" movie, we initially presumed that it might be another recruiting piece for inspiring further mass murders. Heath Ledger's Joker character may have possibly inspired or contributed to a June 8, 2014 murder spree by 22-year-old LaFayette, Indiana native Amanda Miller and her 31-year-old husband, Jerad.

Jerad Miller had been known to dress as the Batman character, Joker. His wife would sometimes portray "Harley Quinn." While residing in Las Vegas, they shot to death two police officers and a good samaritan who attempted to stop them.

Jerad and Amanda entered iCiCi's Pizza on June 8, 2014, shouting, "This is the start of a revolution!" and then shot and killed Alyn Beck, 42, and Igor Soldo, 32, police officers who were having lunch. The killers stole the officers' ammunition and weapons and placed a swastika on one corpse and an American Revolutionary type of "Gadsden flag," depicting a snake and the words "Don't Tread on Me," on the other.

Jerad and Amanḍa Miller

Afterward, they headed to a Las Vegas-area Wal Mart where they waved their guns and spouted their trademark slogan, 'The revolution's begun!"

Joseph Robert Wilcox, 31, a Wal Mart customer, drew his concealed handgun in an attempt to disarm Jerad Miller, but was shot from behind by Amanda. Mr. Wilcox died at the scene.

Police arrived and engaged the couple in an exchange of gun fire. Both the Millers were hit and seriously wounded. Amanda shot her husband (accounts differ, with some reports saying he died of wounds inflicted by the police, rather than her). She allegedly shot herself in the head.

The media claimed investigators were looking into "possible links" between the killer couple and Right wing groups which had defended rancher Cliven Bundy's property in Nevada, in a tense confrontation that month with Federal agents. Some reports indicate that the Millers were present at the stand-off and were asked to leave by the Bundys, due to the intemperate rhetoric and violence they were espousing at the time, which reminded some of agent provocateurs or Manchurian candidates. The Millers' persona online was that of "militia patriots," but they behaved more like heavily programmed, or demon-possessed individuals.

At age 28 actor Heath Ledger died tragically of a drug overdose in the year of the release of "The Dark Knight."

The Joker character he portrayed is utterly merciless and relentlessly sadistic, someone who kills even his own comrades and partners. There is no rationale for his violence. It is purely demonic, the personification of what William Butler Yeats termed the "blood red tide" which drowns "the ceremony of innocence." [1]

Many of the actual mass shootings in America, whether inspired by Hollywood or not, have been in line with the Joker's violence in "The Dark Knight"—that of cold-blooded, anarchistic mega-atrocities against innocent persons, including school children, exhibiting a diabolically heinous disregard for human life.

The "Joker" movie of October, 2019 however, is something else altogether. It is disenchanting and anti-occult. The protagonist in "Joker" is Arthur Fleck, played by Joaquin Phoenix as a mentally disturbed man whose every benevolent act is misunderstood. He attempts to overcome his affliction, but the circumstances of his life and chosen occupation (clowning and standup comedy) conspire to obstruct his intentions.

There is no depiction of "random mass shooting" in this "Joker" movie. The only occasion when multiple people are shot is in a scene in which Arthur is brutally assaulted by three intoxicated executives in suits, on a subway train. The beating they administered was serious enough to paralyze or kill him,

---

[1] Another fictional character of that description in American pop culture is "Trevor Philips," a perverted, homicidal anti-hero in the "Grand Theft Auto" video game series. After 14-year-old Eldon Samuel shot and killed his father and 13-year-old autistic brother in Coeur d'Alene, Idaho in 2014, he informed police during his interrogation that "Trevor Philips" was his role mode. The media noted his statement and then dropped it without further investigation or editorial comment. Depraved video games which psychologically imprint impressionable players by simulating extreme violence and glorifying nihilism, are a multiple-billion dollar industry that seems to be invulnerable to censorship or moderation. The responsibility of these "games," along with prescription psychiatric medications, in contributing to a state of mind that leads to "senseless shooting massacres" is minimized by the corporate media.

had it continued. It does not continue because Arthur saves his own life by drawing his revolver and shooting all of his attackers. Only because he is wearing clown makeup (as part of his employment), do the media (in the movie) exploit the incident and sensationalize the shooter as a clown-killer who murderes innocent bystanders.

Some mass shooters pen suspiciously eloquent "manifestos" somehow timed precisely for release online, either shortly before or during the execution of their crimes. Supposedly this was true of Patrick Crusius.

El Paso *Cielo*

That was alleged to be the case with the August 3, 2019 massacre at a Wal-Mart in El Paso, Texas. The alleged El Paso killer is supposed to have issued a well-crafted "racist manifesto" shortly before his anti-immigrant murder spree. We have not seen any extensive reporting on the fact that the supposed Mexican-detesting shooter, Patrick Crusius, was himself of Mexican descent on his mother's side.

Our colleague Tim contributes the following insights concerning the symbolism of the El Paso slaughter:

"If you take the address listed on the Internet for Patrick Crusius' mother's house and plug it into a driving distance calculator to the Cielo Vista mall (site of the murders) in El Paso, you get three different routes ranging from 657 miles to 668 miles—the Cryptocracy doesn't always need things to be exact. And, if you take the numbers reported in various news stories connecting the August 4 Dayton, Ohio shooting deaths of nine people, with the one in El Paso, we're told that, 'Dayton is roughly 1500 miles from El Paso…'

"Taking the number reported for the distance from Crusius' Allen, Texas residence to El Paso — 600 miles — and the 1500 miles from El Paso to Dayton, we get 2100. Crusius himself is 21 years old. Michael Hoffman has written about the 21st century as the 'gateway' to that great game of metaphysical 'Black Jack" and, as luck would have it, the alleged shooter in Dayton is one Connor Betts—are all bets off at this point?

"The name, 'El Paso' denotes 'The Passage.' If you look at a map for Cielo Vista mall, you'll see that it is bound by 'Gateway Boulevard.'

"Cielo' means 'heaven' or 'sky.' So, we have a 21 year old shooter of Hispanic descent that drives roughly 666 miles to 'The Passageway' to conduct a race war at the 'heaven' mall along the 'gateway' to...Dayton?

"Why Dayton? In Dayton the shooting that was perpetrated supposedly by Connor 'all Betts are off,' was near Ned Peppers[2] Bar, bounded by Gates Street on one side, by Pine on another side (pine box anyone?), and 5th Street in the back—does the law of fives strike a discord?

"Cielo Drive has connections to the fable of Charles Manson's Helter Skelter race war that supposedly was the motivation for his gang having killed Sharon Tate and others at 10050 Cielo Drive in the City of the Angels. August marked the 50 year anniversary of the crime. There is a movie theater at Cielo Vista Mall in El Paso. The movie playing there during the massacre was Quentin Tarantino's paean to the legend of the Manson murders ('Once Upon a Time in Hollywood'). What are the odds of that?

"A supposed white supremacist opens fire at the Cielo Vista in Texas to initiate a race war. Just down the way from his shootings, a movie is playing about 50-year-old ritual murders on Cielo Drive, which supposedly were intended to ignite a race war. One of the killers was named 'Tex.'"[3]

In the 2019 "Joker" film, lead character Arthur Fleck's only "manifesto" is his battered notebook filled with crossed-out, barely legible scrawls and sentence fragments which he reads aloud at a dive that's hosting an Open Mike night. It's as if the film-makers were mocking the media's cooperation with the "manifesto" aspect of the Cryptocracy's surreal accounts of real-life shooters.

---

[2] "Lucky Ned Pepper" was a killer outlaw character in the 2010 remake of the western movie, "True Grit."

[3] We have seen no compelling evidence that Charles Manson ordered the Tate or LaBianca killings. Tex Watson and Susan "Sadie" Atkins may have been the prime movers. Manson did not mount a defense at his trial, succumbing to a role as jester and scapegoat. He may however, have been guilty or at least complicit in the murders of ranch foreman Donald "Shorty" Shea and musician Gary Hinman. William N. Grimstad in his recorded "Sirius Rising" lectures, pondered a possible connection between the Apollo Moon Flight and the mysterious, symbol-laden "Manson" murders on Cielo Drive, which followed less than 3 weeks later. He entertained the possibility that the killings might have been some sort of ritual expiation for the "defilement" of Luna with the astronauts' boot tracks and rubbish, which if true, would perhaps imply that higher-ups orchestrated the ceremonial killings, beyond "Charlie, Sadie" or "Tex."

Eventually Arthur discovers a parlous act of disloyalty. He learns that in his past he was repeatedly brutalized with the connivance of his mother, who up to that point, he cherished and trusted implicitly, and who persuaded him of the veracity of her tale of his exalted patrimony, via his alleged true father, Gotham socialite Thomas Wayne. With the realization that his mother betrayed and lied to him, Arthur's psychological state deteriorates, along with what is left of his composure.

The handgun he wields was forced on him by a manipulative and sinister co-worker. In a key scene, he takes revenge on the co-worker while mercifully sparing the life of another with the statement, "You were the only one who was good to me."

If this had been a film in the "Dark Knight" Batman mold, Arthur would have committed a grotesquely depraved act and gone ahead and shot the person who had been good to him. The mercy he dispenses is a significant marker separating him from the character portrayed by the late Heath Ledger, as well real life gunmen who have made the news in remorseless massacres bearing distressing similarities to the unrelievedly evil Joker character as depicted in the "Dark Knight" movie.

"Murray Franklin," the Johnny Carson-type evening television host in the 2019 film, is portrayed by Robert De Niro. The Franklin character wears the mask of 1970s pop culture respectability, yet is exploiting Arthur for callous audience amusement, as Hop Frog was exploited in Edgar Allan Poe's retributive story of that name. Like Hop Frog, Arthur strikes back, and does so on national television. It is at this juncture that we see director Todd Phillips' "Joker" stepping outside the occult clown-shooter genre and holding a mirror up to our society, as Oliver Stone did in "Natural Born Killers," a film which depicted the corporate media as complicit in the violence of the feral pair of shooters at the center of the action.

Phoenix portrays Fleck (rhymes with Speck, as in Richard)—who will morph into "Joker" toward the end of the movie—as an emaciated, chain-smoking mental patient (eerily resembling in appearance the real life French poète maudit and theatre-of-cruelty theorist Antonin Artaud).

Arthur Fleck, in spite of his mental anguish, is attempting to recover his humanity in the midst of inhuman circumstances. There is little that is occult here. Fleck is someone Artaud might have termed, "The man suicided by society." This is not to negate anyone's responsibilities for their actions, or to grant a homicidal prerogative to the mentally ill. Life in the American big city "Gotham" of the 1970s, and more so today, was a dehumanizing and degrading experience for the poor and disadvantaged.

By the conclusion of the movie, a mob inspired by a degenerate urban youth culture that Fleck did not create, has made him a sardonic hero, "Joker."

In these scenes Joaquin Phoenix's character becomes markedly more youthful underneath a now well-tailored, suit-and-tie clown attire and expertly-applied makeup. Much of the agony in his now more youthful countenance has vanished.

The blood he has shed and the notoriety he has gained seems to strip away years of age and grief as he dances a choreography that celebrates his transformation from a troubled human struggling to do well and be understood, into a figure of almost superhuman agency and potency, having managed to "succeed" the American Way, by gaining entrance to society's demented pop culture celebrity circus, whose suit-and-tie clown grandees, like De Niro's Murray Franklin, are more malevolent than the Joker.

The movie ends with a vaguely unsettling Charlie Chaplinesque slaptick chase in the halls of a mental hospital — as if to say, it's all grist for the entertainment mill.

Production values are high. Cinematography, acting, sets and costumes are all accomplished and well staged. The soundtrack by Icelandic composer Hildur Guðnadóttir jabs the audience with a relentlessly propulsive gloom, transmitting a melancholy that is a sonic migraine for dead souls.

Unlike the second installment in Christopher Nolan's Batman movies, this 2019 Joker origin story, is not a movie that worsens our collective mental health, or immerses us in the shadowy Twilight Language of the Cryptocracy. Rather, it is a toxicology report on the effects of fermentation in the pernicious brine that is "life in the American cosmopolis."

It is art and has validity on that basis, without didactically messaging a remedy. It is a cinematic document about one rejected and scorned person from our nation's recent past, a kind of everyman who could be any one of us if we were so unlucky. It necessarily foreshadows our future, should America choose to continue on its grossly materialistic, fantastically cruel (mass abortionist), Christ-less path. [4]

To mistake this sobering reflection on the decayed state of our nation, with a cryptogram from the Deep State, would be a significant failure of perception, intuition and detection.

Satanic Pederast Sex Rings in Legend and Reality

One iconic scene in the 2019 "Joker" movie shows a troubled man transformed into the Joker character as he dances on a set of outdoor stairs, to a tune by British rock musician Paul Gadd, whose stage name was "Gary Glitter." Gadd/Glitter's "Rock and Roll (Part 2)" was a 1972 hit tune which was broadcast in sports stadiums as an anthem (popularly known as "The Hey! Song"). It can be heard on the soundtrack of at least two Hollywood movies, "The Replacements," and "Meet the Fockers" (starring Robert De Niro).

In October, 2012 evidence emerged in Britain that Glitter had been part of Sir James "Jimmy" Savile's child sex ring. The now elderly Glitter is in prison serving a sentence of 16 years after conviction on four counts of indecent assault and one count of having sex with a girl under 13. He was first jailed in 1999 when he admitted to possessing images of child pornography. He has been accused of dozens of acts of molestation in Asian countries. In 2008 Glitter finished serving nearly three years in a Vietnamese prison for molesting two children. [5]

The Sex Ring Master and the Queen

Savile (1926-2011) was a demonic child molestor. The Queen of England awarded him the Order of the British Empire in 1971. She knighted this ghoul in 1990. For decades Savile supplied children to elite members of British society for sexual exploitation. We're expected to believe that during Savile's lifetime neither the British monarch nor her son Charles, the

---

[4] "Christ-less" here is a reference to both the barbaric secular culture which denies human rights to unborn human beings, as well as the proliferation of the institutions of Churchianity, those temples of artificial contraception, usury, and accommodation with the military-industrial state, for the sanctification of *Homo economicus.*

[5] *New York Times,* Aug. 21, 2008, p. E5.

Prince of Wales, never once received intelligence from the Crown's MI5 domestic spy service or the Metropolitan Police concerning his heinous crimes.

The Sex Ring Master and the Prince

In 1984 Savile was accepted as a member of the Athenaeum, a high society gentlemen's club in London's Pall Mall, after being proposed by "Catholic" Cardinal Basil Hume. Another clerical member of Savile's pederast ring was the Anglican Bishop of Gloucester, the Rt. Rev. Peter Bell, who was deeply connected to the royal family including Queen Elizabeth and Prince Charles, heir to the British throne. [6] During this time Savile was known to perform necrophliac acts on corpses and wore rings fashioned from glass eyes taken from the dead.[7]

Sir James Savile met Prince Charles through "mutual charity interests." The Prince reportedly conveyed gifts to Savile on his 80th birthday, along with an enigmatic note reading, *"Nobody will ever know what you have done for this country, Jimmy. This is to go some way in thanking you for that."*

The Sex Ring Master and the Prime Minister

Savile was also a close friend of the "upright conservative" British Prime Minister Margaret Thatcher: "Correspondence showing the depth of the friendship between Sir Jimmy Savile and former Prime Minister Margaret Thatcher is unveiled today in a secret Downing Street file that has been *heavily redacted by civil servants* following revelations about sexual abuse by the late entertainer. The 21-page dossier released under the 30-year rule by the National Archives shows Savile's access to the highest echelons of British society." [8]

"Thatcher and Savile met quite often...*Some papers and sections of the government file on Thatcher's relations with Savile remain withheld from public scrutiny for another 10 years.*" Prime Minister Thatcher is suspected of having

---

[6] "Jimmy Savile and Prince Charles' very close friendship with sex abuse bishop Peter Ball" (*Daily Mail*, October 8, 2015).

[7] "Revealed: The glass eye Jimmy Savile stole from a corpse and made into a necklace that he wore on final Top of the Pops - where he also groped a child" (*Daily Mail*, June 27, 2014)

[8] Owen Bowcott, "Savile's Extraordinary Access to Thatcher detailed in secret files," *The Guardian* (UK), December 27, 2012; emphasis supplied.

concealed a child-rape ring operating among high officials of the British government. [9]

Gary Glitter (left) and Sir Jimmy Savile

In 2017, Nico Hines, London editor of the "Daily Beast" blog (thedailybeast.com), reported as follows:

Don Hale, "...a newspaper editor was handed startling evidence that Britain's top law enforcement official knew there was a VIP pedophile network in Westminster, at the heart of the British government....

"Leon Brittan, Margaret Thatcher's Home Secretary, was fully aware of a pedophile network that included top politicians...the following morning, police officers from the counter-terror and intelligence unit known as Special Branch burst into the newspaper office, seized the material and threatened to have Hale arrested if he ever reported what had been found...Brittan, a protégé of Prime Minister Margaret

---

[9] Terrence McCoy, "A 'big political cover-up' of 1980s pedophile-ring in U.K. Parliament?,"*Washington Post*, July 7, 2014.

Thatcher, had been promoted to Home Secretary at the age of 43, making him (among) the youngest person(s) to preside over Britain's domestic law enforcement and national security apparatus...

"...allegations included in the Home Office papers that about 16 Members of Parliament and members of the House of Lords, and 30 high-profile figures from the Church of England, private schools, and big business, were members of, and advocates for, the 'Paedophile Information Exchange.' The shadowy group, which operated partly in the open, campaigned for the age of consent to be abolished and incest to be legalized.

"...There is growing evidence that MI5 and MI6, Britain's security services, repeatedly blocked investigations...

"The longtime deputy director of MI6, and former High Commissioner in Canada, Peter Hayman, was himself allegedly a pedophile, and was ultimately named as such in parliament by Geoffrey Dickens. Hayman had been caught with explicit material in 1978 but no charge was brought.

"Secret files discovered at the National Archives this year revealed that the attorney general at the time believed it wasn't in the public interest for Hayman to be prosecuted.

"Prime Minister Thatcher ordered his depravity to be concealed from the public. Thatcher must also have known about the allegations against her Home Secretary, Leon Brittan...

"Another of her most trusted lieutenants, Sir Peter Morrison, had also abused underage boys. She appointed Morrison to run her 1990 re-election campaign, regardless." [10]

"Maggie" Thatcher is a heroine to British Tories and America's "Reagan conservatives." Her legacy was enshrined in an adoring 2011 Hollywood film, "The Iron Lady," for which Meryl Streep won an Academy Award. [11]

Beginning as early as 1955, and throughout his lifelong career as a rapist of hundreds of young people, heading a ring that supplied them to highest rank of the British government,

---

[10] "How Thatcher's Government Covered Up a VIP Pedophile Ring," thedailybeast.com Also see: "A 'big political cover-up' of 1980s pedophile-ring in U.K. Parliament?" *Washington Post*, July 7, 2014.

[11] "Meryl Streep praises Margaret Thatcher as 'figure of awe,'" *The Guardian* (UK), April 9, 2013.

aristocracy and society, *Savile enjoyed total immunity from police arrest, Crown prosecution, and imprisonment.* Sex crimes were committed by Savile on at least 450 persons (328 being minors at the time) across England and Scotland, and also in Jersey, *for six decades.* [12] In 2013 Britain's National Society for the Prevention of Cruelty to Children described Savile as one of the most prolific sex offenders in its 129-year history of investigating molestation. [13]

He died a multi-millionaire, respected and honored; the favorite of the queen, the future king, the prime minister and countless accomplices and enablers among the police, intelligence agencies, parliament and the press. [14]

In 2009, in a taped interview with his biographer, Savile defended Gary Glitter, convicted in 1999 of possession of child pornography, who he described as a celebrity being vilified for watching: "...dodgy films...It were for his own gratification. Whether it was right or wrong is up to him as a person... they (those who possess child pornography) didn't do anything wrong but they are then demonized.' The interview was not published at the time, and the recording was not released until after Savile's death." [15]

Child sex rings operating among the "best circles" of society, including governments and their intelligence agencies, are sign posts pointing to the existence of extraordinary malice in high places. Child molestation rings operating at elite levels of government and entertainment are an explosive reality that can (and should) detonate the people's faith in the ruling class. The Right wing is often as guilty as the Left in these crimes.

---

[12] "Giving Victims a Voice," (2013).
lib.latrobe.edu.au/research/ageofinquiry/biogs/E000070b.htm

[13] "Jimmy Savile spent 'every waking minute' thinking about abusing boys and girls." The Daily Telegraph, January 11, 2013. "Jimmy Savile abused boy aged eight and dying child: decades of abuse revealed," *London Evening Standard,* January 11, 2013. "Jimmy Savile abused children at 14 hospitals across six decades – report," *The Guardian,* January 11, 2013.

[14] As far back as 1978, punk-rocker John Lydon ("Johnny Rotten") did an interview with the BBC radio service, during which he accused Savile of being "into all sorts of seediness. We all know about it but we're not allowed to talk about it." Speaking in 2015 to journalist Piers Morgan, Lydon said: "I'm very, very bitter that the likes of Savile and the rest of them were allowed to continue. I did my bit, I said what I had to. But they didn't air that. I found myself banned from BBC radio for quite a while."

[15] "Jimmy Savile claimed paedophile Gary Glitter 'did nothing wrong" (*Daily Telegraph* [UK], Oct. 1, 2012).

Any sustained examination of the life of Gary Glitter turns up the name of Sir James Savile. From there, one overturns one rock after another concealing venomous snakes who our civilization venerates as the worthiest and most respectable people among us: monarchs, prime ministers, presidents and Hollywood moguls. The notoriety of pederasty rings led by people in power waxes and wanes. Some of this is due to the Cryptocracy planting in Right wing circles false accounts of pederasty rings mixed with half-truths, and then, through this calculated misdirection, infiltrating "useful idiot" conspiracy theorist movements so as to induce them to cry wolf and discredit the existence of the actual operations with flimsy accusations which appear in the media as opera bouffe. [16]

Cass R. Sunstein, one of the Cryptocracy's leading counter-intelligence and behavior modification specialists, co-authored a Revelation of the Method manifesto stating:

"Because those who hold conspiracy theories typically suffer from a 'crippled epistemology'...the best response consists in *cognitive infiltration* of extremist groups...our main policy idea is that *government should engage in cognitive infiltration of the groups that produce conspiracy theories.*" [17]

QAnon and the Republican nincompoops who allegedly laid the groundwork for the January, 2021 assault on the Capitol, and the sabotage (by instilling voter apathy among Republicans), allegedly by L. Lin Wood and others, of the U.S. Senate run-off in Georgia, fit the profile of groups and individuals cognitively infiltrated by the Sunstein control stratagem of the Cryptocracy. Online, we estimate that more than half of the conspiracy theorists, particularly those who put forth dates and times for catastrophes and upheavals that don't take place, and who advocate violence or hatred, are persons processed by *cognitive infiltration*.

Mr. Sunstein is a Harvard Law professor and former official in the administration of Barack Obama, having served as President Obama's Director of the White House Office of Information. Sunstein's specialty is psychological warfare contra populist and traditional Christian leaders and

---

[16] rollingstone.com/feature/anatomy-of-a-fake-news-scandal-125877/

[17] Cass R. Sunstein & Adrian Vermeule, "Conspiracy Theories" (John M. Olin Program in Law and Economics Working Paper no. 387 [2008], Coase-Sandor Institute, University of Chicago Law School); emphasis supplied.

organizations. In 2020, the World Health Organization appointed him chairman of its technical advisory group on "Behavioral Insights." [18]

Prof. Sunstein is married to Samantha Power, Professor of Public Policy at Harvard and former U.S. Ambassador to the United Nations under Obama. In 2021 President Biden appointed the aptly named Power as Administrator of the United States Agency for International Development, a government bureaucracy which often serves as a front for C.I.A. operations.

How do unpunished atrocities against children by our society's exalted paragons of virtue, fame, power and wealth, fade from our collective memory? It is a fact of our media-saturated lives that we often suffer from attention deficit, as well as compassion fatigue, and what alarmed us yesterday is mostly down the memory hole today, despite the appalling consequences of this amnesia.

The Crown of England, captured by the occult in the sixteenth century, has been invulnerable to revolutionary overthrow, with one exception—the victory of Republican forces under Oliver Cromwell, which led to the trial and execution of King Charles I in the seventeenth century.

It looked as though things were coming apart at the seams for Elizabeth II in 1992, a year the queen termed *annus horribilis* in the wake of Princess Diana's threats to reveal what she knew about the "darkness" in the royal family (Diana would be dead in less than five years). Those revelations were snuffed out with her murder (which she predicted), a killing disguised as an automobile accident caused by her supposedly "recklessly inebriated driver."

---

[18] In 2020 the World Health Organization (WHO) announced the staff of the Technical Advisory Group (TAG) on Behavioral Insights, chaired by Cass Sunstein. It is a who's who of "behavior modification and intervention" authorities, and psychological warfare experts: Dr Tim Chadborn, Dr. Maria Augusta Carrasco, Dr Varun Gauri, Dr Fadi Makki, Dr Shahinaz Ibrahim Mekheimar, Professor Susan Michie, Professor Saad B. Omer, Professor Rajiv Rimal, Ms Jana Smith, Dr Chiara Varazzani, Ms Archna Vyas.

To give some examples, according to WHO, Prof. Omer's "research portfolio" "includes behavioral interventions to increase demand and acceptance of COVID-19 interventions." Prof. Rimal "is an expert in the use of social norms theory for promoting social change." Dr.Varazzani "is a leading specialist in applying behavioral science to government and public policy. She has set up and led units of behavioral scientists in government-designed behavior change interventions..." No accusation of wrong-doing is here imputed to the aforementioned persons. Our profile is predicated on information found at the official website of the World Health Organization as of November, 2020.

Queen Elizabeth II and Prince Charles, together with conservative heroine Margaret Thatcher, appear to have enabled the massive crimes against children perpetrated by "Sir Jimmy" and his filthy cohort. Moreover, molestation of underage boys is a huge problem in Hollywood as well. [19]

Beginning around 2016, "QAnon," an organization heavily publicized by the corporate media, came to prominence. It was supposedly created to fight international Satanic child-trafficking rings that were allegedly conspiring to bring down President Donald Trump. During Mr. Trump's presidency, Jeffrey Epstein, the man who led one of the most extensive of those sex rings, was arrested and subsequently incarcerated in a Federal jail in New York City.

**Photo published worldwide in July, 2019
after Jeffrey Epstein's incarceration in New York**
Note the Middle Eastern motif of the temple architecture, with its golden tutelary deities (on the roof and the ground around the structure), on pederastic Little St. James island, privately owned by Epstein until his death (part of the U.S. Virgin Islands).

Epstein was facing life in prison and was being pressured to accept a plea bargain in return for naming the powerful men (former President Bill Clinton, Prince Andrew, son of Queen Elizabeth, and dozens more) suspected of having been serviced

---

[19] "The Lost Boys: How Hollywood paedophile ring behind child abuse 'as horrific as Jimmy Savile's' could finally be exposed in wake of Weinstein scandal" (*The Sun*, October 19, 2017).

by the sex slaves Epstein furnished. Not long afterward Epstein was found dead in his cell, while the surveillance cameras in the jail "malfunctioned" and his guards "fell asleep."

Mr. Trump's Attorney General, William Barr, swore he would get to the bottom of the blatantly obvious foul play that was in truth Epstein's murder while in "protective Federal custody." In the end Mr. Barr, with Mr. Trump's acquiescence, did nothing of the kind, and signed off on Epstein's death as a suicide. It was said that the cameras and the guards were out of action due to "incompetence." A few mid-level officials received reprimands or were demoted. A bald fact: *Epstein's killing on Trump's watch was not prosecuted by the Trump administration. The killers went free.* Cui bono?

The insiders who systematically abused and exploited the girls and women provided by Epstein, surely breathed a huge sigh of relief thanks to Donald Trump, the man laughably honored by QAnon's useful idiots, as the number one nemesis of international Satanist child-trafficking rings. What reward did Trump and Barr receive for covering up the homicidal silencing of Epstein?

As further testimony to his charlatanry, we make note of Donald Trump in his last days in office having refused to pardon Julian Assange or Edward Snowden, yet he issued a pardon to the Israeli spy Aviem Sella, who had recruited Jonathan Pollard to steal U.S. military secrets for the Israelis. The Israelis in turn conveyed those secrets to Pakistan.

Trump put Mossad asset Jared Kushner in charge of infiltrating U.S. Intelligence and Defense. In 2020 Trump campaigned on the claim that Hunter Biden was a Chinese agent, but the president made no mention of Charles Kushner (Jared's father), who allegedly served as an agent of China's Anbang Insurance, a Communist front.

Memo to U.S. servicemen and women wounded and maimed in Afghanistan, and the families of American troops killed by the Taliban: in 2019 "your" government, under super-patriot Trump, ordered Joint Special Forces Command to *ally with the Taliban and provide air support on behalf of the Taliban* in their battles with their rival, Islamic State Khorasan.

Exhibiting the marks of cognitive infiltration, "Constitutional patriot" General Michael Flynn, after the November 2020 election, advocated suspending the Constitution and imposing martial law. Trump cronies Sidney Powell and L. Lin Wood, both prominent Right-wing attorneys, created an atmosphere of militant confrontation after the November, 2020 presidential election. This in turn contributed to the milieu in which Trump dispatched his loyal followers on January 6, 2021 when they marched into a trap at the Capitol, instigated that day by Trump and former New York Mayor Rudy Giuliani, a principal in the 9/11 conspiracy coverup. [20]

Leaked Insider Recording From ABC News Reveals Network Executives Killed Bombshell Story Implicating Jeffrey Epstein

ProjectVeritas.com, November 5, 2019

Amy Robach, 'Good Morning America' Co-Host and Breaking News Anchor at ABC, explains how a witness came forward years ago with information pertaining to Epstein, but Disney-owned ABC News refused to air the material for years. Robach vents her anger in a "hot mic" moment with an off-camera producer, explaining that ABC quashed the story in it's early stages. Robach describes how she interviewed a woman who had the courage to come forward "years" ago about Epstein: "She had pictures, She had everything. She was in hiding for twelve years. We convinced her to come out. We convinced her to talk to us."

"I've had this interview with Virginia Roberts (Now Virginia Guiffre) [alleged Epstein victim]. We would not put it on the air. Um, first of all, I was told "Who's Jeffrey Epstein? No one knows who that is. This is a stupid story." She continued, *"The Palace found out that we had her whole allegations about Prince Andrew and threatened us a million different ways."*

Robach goes on to express her belief that Epstein was killed in prison saying, "So do I think he was killed? 100% Yes, I do... He made his whole living blackmailing people... Yup, there were a lot of men in those planes. A lot of men who visited that Island, a lot of powerful men who came into that apartment."

Robach repeats a prophetic statement purportedly made by Attorney Brad Edwards, "There will come a day when we will

---

[20] Cf. *Revisionist History*® no. 112 (January, 2021), "Downfall: Trump's Debacle in D.C." The "Unite the Right Rally" in Charlottesville, Virginia, August 11-12, 2017 also exhibited aspects of cognitive infiltration. Like at the Capitol in January, 2021, the Charlottesville debacle paid huge dividends to the Cryptocracy.

realize Jeffrey Epstein was the most prolific pedophile this country has ever known," and disgustedly Robach states "I had it all three years ago." (End quote; emphasis supplied).

Another Wayne
Child Sex Trafficking Networks Associated with John Wayne Gacy

There is Bruce Wayne and then there is John Wayne Gacy, the monster dubbed "Joker" and "the Killer Clown." He murdered 33 boys and wore a security lapel pin conferred upon him by the U.S. Secret Service in a 1978 meeting with First Lady Rosalyn Carter. Gacy sometimes posed as a policeman and flashed police credentials. He released a few victims of his attacks without taking their lives.

From 1972 to December 1978, it seems he may have possibly been immune from arrest for homicide until such time as he had killed his 33rd victim. Either that, or the Chicago-area police were among the most incompetent in the nation.

Wayne Gacy hunted for some of his vagrant victims in Chicago's "Bughouse Square."

According to *Chicago Tribune* (May 16, 1977), Phillip Paske (1953-1998), operated a child sex trafficking ring called the "Delta Project" while the ring's "mastermind," John D. Norman (1927-2009), was inside serving a prison sentence. Norman had previously controlled a child pornography operation in Dallas, Texas, known as the Odyssey Foundation.

Paske was also an employee of John Wayne Gacy's PDM Construction company. Like Gacy, Paske and Norman seemed to have lived a life of crime with near impunity, at least for a time. Norman served only a few years in prison on separate occasions for major felonies, including forcible sodomy and repeated child sex trafficking over many decades. At least one witness against Norman was killed. At one point Norman published *"Hermes,"* a child-sex networking newsletter.

Paske was a murderer who was granted significantly reduced charges and sentence reductions. At least one Gacy victim who was made a captive but was not killed, reported seeing a man matching Paske's description observing Gacy as he tormented and imprisoned the man inside Gacy's residence.

It may not be significant but it is worth noting for the record that according to the findings of the House Select Committee on Assassinations, Volume IX, V, in 1962 John F. Kennedy assassination conspirator Jack Ruby gave a $40 deposit on an apartment in Dallas to a landlord's agent bearing the name "John D. Norman."

The extent of the reach of the John Norman/John Wayne Gacy pederast network is unknown; that it enjoyed a fairly remarkable freedom of operation during the time it fulfilled its appointed mission would seem to indicate high level protection.

"Wayne County" is the stage name of a headliner in various 1970s-era transvestite rock music acts (one of which was called "Queen Elizabeth"). The Fox Sisters' seance-faith of Spiritualism, a nineteenth century American religion, was born in Wayne County, New York. In the town of Manchester, bordering Wayne County, Hill Cumorah, which is situated on the 42nd degree line of latitude, is the place where the Mormon Church says Joseph Smith received "golden plates" from the Angel Moroni, from which he translated the *Book of Mormon*.

At the conclusion of "The Dark Knight Rises" Bruce Wayne (played by Satanist Christian Bale),[21] is shown relaxing at an outdoor restaurant in Florence, Italy, one-time occult citadel of the Cryptocracy when it began to take power through the Church in the early Renaissance. Wayne's British (Intelligence) factotum/handler, "Alfred" (Michael Caine), frequents Florence and "stumbles" upon Batman and Catwoman there.

As the 2012 Batman film premiered nationwide in Aurora, Colorado and elsewhere, it was preceded on the screen, as is customary, by previews for other movies. One of these was for the forthcoming 007 movie, "Skyfall." Another trailer, this one for the movie "Gangster Squad," was also shown in theaters that were screening "The Dark Knight Rises." 2:03 minutes into the trailer, four men are depicted standing behind a movie screen, walking toward the audience, shooting at them.

"Gangster Squad" is based on the life of Los Angeles organized crime boss Meyer "Mickey" Cohen, whose girlfriend for a time was Juanita Slusher, otherwise known as "Candy Barr," the famous stripper and courtesan befriended in Dallas by that man of all connections, Jack Ruby.

---

[21] "Thank you to Satan for giving me inspiration for playing this role." — Christian Bale, Golden Globe award acceptance speech, nationally televised January 6, 2019. Yes, it's *assumed* he was making a joke (in the age of "woke," when little or nothing is).

Route 91 Harvest Massacre
The Haunting Of America
Beamed from the Vegas Strip

The map of our collective dream world
is being perpetually redrawn

"Ship me somewheres east of Suez,
where the best is like the worst,
Where there aren't no Ten Commandments
an' a man can raise a thirst;
For the temple-bells are callin', an' it's there that I would be
By the old Moulmein Pagoda, looking lazy at the sea;
On the road to Mandalay."

— Rudyard Kipling, "Mandalay" [1]

---

[1] Rudyard Kipling was initiated into Freemasonry in 1886 at the age of 20, in the Hope and Perseverance Lodge, No. 782; Lahore, India (now Pakistan).

Sin City quickly returned to business as usual shortly after the October 1, 2017 "Harvest Festival" mass murder of 61 of their fellow Americans (411 shot and wounded), [2] a slaughter which has been attributed to Stephen Paddock [3] and which occurred in the immediate vicinity of the Mandalay/Luxor site on the Las Vegas Strip.

The *Wall Street Journal* reported, "...the mood on the Las Vegas Strip lifted as the week progressed. Monday evening (October 2) was eerily quiet, with festive public displays such as the Fountains of Bellagio turned off out of respect for the victims. But by Thursday night (October 5), boisterous crowds were back. Groups of revelers strolled with three-foot-tall daiquiris strapped to their necks. Scantily clad women in police costumes were handcuffing passersby, angling for paid photos. Beer pong tables were full at O'Shea's Casino close to the Strip. Kevin Riley had been in town since Sunday, part of a two-week motorcycle excursion from Chicago to Los Angeles. Standing in front of the Bellagio fountains, the Australian marveled at how the Strip felt no different than other times he's visited. "The way it came back the night after the event, that said, 'Nothing's going to dampen this town,' Mr. Riley said."

On October 2, less than 24 hours after the bloodbath, the NFL's nationally broadcast "Monday Night Football" extravaganza, with a stadium full of raucous fans, was underway as usual.

S.K. Bain notes that the *Route 91* Harvest Massacre took place with *91 days left in the calendar year*. The countdown had begun. "Conspiracy theorists spread false information"—this was the headline at Snopes.com and—heavily promoted by Google on October 5. *Wall Street Journal* headline: "YouTube Tweaks Search Results as Las Vegas Conspiracy Theories Rise to Top."

---

[2] Casualty figures among the 22,000 Country and Western fans continue to vary, with the number of dead from official sources and the corporate media listed at 58, 59 or 61.

[3] August 3, 2018 the *New York Times* reported, "Mr. Paddock left no suicide note...There was no evidence he belonged to any terrorist organizations or hate groups, and he had no criminal record. While his financial assets had diminished before the attack, he was indebted to no one and had paid all his gambling debts.' In the ensuing years it was apparently determined that Paddock's life was not sufficiently sinister to render credible the homicidal maniac persona assigned to him. Hence, more recently a back story alleging "anti-government fanaticism" has been added to the official tale of his "lone nut" culpability.

The *Journal* reported October 5 that YouTube (owned by Google), was falsifying (i.e. "tweaking") search results — to move readers away from alternative sources and toward mainstream media's "authoritative" sources, while associating investigations outside that narrow aperture with "hateful messages" and "misinformation."

The *New York Times* reported that Las Vegas Sheriff Joe Lombardo in a briefing on Wednesday (October 4) questioned the veracity of the lone nut conclusion:

"Do you think this was all accomplished on his (Paddock's) own? Face value, you've got to make the assumption that he had to have some help at some point, and we want to ensure that that's the answer. Maybe he's a super guy, a superhero — not a hero. Super, I won't use the word. Maybe he...was working out all this on his own. But it would be hard for me to believe that."

Script Change: It was reported for days after the shooting that a hotel security guard was shot by Paddock *after* Paddock committed the massacre, and this was the encounter that led the perpetrator to abort his mass murder spree. A host of media tales about what happened in connection with that supposed *post-massacre* assault on the guard were retailed to the public by what the Establishment terms the "credentialed" media. *Los Angeles Times*: "They (police) had credited (Jesus) Campos, who was shot in the leg, with stopping the 10-minute assault on the concert crowd by turning the gunman's attention to the hotel hallway, where Campos was checking an alert for an open door in another guest's room.

By October 9, the official reason that the shooter halted his gunfire after ten minutes needed to be revised and a new official reason substituted, so there was a script change. Clark County Sheriff Joe Lombardo now was asserting (October 9) that Paddock shot Campos *before* his alleged mass shooting spree — at 9:59 p.m. — and *they now didn't know why Paddock stopped his attack on the crowd*. "Police Alter Timeline of Vegas Shooting" (Valley News via Los Angeles Times, Oct. 10, 2017):

"Police have dramatically changed their account of how the Las Vegas massacre began on Oct. 1, revealing on Monday that the gunman shot a hotel security guard six minutes before opening fire on a country music concert — raising new questions...Investigators previously said that the security guard was shot after Paddock had already spent 10 minutes firing into the crowd of concertgoers gathered below the hotel. In a timeline released last week, investigators said Paddock had stopped firing at the concert across the street at 10:15 p.m., and the first police officers arrived on the floor at 10:17 p.m. and encountered the wounded Campos at 10:18 p.m., who directed the officers to Paddock's suite. Police were not in a hurry to enter Paddock's suite because the security guard's arrival had halted the shooting, police implied in previously describing the timeline. Paddock had killed himself by the time officers entered the room, they said.

"In a news conference Wednesday (October 4), Lombardo said it was his 'assumption' that Paddock stopped his shooting spree because the gunman, using his spy cameras, 'observed the security guard, and he was in fear that he was about to be breached, so he was doing everything possible to figure out how to escape at that point.'

"In another news conference last week, Clark County Undersheriff Kevin McMahill said Campos 'had notified his dispatch, which was absolutely critical to us, knowing the location, as well as advising the responding officers as they arrived.' But on Monday, the timeline changed. Mr. Campos was encountered by the suspect prior to his shooting to the outside world,' Lombardo said at a Monday news conference...A police spokesperson did not immediately respond to several follow-up questions from the *Los Angeles Times* seeking clarification on the new timeline. Charles 'Sid' Heal, a retired Los Angeles County sheriff's commander and tactical expert, said the new timeline 'changes the whole perspective of the shooting." (End quote from the *Los Angeles Times*).

We were expected to believe the original timeline and not doubt it, because to do so renders one a "conspiracy theorist." Yet later the Establishment media told us *not* to believe the officially-promulgated initial timeline. All obedient Americans were then required to believe the new timeline and discard the old one. In the days ahead our trustworthy news media and government officials told us more of what we were to believe and what we shouldn't believe about the Route 91 Harvest Massacre. Here's the message: however much the script is reversed in the future, obey it without question if you don't want to be stigmatized as a "paranoid conspiracy theorist," or a "Grassy knoll nutcase."

"Paddock used more than 10 suitcases to bring at least 23 weapons, mostly rifles, into his Mandalay Bay hotel room. Over the last 12 months, Paddock bought 33 guns...In the last year, Paddock had made chip purchases in Nevada casinos in excess of $10,000 a day..." (*Los Angeles Times*, October 5).

Washington Post online, October 2, 5:10 p.m. Pacific: "After the shooting, officers found Stephen Paddock dead with 23 guns on the 32nd floor..."

"23" and "32" are significant numbers.[4] The *Las Vegas Review Journal*, October 4, 2017 added two more significant numbers to the cauldron: "The attack lasted between nine and 11 minutes..." (9/11).

It was said that Paddock had stopped shooting on the crowd after approximately ten minutes. Los Angeles Times, October 5: "Officers decided he was no longer an active shooter, and decided not to enter the room immediately...Officers blew down Paddock's door at 11:20 p.m., 75 minutes after the shooting began." For more than an hour the police left Paddock alone with an arsenal of weapons in his hotel room overlooking the dead and wounded victims and first responders, during which time he could have resumed shooting at any moment.

The monotonous silhouette of the lone nut fable began to be set in stone almost immediately. On October 2 the media chimed: "Police believe Paddock acted alone in executing the deadliest mass shooting in modern U.S. history." *Less than a day after the atrocity, when a thorough investigation should have just begun, the media announced that the authorities were certain that Paddock acted alone and had no help whatsoever.* How could they know this? On what basis could this clairvoyant conclusion be reached so soon, without a thorough investigation that would take days or weeks? The lone nut meme was being implanted in the Hive Mind less than twenty-four hours after the massacre.

Then Sheriff Lombardo dissented. BBC News called it, "A twist in the investigation."

October 5: "The possibility that Paddock could have had an accomplice is the new angle." In the aftermath of the shooting officials described Paddock as 'a lone wolf' and said he was

---

[4] The August 12, 2019 *Washington Post* published online the headline: "23 Bizarre Conspiracy Theories Trump has Elevated." There are hundreds of additional examples of the assignment (or "coincidental" connection) of number 23 to anomalies.

'solely responsible for this heinous act.' Then came the 'twist.' The sheriff stated that "while there were two cameras on a room service cart outside Paddock's room as well as the door peephole and inside the general family area of the hotel room, *none of those cameras were recording.*" [5]

Ann Coulter, October 4: "Who was the woman shouting, *'You're all going to die!'* right before the concert? [6] Is any reporter interested in finding out? Probably a random crazy lady, but that's not typical pre-concert behavior. Why is it taking so long to find out if anyone else went into Paddock's hotel room since he checked in last Thursday? I'm perfectly prepared to accept that he was the only one who entered that room, but can we see the surveillance video?..."

Truths on the Road to Arlington: In the movie "Arlington Road" (described as a "gripping contemporary thriller about the terrible truths that can hide behind everyday appearances"), Michael Faraday (Jeff Bridges) is a man attempting to prevent a catastrophic massacre in Washington D.C. He *unknowingly* delivers the terror bomb that causes the massacre that forever-after brands this innocent individual as one of the most heinous terrorists in American history.

We ask the following question: what if Stephen Paddock was not the shooter? What if he was only a fall guy?

Let's ponder an alternate scenario: Paddock was somehow incapacitated in his hotel room while an expert marksman (or marksmen), gunned down the 61 people and wounded 411 in a mere "9 or 11" minutes. After the massacre, a gun was forced into the unconscious or paralyzed Paddock's hand. Someone else pulled the trigger on the handgun and he died by "suicide," and entered the media's gallery of "anti-government" terrorists who are actually Arlington Road patsies.

On October 5 news.com.au (News Australia) reported that Eric Paddock wondered whether his brother Stephen actually

---

[5] None of the cameras outside Jefrey Epstein's cell the day he died "were recording."

[6] "In 1974, retired LAPD officer Paul Sharaga told a newsman with KMPC in Los Angeles that as he was responding to the shooting (of Robert F. Kennedy) in the hotel, an elderly couple reported to him that they saw a couple in their early 20s, one of whom was a woman in a polka-dot dress. The couple were smiling and shouting, 'We shot him... we killed Kennedy...we shot him...we killed him.' Sharaga also stated that he filed official reports of the incident, but that they disappeared and were never investigated. (*Santa Monica Evening Outlook* Dec. 23, 1974, p. 5).

committed the crime, or whether an impersonator was involved:

"Eric said he hopes police find a 'tumor in his (brother's) head or something' when they do an autopsy in order to explain what happened. 'If they don't, we're all in trouble,' he said. 'I'm praying for at least some data points. Because otherwise, the bug in 'Men In Black' put on a Steve suit and went and did this. There's no other rationalization." ("The bug" is an alien and the main antagonist in the first "Men in Black film." While on earth, he impersonates a human).

Until we know more, all angles with some potential for having occurred, should be considered. Pardon our skepticism, but we would not be at all surprised if the crazed forces in our own government who brought down the Twin Towers on 9/11 by controlled demolition, killed and maimed hundreds of their fellow citizens in Las Vegas in order to propitiate the eldtritch entities symbolized by the Strip's Pharonic graven images.

Daddy Paddock, The Teflon Career Criminal

Benjamin Hoskins Paddock II (a.k.a. "Chromedome," a.k.a. "Bingo Bruce Ericksen"), was once on the FBI's "Ten Most Wanted" list of fugitives. He was the father of Stephen Paddock. What strikes this writer about the biography of the shooter's father, a one-time hunted fugitive wanted for bank robbery, prison escape and attempted murder of an FBI agent, was the ease with which, like John D. Norman, he obtained in more than one instance, *partial and episodic immunity from the government for his major felony crimes.*

Benjamin Hoskins Paddock was not required to serve the remaining eleven years of the bank robbery sentence he had evaded by escaping from prison; nor was he punished for a subsequent bank robbery, or attempting, in Las Vegas, to kill an officer with his car — beyond a relatively short jail sentence.

Subsequent financial crimes he committed years later, involving racketeering, also proved to have little consequence for the alleged Las Vegas shooter's father who, it can be said, seems to have lived a fairly charmed life.

Like his Dad, Stephen Paddock appears to have lived a charmed life prior to allegedly machine-gunning the patrons of the Harvest Festival in Las Vegas. Benjamin Hoskins Paddock II was born in Sheboygan, Wisconsin in 1926. He served in the Navy during World War II.

**Benjamin "Bingo Bruce"
Hoskins Paddock II**

I. His life of crime commenced in 1946 at age 20, with a conviction in Illinois on ten counts of auto theft and five counts of running a confidence game.

"Married in Reno, Nevada in 1952 and fathered Stephen, before being imprisoned in 1953 for a fraudulent check scheme...When he got out in 1956, the Paddocks moved to Arizona and Stephen's parents started going by different names: Benjamin became Patrick, and his wife, Irene, became Delores..." [7]

Benjamin Hoskins Paddock was hunted by the FBI in Las Vegas and at the time of the arrest in 1961 he tried to run down an FBI agent with his car: "Benjamin 'Chromedome' Paddock, Ex-Tucsonian, Makes FBI List Of 10 Most Wanted" by Gilbert T. Matthews, *Tucson Citizen Daily*, April 27, 1971:

"Known to his associates as 'Chromedome, Old Baldy,' and 'Big Daddy,' Benjamin Hoskins Paddock is Tucson's contribution to the FBI's list of 10 most-wanted fugitives. He made the list after escaping on Dec. 31, 1968, from the Federal

---

[7] *New York Times* October 4, 2017, p. A16.

Correctional Institution at La Tuna, Tex., where he was serving a 20-year sentence for robbing a Phoenix bank in 1960. Paddock—alias Perry Archer, Benjamin J. Butler, Leo Genstein, Pat Paddock and Patrick Benjamin Paddock— hasn't been seen or heard from since. At the time of the robbery, Paddock lived in Tucson with his wife and four children. Neighbors said they couldn't believe that the colorful businessman, then 34 years old, was involved in crime. Paddock sold garbage disposal units here under the business name of Arizona Disposer 'Chromedome' Co. He called himself 'Big Daddy' in connection with a night club operation on North 1st Avenue. Before selling the disposal units, he operated an East Broadway service station and also sold used cars.

"Although he was imprisoned for the...holdup of a branch of the Valley National Bank in Phoenix, Paddock also had been accused of two other bank robberies. Those charges were dropped after his conviction. Palmer M. Baken Jr., agent in charge of the Phoenix FBI office described Paddock as being 'A glib, smooth-talking man who is egotistical and arrogant.'"

The *Eugene-Register Guard* (Oregon) September 15, 1978: "A Springfield bingo parlor manager arrested last week as a long-sought federal prison escapee was ordered to San Francisco to face a 1960 robbery charge. Benjamin Hoskins Paddock, 51, manager of The Bingo Centre at 612 Main St., received the order in an appearance before US Magistrate Michael Hogan in Eugene. Paddock is charged with the armed robbery of a San Francisco bank on June 4, 1969, about six months after his escape from a federal prison in Texas....He lived in the Eugene-Springfield area for several years under the name Brice Werner Ericksen. He managed to escape detection by changing his appearance and avoiding contact with law enforcement agencies that might have resulted in fingerprinting, according to the FBI."

His extensive rap sheet: "Over an 18-month span in 1959 and 1960, Mr. Paddock hit two branches of the Valley National Bank in Phoenix —one of them twice —and made off with $25,000, according to *The Arizona Republic*, citing an indictment. Each time, the report said, he showed the teller a snub-nosed revolver tucked in his belt, and fled in a stolen car that he abandoned a few blocks away to switch to the family's new Pontiac station wagon. When the F.B.I. finally caught up with him at a gas station in downtown Las Vegas, he tried to flee, nearly ramming an agent, before an agent fired a bullet through his windshield. He surrendered unharmed. Mr. Paddock was convicted in 1961 and sentenced to 20 years in prison. He escaped from the penitentiary...and made his way to San Francisco, where he robbed another bank." [8]

After his capture in 1978 Benjamin Hoskins Paddock was paroled circa 1979, serving merely a year for multiple bank robberies, attempting to run over a Federal officer, and prison escape. He was not required to serve the remaining eleven years of the prison sentence he had avoided by escaping. *In other words, he was rewarded for having escaped from prison.* For his long list of felonies he received a brief sentence in jail and was then paroled. His parole application was supported by the City Mayor and the County Commissioner. *No one in the government ever seemed to try very hard to make charges stick when it came to Teflon Paddock.*

Eight years after extricating himself from bank robbery, attempted murder and prison escape convictions, he experienced another almost miraculous slap on the wrist: "In 1987 Benjamin Hoskins Paddock was again arrested. He was charged with penalties amounting to $623,000 for racketeering. Circuit Judge George Goodrich reduced Paddock's fine to $100,000 and no jail time."

"Bingo Bruce Ericksen" (Paddock) died in Texas eleven years later in January, 1998 at age 77. His live-in companion since 1988 had been Laurel Paulson, a woman he'd met in Eugene. [9]

What is the significance (if any) of the elder Paddock's charmed life? One wonders if he had a protective "connection" inside the Cryptocracy. If so, why was the protection in place? Had their been a quid pro quo? Did it take the form of missions "Bingo Bruce" undertook for the government?

According to the October 3, 2017 *Wall Street Journal*, in the 1970s Stephen Paddock had been employed by the U.S. government, in the Internal Revenue Service (IRS). Lockheed Martin, the defense giant, said that Paddock worked for them for three years in the 1980s.

---

[8] *New York Times*, op.cit.

[9] Cf. *Eugene-Register Guard*, February 9, 1998.

"He was worth more than $2 million, relatives said. Before retiring, he made a small fortune from real estate deals and a business that he and (his brother) Eric Paddock sold off. Eric Paddock...recalled one time when the entire family took over the top floor of the Atlantis at the casino's expense."

The Pharaonic Egyptian mise-en-scéne at the site of the Las Vegas mass sacrifice

The Route 91 Harvest Festival, whether by design or coincidence control, was a harvest of human beings.

In pre-Christian nature religions humans were sacrificed to the dark gods during the autumn harvest. Another aspect of pagan propitiation of these gods is cult prostitution. Given the proliferation of huge Egyptian cult objects in "Sin City," it may be likely that, together with the post-modernist animus toward Biblical morality, some Las Vegas harlots engage in *qedeshah* (cult prostitution, cf. Deuteronomy 23:17), which historically has been part of the sex-and-sacrifice rites of certain pagan sects, and which continue to be regarded as a means of invoking dark forces.

According to advertisements, the "Route 91 Harvest" was "powered by Sirius," i.e. Sirius XM radio. [10] The obelisk, the control icon of Pharaonic Egypt which hallowed Sirius, squats adjacent to the Mandalay hotel on the "Vegas Strip." Next door from the massacre site, at "Luxor," is the ominous Egyptian pyramid replica (646 feet at its base and 350 feet tall). The Country and Western fans in "Sin City" were slaughtered, like an obeisance to the dark gods, in proximity to these Pharaonic death cult objects.

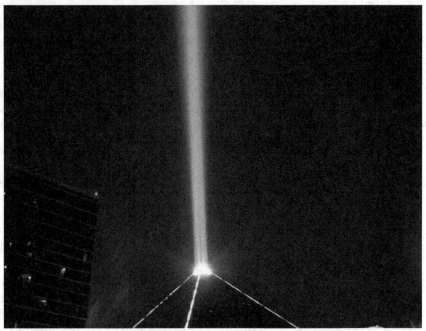

In the videos of the attack one can see the Luxor Sky Beam, the most powerful beam of light in the world, visible in outer space, being emitted out of the top of the Las Vegas pyramid.

According to the *Oxford English Dictionary*, the name "Paddock" is another word for "a familiar spirit in the shape of a toad."

In Shakespeare's *Macbeth* (act 1, scene 1), the three witches speak: "I come, Grimalkin Paddock calls anon. Fair is foul, and foul is fair, Hover through the fog and filthy air."

---

[10] No accusation of wrongdoing is being leveled against Sirius XM, its owners, employees or affiliates.

We have often pointed to a civic magic that is being revealed publicly with little noticeable counter-reaction from the people. In the wake of the 9/11 terror attacks, the mass open air occult process has increased dramatically, as the processing has increased.

Every year the U.S. government "accidentally" kills hundreds of civilians in the Middle East and western Asia at rural weddings and in cities, as part of our "wars against terrorism" which often terrorize civilians, and then in turn act as recruiting devices for additional terrorists to "fight America." The terror and counter-terror cycle has no end in sight. Murder by government, and corporate media lies, are piling ever higher, along with "random" killings.

The mainstream media's purveyors of conformity will frown on our occult analyses and denounce them as the sin of conspiracy theorizing. These editors and reporters who act as the System's gate-keepers, would not dream of exploring occult symbolism in spectacular crimes. It isn't done, *unless it's in connection with fictional Hollywood films*. In the October 2, 2017 *New York Times* online, movie critic A.O. Scott approved of occult investigation—when it concerns fantasy movies. Concerning the film "Blade Runner" he writes, "One of my fondest memories as a father and a film critic is of an impromptu post-screening seminar with two 11-year-olds about occult meanings and hidden clues in the director's cut."

"Occult meanings" and "hidden clues" in America's epidemic of mass shootings? It wouldn't be politically correct to look for them. Establishment-approved conformists and media-certified "good people" believe official tales, succumb to confirmation bias and keep silent concerning anomalies in the script. Some of us, however, hear the cries of the dead for justice. Our eyes are open and we refuse to be silent.

Eyes Wide Shut

III

PHARMAKOS

The Greeks practiced a scapegoat ritual, employing a human sacrifice, the *pharmakos*, who was beaten and paraded in the streets before being executed. "The Athenians regularly maintained a number of degraded and useless beings at the public expense; and when any calamity such as plague, drought or famine befell the city, they sacrificed two of these outcasts as scapegoats." [1]

The scapegoat is found in Leviticus and I and II Kings, as well Revelation 2:20, 9:21, 18:23, 21:8 and 22:14-15. In the New Testament the Ionic/Koine Greek noun *pharmakos* is synonymous with enchantment and crippling through drugs and sorcery. [2]

James Shelby Downard viewed himself as having been on the receiving end of both pathologies. He had compassion for dissidents and sleuths who he believed had undergone a similar scapegoat ordeal after having attempted to proclaim or disclose an inconvenient truth about the Cryptocracy, which he denominated in terms of the secret society of Freemasonry, the "Invisible Empire" of the Ku Klux Klan, and the FBI ("Federal Bureau of Inverts")—for which he harbored special antipathy. [3]

---

[1] Sir James Frazer, T*he Golden Bough: A Study in Magic and Religion, Part IV: The Scapegoat* (New York: Macmillan, 1935), p. 253.

[2] In the New Testament sorcery *and* scapegoat are both connoted by *pharmakos* and its derivatives. In Revelation 22:15 *pharmakoi* are the sorcerers associated with dogs: "Outside the city are the dogs—the sorcerers..." Whether this is a reference to Anubis is unclear. In the ancient Greek denotation, *pharmakoi* are scapegoats, In Revelation a *pharmakos* is enslaved through drugs and sorcery perpetrated by *pharmakoi*. For example, in 2 Kings 9:22 and Rev. 2:20 Jezebel is a *pharmakos /pharmaka* (sorcerer). She scapegoats the prophets and then kills them (I Kings 18:4).

[3] Mr. Downard believed his estranged wife had been coerced by FBI agents into playing the part of the "Great Whore" in *magica sexualis* rites at Mount Palomar, and in bungalows at the Hotel Del Charro in LaJolla, California, It was there, from 1953-1971, that J. Edgar Hoover was the non-paying guest of the hotel's owner, mobster Clint Murchison. The Del Charro was located 14 miles from the Del Mar Turf Club, where Mr. Hoover placed wagers on horse races and conferred with members of the Mafia.

> "...eugenic abortion...countries like Iceland boast of having 'eliminated' the condition (Down syndrome) — not via therapy, but by destroying those who have it." [4]

Extermination of Down syndrome humans degraded into the status of *pharmakoi,* is the pagan Neo-Nazism of our time; another dare-not-be-spoken truth.

Other humans designated as *pharmakoi* by the Cryptocracy are the Palestinian, Lebanese, Syrian, Iraqi, Afghan, Yemeni and Iranian people, as well as the much-despised hillbilly and redneck "deplorables" of rural America.

Black people became *pharmakoi* in the eyes of North African Muslims, [5] Queen Elizabeth I and her pirate slavers John Hawkins and Francis Drake, and among their intellectual and spiritual heirs in the slave-holding and Jim Crow American South, due in part to the influence of the ruling in the *Guide of the Perplexed* [6] by Moses Maimonides, the renowned medieval rabbinic law-giver and physician, who was esteemed by papal, Islamic and Protestant theologians alike.

---

[4] Charles A. Donovan and Robert G. Marshall.

[5] Maimonides was the court physician to the family of the Sultan of Egypt. His *halakhic* magnum opus is the *Mishneh Torah*. See the note below.

[6] Few pronouncements have caused black people more misery than that of Maimonides, who ruled they are "irrational animals" (cf. *Guide of the Perplexed*, the uncensored Shlomo Pines translation, University of Chicago Press [1963], vol. 2, pp. 618-19). According to Maimonides' virulently racist teaching, the fact that black people can speak places them "above the apes but below the level of man." This bigotry was transmitted to the western intelligentsia. Paraphrasing Maimonides, Voltaire wrote, "Blacks are not men except in their stature, with the faculty of speech..." (Kwame Appiah, *New York Review of Books* May 9, 2019, p. 40). Many Judaic people are not aware of Maimonides' statement. In our experience those Judaics who do know of it repudiate it and consider it abhorrent.

In pre-Christian Greece *pharmakos* was defined variously as someone created to be thrown away; she or he who is valueless; refuse; trash. It simultaneously denotes an expiatory offering, such as the long ago slayings of the *pharmakos* at the annual Athenian festival of Thargelia, held in the early summer.

In ancient Greece the *pharmakos* was regarded as the very least of men, someone whose human dignity was so completely lost that that their execution was made a public spectacle and entertainment. [7]

---

[7] Patsy, n. slang (orig. U.S.). [Origin unknown.] A person who is ridiculed, deceived, blamed, or victimized (*Oxford English Dictionary*).

"In his last year, one locale Shelby wanted to visit before he became too ill to do so, was Lincoln, Montana on the Continental Divide, adjacent to the Scapegoat Wilderness, the final residence of Ted Kaczynski before his lifetime incarceration. There was a Scapegoat Cafe in Lincoln, and Shelby examined the site of Kaczynski's cabin on a map. It had been situated on terrain marked "Scapegoat," which made a big impression on him." [8]

---

[8] Information in an e-mail from Michael Hoffman to Charles Saunders, regarding James Shelby Downard, April 15, 2016. Kaczynski had been groomed as a *pharmakos* from his days as a university student: "During Kaczynski's sophomore year at Harvard, in 1959, he was recruited for a psychological experiment that, unbeknownst to him, would last three years. The experiment involved psychological torment and humiliation, a story I include in my book *Mind Wars: Brain Research and the Military in the 21st Century*. The Harvard study aimed at psychic deconstruction by humiliating undergraduates and thereby causing them to experience severe stress....The man who conducted the humiliation experiment was the brilliant and complex Harvard psychologist Henry A. Murray...Murray was...the pioneer of personality tests that are now a routine part of industrial management and psychological assessments...In yet another odd twist...while Kaczynski was undergoing those humiliation experiments a young Harvard researcher named Timothy Leary was beginning his research career on psychedelics. In 1960 Leary returned from a vacation in Mexico with a suitcase full of magic mushrooms. Murray himself is said to have supervised psychoactive drug experiments, including Leary's. According to Alston Chase, author of *Harvard and the Unabomber*, Leary called Murray "the wizard of personality assessment who, as OSS chief psychologist, had monitored military experiments on brainwashing and sodium amytal interrogation." (Jonathan D. Moeno, PhD., *Psychology Today*, May 25, 2012. PsychologyToday.com).

The spectacle "Possess(es) all the means necessary to falsify perception; the spectacle is the absolute master of memories, just as it is the unfettered master of plans which will shape the most distant future...

"Since no one may contradict it, it has the right to contradict itself, to correct it own past...

"Expressions of hypocritical regret for the passing of real life...and superficial concerns with the technological...developments which accelerate the cycles of...simulation, are voiced in an empty debate conducted by the spectacle itself..." [9]

---

[9] Guy Debord, *Comments on the Society of the Spectacle* (1991), pp. 4, 6, 10 and 28.

"...This demonstrates one of the simpler methods used by the occult conspiracy groups. Realizing that their activities will sooner or later come to light, they structure their activities so that as conspiracy researchers unravel their activities, they will release information into the public consciousness in such a way that it mirrors the groups' initiatory procedure.

"In this way, the more they are investigated, the more masses of people are psychologically processed by the very people who seek to expose them.

"The meme, or idea pattern, that constitutes the essential structure of the group is then successfully mimicked within the consciousness of those who speculate about it. Success can be measured precisely to the extent that the conspiracy has been exposed." [10]

---

[10] *London Psychogeographical Assoc. Newsletter,* no. 15 (London, England, 1996), p. 3.

Jesus said, "My coming into this world is itself a judgment: those who cannot see have their eyes opened, and those who think they can see become blind."

Some of the Pharisees near him overheard this and said, "So we're blind too?"

"If you were blind," Jesus replied, nobody could blame you, but as you say, 'We can see'—your guilt remains."

John 9:39-41

Plaincourault Chapel, France, 1291 A.D.

This page is for the reader's notes